The English Book

to Jack and Elizabeth

and for anyone living in grief

To Jemima
with every good wish
Dave Martin ♡

Marcela Books, Bournemouth UK 2019

www.englishbookofthedead.com

CONTENTS

Introduction

I've seen this happen in other people's lives,
Now it's happening in mine.

The Smiths, *That Joke Isn't Funny Anymore*

In the early hours of December 4th 2009, Debbie my wife wakes me suddenly from my deep sleep. Her voice is more urgent and serious than I've ever known: '*It's Jack: he has had an accident. They've taken him to hospital. We have to go*'. Our only son is in a coma. Thirty-six hours pass and he is dead. Debbie, our daughter Rosie and Jack's aunt Denny take turns to bend and kiss Jack goodbye, his body lying on a bed in the Civic Hospital in Palermo, Sicily. He has not long turned 21.

Until this moment I had kept a warped sort of affection for death, seeing it as mortality's last and best laugh, the ultimate punchline. Now the joke was lost on me. Now the joke was on me. The thing I'd feared most has happened. I look across to Debbie and to Rosie. Their eyes are haunted by pain. I say out loud, but probably to myself, '*We'll be lucky if we survive this*'. Or unlucky even. Death is now no longer an amusing passing acquaintance, but a heartless fixed companion.

In coming across people in the weeks and months that followed Jack's death, a disturbing theme emerged. While some were able to talk to Debbie and me directly about our loss, others – many of whom had known us for years – stayed away from the subject, despite our obvious distress. We were left feeling we had somehow done wrong: we'd brought death into their world. When meeting us on the street or in Tesco's, they kept an arm's length back, out of touching distance. Death, it seemed, was contagious. Sometimes when they saw Debbie or I coming they'd cross the street, as though side-stepping the grim reaper. One time, I was walking on a local hilltop towards steps that unwound downhill to a village below. Just to my left I saw Sally, out with her dog. I had known Sally for years. We had even worked together. She, like me, was headed towards the steps. On seeing me, Sally gave a start as if she'd seen a ghost and almost sprinted down the hill. I'd never known her run before. Nor, clearly, had her Labrador: he was left static, marooned on the hilltop with his owner already out of sight. Mystified, the dog looked up at me. '*I can't figure it either mate,*' I said, shrugging my shoulders.

Talking to other bereaved parents from across the country, we found that this was a common experience. Yet the Scots and Irish didn't seem to have this problem. What, I wondered, had made death such an English taboo? And, now death has claimed my only son, what exactly is it? What do we know about death? This book is an attempt to provide some answers. Because these are important questions, I won't lie or look to mislead you. But I may offend you. Death can be offensive.

Jack

*I have curly hair, I'm very slightly above average in height so as to make
short people look short but tall people look tall, I'm fairly lazy, but
loveable rogue lazy, not fat and ignorant lazy. Still lazy though. I play for
Tisbury Dynamites FC, who are currently languishing mid-table in the
Salisbury and district Sunday league division 3. Have I let success go to
my head? Has hitting the big time changed me? Probably.*

Jack Marteau, age 19, Student Direct Magazine 2008

At 27 I decided the computer business was no longer for me and instead
enrolled as a student mental health nurse in Gloucester. I was still seven
months from qualifying when Jack turned up in September 1988, our
second and last child. His sister Rosie was 28 months his senior. She
struggled a bit with a new face on the scene, and Deb and I struggled more
than a bit with low income, loss of liberty and little sleep. Before parenthood
Deb and I had pleased ourselves, moving around Britain, India and the USA,
living briefly in California. If we felt ourselves getting in a rut, we'd work
extra jobs, save hard, pack it all in and go away. Suddenly, we had two small
children, a mortgage and no prospect of doing precisely as we wanted; an
easy life set hard. We argued more than we knew was enough, and then
fretted these tensions would make Jack a serious boy. For the first year of
his life that seemed true, but once he'd learned to walk and begun to talk,
he became more fun-loving, lighter. When Jack was three Debbie went off
to college to study horticulture full time for a year. I became Jack's main
carer, and as much as I felt my brain developing malnutrition from a
constant diet of Thomas the Tank Engine and Postman Pat, I loved
showing Jack the world and seeing its wonder through his eyes. We'd catch
frogs, study insects and climb on fallen trees. I'd work the weekends, leaving
Deb in charge of Rosie and Jack, and come Monday morning I'd be back
on duty.

The year we spent together tightened the bond between Jack and me. Looking around, I saw plenty of dads who complained their sons were too distant from them, but none made the connection that through work or fecklessness, they'd been too distant from their boys. I congratulated myself on not making that mistake, and immediately grew complacent. As a privileged baby-boomer I'd had it easy – free education and healthcare, ready employment – but working nights caused me to become biologically grumpy. I'd also started a tee-shirt business that had failed. These factors combined to make me feel terminally fed up and declare to Deb that our marriage had become a source of unendurable misery, and I was leaving. Enough of our contemporaries were splitting up, so why not us? I fixed up a rented room across town and started packing my bags. Confused and frightened, six-year-old Jack picked a stone up from the garden and took it to his room. '*Why have you done that?*' asked Deb. '*To keep by my bed, so I won't forget dad,*' said Jack. When I saw the pain and panic in his eyes, I stepped off my high horse, cancelled the rent and never again threatened to leave.

Jack continued to be thoughtful boy, aware of his and others' feelings. One days there was an odd number of us at home, family and friends, debating whether to go to the swimming pool or the park. We couldn't agree so put it to a vote. The scores were tied, with only Jack left to state his preference. '*You've got the casting vote,*' we told him. Jack sat for a while then said, '*I don't want to say what I want to do because then some of us aren't going to get to do what they want to do.*' He was only eight years old. He stuck to his guns and we ended up staying in. Sticking to his guns was a trait he'd keep for the rest of his life. '*You never held back on your opinions and without doubt stuck to your principles, with might I say some hilarious consequences,*' wrote his fellow student Rowan Smart in a University book of tributes. Jack could get on with most people, but occasionally he'd take a dislike to someone. Rather than compromising via exchange of small talk, Jack's policy was never to speak to them, and he kept this rule even if they were three feet away and talking to him. '*Why should I talk to him? I don't like him,'* was Jack's watertight reasoning. People might petition on the unfortunate fella's behalf, but Jack would not shift. Sometimes no-one liked an individual who tagged on to their group on a night out, but no-one would tell them to their face. Jack's good friend John recalled an evening with just such a hanger-on. After ignoring the bloke for some time and seeing this strategy fail, Jack lost patience and simply asked him, *'Why are you still here?'* There was no implicit aggression in his words — Jack was incapable of violence — but expecting exactly that the group caught its collective breath. The irritant, unable to give an answer to a straightforward question, turned around and left.

Speaking up and never backing down are admirable traits, but people don't always love plain speaking, and defensive angry people can really dislike it. Jack's unwillingness to yield to the school bullies led to him being attacked by them. He was kicked, punched and even had his head rammed down a toilet. This didn't change him; he was temperamentally incapable of acting insincerely, even when other people beat him for this stance. In the end Jack had enough and decided to leave the school. Being a bright kid, he wondered if a grammar school might take him. It would be less rough there he reasoned, and he wouldn't stand out as the clever one. Having been to and disliked similar schools ourselves (I went to a grammar in north London and Deb was awarded a scholarship place at a public day school in Croydon), we tried to talk Jack out of this, but of course that was futile: he made his own application to a grammar in Salisbury and come September he was in and free of the neighbourhood bullies.

He took to it straight away, although he didn't totally fit in — the school was deeply conventional, the pupils looked like they'd been born in their oversized black woollen blazers. Jack, by contrast, wore a tight-fitting blue jacket from Oxfam and turned up one day with his light brown hair dyed crow-black. Livid, the head of year sent him home and phoned us to say Jack couldn't come back unless his hair was returned its normal colour. The dye was permanent, and if bleached would turn bright orange, so we put it to Jack that the only viable option would be to shave the lot off. He was fine with that, but it was no shock when the next day the head of year reverted to apoplexy. But bald himself, he lacked the essential commodity to punish Jack further.

Trouble with authority was rare though; Jack never skipped school and had a poor appetite for outlaw behaviour. When a couple of mates started smoking weed and dropping out, Jack stepped back and aligned himself with his less rebellious friends. At thirteen years old, he had started a band with other lads from school. They rehearsed at a youth centre and played pop-punk and ska tunes in a few gigs around Salisbury. Consistent with his habit of finding the least demanding route to any objective, Jack opted to play the bass because, he told me, it was lighter to carry than drums and easier to learn than guitar. Time moved on, the band broke up, and Jack saw no need to repeat the experiment. He started going out with Beth, but enthusiasm for the relationship was one-sided: Jack was dismissive of teenage friends who had immersed themselves in committed relationships, regarding them as having surrendered their liberty just as the party had started.

An able student, Jack collected ten GCSEs without much visible effort, and carried on to sixth year. Over a drink in the local pub he and some friends from primary school days decided to form a football club from scratch. Rather than the fantasy evaporating like so much pub talk, they managed to collect a squad of players, find a kit sponsorship deal and get accreditation from the local Sunday league committee. As an ironic reference to an explosive style of football that no teenagers were likely to accomplish after a heavy Saturday night, they named the club Tisbury Dynamites FC. Jack had just passed his driving test and his grandparents chipped in with him to buy an ageing red Peugeot. He'd take it to matches every Sunday and although the Dynamites would generally get beaten, he didn't mind.

Three years later, he told me, ' *The happiest I've ever been in my life is when I was seventeen, driving down to play for the Dynamites. I know,*' he added,

'*I'll never be as happy again.*' He wasn't in the least depressed when he said this, just matter-of-fact. He could see and feel the grown-up world of responsibility and obligation closing around him. He didn't delude himself that he might escape the constraints of adult life, nor did he hold to a notion that reduced liberty could produce equal pleasure. He said to Deb, with a smile, '*I never want any responsibility.*' He wasn't irresponsible: he could stick at things (University, amateur journalism, Tisbury Dynamites), and if he'd started a family Deb and I felt he would have made a dependable parent. No, through studying the lives of others, he had glimpsed a future, and this perspective was uncoloured by romanticism. Jack was a realist. He would never say it how it wasn't: '*You've been funny, kind, impossibly intelligent. You've derided my socialist views and taken sarcasm to new (and often disturbing) levels – you have been, in short, unforgettable,*' wrote Angela, one of Jack's University friends.

Was his scepticism about life generated by self-doubt, a personal defeatism that drove him to get in first, reject the world before it rejected him? Not really, he had too much appetite for life for that to be true. '*You were one of the few people I know who took every opportunity that they came across,*' was how his friend Luce viewed him. In fact, with some significant exceptions (getting up early, hard physical graft, a small number of people), Jack enjoyed life, particularly laughter and pop culture: '*All the time I knew you I never stopped laughing...I never ceased to be amazed at your ridiculous general knowledge, you may have been 20 but you still knew the names of all 152 Pokémon,*' wrote his good friend Jamie Ison. Jack, who loved to play with the double bluff of false immodesty, had his own highly positive view of himself: '*I know I'm good because I have good taste, and I like myself.*'

Jack was hard to tell off. He would own his part in any trouble, apologise and offer no passive aggression, shame or indignation. Deb and I were away one night, leaving 17-year-old Rosie in charge of the home. Jack managed to convince Rose that it would be fine if some of his mates came around for the evening. Events soon slid out of his control, and the thing turned into a full-on party. He cleared away the breakages, but Debbie knew exactly what had gone on as soon as she stepped through the door. She hit the roof, tearing into him for his dishonesty and recklessness. When she finally finished shouting, Jack replied that he'd wished he'd never thrown the party as he had been in a state of high anxiety throughout the entire event. On another occasion, he and his mates dropped a hot coal from a hookah which burnt straight though some new vinyl floor. Once again, his mum hit the roof. Jack gave a calm apology and added, '*I knew you'd go ballistic Deb, but you've excelled yourself this time.*' She had. That pretty well closed the matter. Another time, in a standard event of adolescent thoughtlessness, Jack had failed to do something he should have, or done something he really shouldn't: I forget the detail. For some reason I really lost my temper with him, and ranted on for longer than necessary, shouting '*Get your fucking act together Jack!* He stayed calm. '*Sure enough I did wrong Dave, but there's no need for that.*' The moral high ground crumbled beneath my feet. '*You're probably right,*' I heard myself say.

David, his head of year at University, summoned Jack to his office for not turning up for a lecture or two. Jack offered no excuse, but instead said he couldn't help noticing that while David had chosen to reprimand one of his most active course participants, he had left unsanctioned the lazy many who always turn up and always contribute nothing. Knowing Jack had found his precise weak point, David just had to laugh, and the carpeting disintegrated into farce.

As soon as he could walk, Jack took against the activity. Its most abstracted form, the all-day circular hike, appalled him ('*All that effort to end up where you started,*' he tutted). It was plain to Jack that mechanised transport had made walking obsolete. His university friend Lizzie complained that Jack once made her catch a bus for just one stop. Lizzie had little option; once Jack had made up his mind about something or someone, there was scant reward for any attempt to shift his opinion. There was this kid lived down our street who was, by most people's standards, annoying. Essentially OK,

Jason had little sense of the privacy of others, and was untrustworthy at times. '*I don't like him,*' said Jack flatly. I found myself pleading for the defence: '*You've got to realise,*' I said, '*Jason's had a tough time. His dad left him and his mum's with this bloke who -*' '*I'm not really looking for explanations,*' Jack interrupted, '*I just don't like him.*' I gave up. Despite, or even because of this implacability, Jack could be extremely patient with those he did like. Dan, another lad landed with an unsolicited new dad, would often drift around our place, say or do almost nothing, and not leave for some hours. I guess he was lonely or unhappy or both. Jack felt put-upon ('*Dan's here again,*' he'd complain), but he never treated him unkindly, and as the years passed Dan turned into far more confident and comfortable company. Jack had a few friends, but he was sympathetic enough to become Dan's only friend. The most important thing about Jack, and perhaps any of us, is that he was kind: '*You were always so happy and friendly and would do anything for anybody. I'll never forget that,*' was fellow student Ashton's tribute. '*You were without a doubt the best one of us,*' wrote Clare, a girl who lived in the same university block as Jack.

A little after midnight on 3ʳᵈ December 2009, Jack and his flatmates Ross and James left a student party on the Via Roma in central Palermo. They stepped out onto a zebra crossing just as a speeding motorist was overtaking another oncoming car. Ross made it to the other side, James pulled back and Jack, halfway across, was hit full-on. His fellow student Holly wrote: '*You will remain one of the funniest, most charming people I have ever had the pleasure to know and your absence will be immense. Never change.*'

Grief

Date: Fri, 28 Sep 2007
From: Jack.Marteau@student.manchester.ac.uk
To: davemarteau@hotmail.com

*Fresher's week has left my body feeling less like a temple and more like a
cess pit….*
Miss you guys a lot,
Love Jack xx

It is around two in the morning. Jack has just died. We stand outside the
hospital, gazing out into the night. Rain is falling steadily. Two ambulances
are docked at the bay to the Accident & Emergency department. Their blue
lights are on, and as they flash into the darkness they pick out individual
drops of rain, making freezeframes of suspended sapphires, human distress
crystallised. '*I suppose that's the image we'll always remember,*' says Rosie.
Blue is the deepest colour. And the coldest.

Jack's friend Eveline is at the hospital. She has an old-school camcorder and
has recently been filming fellow students, including Jack. She gives us a USB
stick of six videos. Back home we play the clips on a laptop. We hadn't seen
Jack in three months, but here he is just three days before the accident,
joking around, large as life. He's easy and funny, the effortless centre of
every scene. He radiates happiness. At one point he takes over the camcorder
from Eveline and asks her to say something. '*Hi mum,*' waves Eveline, '*I love
you!* Jack turns the camera on himself and looks straight into the lens. '*I
love you too mum,*' he says. His voice is unsentimental. He's stating a fact.
He is certain Deb will never see the clip. I turn to Deb. Jack's words have
left her stunned, almost concussed. It's too much. But in time she will
treasure this message.

In the days that followed Jack's death I felt like one of those Old Testament
characters who wake to find they have been struck blind. The world had

12

gone dark black. I could see, but my brain was so submersed in sorrow it had no capacity to process or organise visual information. I could see that there was a door to the room I was sitting in, but the four walls that made up that space were indistinct. To leave the room I had to feel my way, touching the wall, not so much for support, more to locate exactly where the wall stood and find where it met the doorway.

My gaze would settle on anything that lay between me and the horizon. I was indifferent to the object; it might be the TV, a tree, a picture on a wall or a boat on the sea. My eyes were open, so objects occupied my visual field, but I had no use for the images that reached the back of my brain. They hung there unattended, like a film playing in an empty cinema.

Closed to the external world, my mind turned in on itself, registering all its suffering and calculating how much more pain it could take. At one point I realised that I had been staring at a light switch for more than quarter of an hour. I was prepared to keep gazing at it indefinitely. There was nothing interesting about the switch, but I kept looking at it anyway. I could do this because the switch had changed in its physical make-up. It was still real but had lost its solidity. It was both there and not there. I was in a dreamworld, a baddreamworld.

Looking into Debbie and Rosie's eyes I could see levels of pain I'd never seen before. They were tormented. In what the poet Michael Rosen calls 'those first, worst days' we clung to each other like orphans, moving from one room to another together, fearing that if one of us were left out of sight, they might, like Jack, simply vanish. A thought settled in my mind: if four of you decide never to leave a room, one day that room will be empty. One by one, all of you must go; it's only a matter of time. I'm amazed and grateful I'd not had this thought earlier in my life.

It's likely there's no pain greater than the pain of losing someone you have always loved. It is absolute. This is an imperfect world; we look for perfection while knowing that it's a fool's errand. The perfect job, perfect

13

partner, perfect holiday destination, perfect home. Yet suddenly here it was: perfection. Free of all impurity, distilled to its absolute essence, 100 per cent perfect pain. It had an almost beautiful simplicity. Agony, unadulterated, unlimited, remorseless, inescapable.

Waking up each morning, I imagined I knew how victims of torture felt: I'm conscious, so I'm in agony, again. Except, unlike the imprisoned torture victim, I could escape. I could stop all the pain in its tracks by simply quitting this world. At times during the day I would picture lifting a gun, putting its heavy barrel to the roof of my mouth and pulling the trigger. Like my sister Elizabeth, I wouldn't have to suffer any longer. In truth, it was only a consoling fantasy. I didn't even know where to get a gun; I'm not from Texas. Yet I wanted to die. The future stretched out in front of me like an endless pan-flat desert. Before Jack died I had worried that my time was running away. I had turned 50 and the months seemed to be flashing past in a blur of work and weekends. Seasons and even years seemed to be tumbling by. If I wasn't careful, it would all be over very soon. Time just kept accelerating.

And then it stopped. Suddenly I was adrift on an ocean of time. I could sense the grinding progress of each second. One hour lasted a day. I could no longer rely on time to turn the clock; it would be down to me to move from one moment to the next. I realised that I would have to walk through the limitless weeks and months that were to comprise the rest of my life.

But time had leapt as well as stopped: over the course of only a few weeks Debbie and I felt ten years older. We hadn't aged physically, but in ourselves, our core, we had been fast-forwarded a decade. People who were our seniors by some years suddenly seemed younger than us, less knowing. By the same token, our former selves were gone forever. We were always a jokey family, poking fun at the world and each other. With Jack's death, a crevasse had opened between people we had been and our new selves. The former us were left stranded on the opposite edge of a great divide, lifeless as waxworks.

14

I'd always known what I wanted to do: get a job, buy a motorbike, leave home, rent a flat, find a girl, go to America. Now I didn't have a clue. Every day, every hour, I was muttering to myself, '*What am I going to do next? What am I going to do next?*' I had no answer. I was lost. I knew I couldn't remain where I was: I was in too much pain. But I couldn't think of a move to make. Standing barefoot on hot coals, I hadn't the wit to jump out the fire. I'd lost the instinct to live.

Jack was dead, and with him part of me had died. In addition to Jack, I was mourning the loss of a former unbroken self. I imagined that this was how someone who is suddenly wheelchair-bound must feel. Except it was my heart, not my spinal cord, damaged beyond repair. For the rest of my life I would be emotionally disabled: I was never going to get over this; Jack was never coming back; my heart was never going to mend. In the days that followed Jack's death I could feel the damage there, a burrowing pain in the middle of my chest. Debbie's heart hurt so much that at moments she would stop breathing. We were experiencing what is known as broken heart syndrome. Extreme grief weakens the heart's muscle, causing one of its chambers to swell out of shape. This gives the sufferer the sensation of mild heart attack. Broken heart syndrome is the body's way of protecting itself, stretching the heart so that the tidal wave of adrenaline that grief launches does not stop it beating. The heart breaks so that its owner doesn't die.

In those first black days I would weep and then stop, stare off into space, start to prepare some food, then weep again. At one point I caught myself in the mirror. My face red and wet with tears. I was appalled. I looked pathetic.

The mayor's office in Palermo could give us no firm date when Jack's body would be released for repatriation. There would have to be a post mortem and, as Jack had been hit by a speeding motorist on a zebra crossing, there was the possibility of a manslaughter charge. Cramped into a tiny hotel room, desperate and at the limit of endurable pain, Rosie, Debbie and I couldn't face even the briefest interaction with people back home. In the meantime, I had Consular officials, lawyers, hospital managers, flight companies and funeral directors to deal with. Rather than call me again, I asked my mum and dad to wait until they heard from me. I told them I would be in touch as soon as I had Jack's body back home and we had a date set for his funeral. For reasons that are still unclear to me, my dad was unable to comply with my request, and after 72 hours he sent me an email urging me to hurry up with arrangements. It was punctuated with censorious exclamation marks, finding fault with the way I was handling the death of my only son. His words stabbed at my heart. Livid, I phoned him up and unleashed a torrent of fury. I told him he and mum were not to contact me again, but I would let him know when the funeral was set. It took another week to get a date and I kept my word, but I resented them for making me feel worse at the lowest point of my life.

I was polite to them at the funeral – I was so dazed that day I was inoculated against any emotion, even grief – but the next morning my pain and anger towards them came scorching back. Maddened by grief, I felt like setting fire to their house. We met for a coffee after three months. They offered apologies for the email, but I think they were bemused by how badly Debbie and I had taken it. I figured that if they couldn't see that they'd done much wrong, they were highly likely to blunder into some other thoughtless act. It was nothing personal, but Debbie and I were teetering on the edge of despair. As things stood, we both wanted to die, and I felt that any further hurtful acts might tip us into suicide. I listened to the apologies but experienced both my parents as a danger. I couldn't bear to stay in their company and left the café.

It sounds crazy, but I blamed Adolf Hitler for the row; Piet had been so traumatised by his experience of fighting in the second world war that anyone dead had to be disposed of as quickly as possible. Or perhaps Jack's death had stirred too many banished feelings around my sister Elizabeth's death. Either way, Piet's instinct to control his offspring rebounded so badly that our relationship was all but destroyed. I was very close to permanently quitting the Marteau family. I stayed out of contact for two years. Piet and I were reconciled before his death, but something had been damaged that we could never really repair: trust.

Jack's death had exploded our lives and there were others caught up in the blast. Two long-standing friendships ended. We had received kindness where we'd least expected it, from people we hadn't known particularly long or well; but we found to our confusion and dismay that some old friends weren't moved to help us very much at all. We reasoned that if a friend couldn't give you a hand when you most need it, the relationship had failed a fundamental stress-test. We stopped all communication with them, and if they persisted in getting in touch, we simply told them we never wanted to see them again. They were deeply hurt, but we didn't care. We couldn't like them anymore, so we couldn't be friends anymore. Such is the logic of grief. I feel neither good nor bad about this. I'd imagined that grief would change me as a person, but I hadn't thought it would make me worse. People talk about 'growing spiritually' after facing up to tragedy, but spiritual shrinkage seemed to be my fate. Interest rates can go down as well as up.

We held Jack's funeral on 21st December. Fitting that we honoured his short life on the shortest day. Christmas Day came and went. We had a sandwich I think.

Four days into the New Year Debbie and I drove through a near blizzard to Cornwall. We had rented the only house in an isolated cove, right by the ocean. More snow fell, and we were trapped, just the two of us and the foaming sea. Temperatures were at their lowest for twenty years. It felt about right. Every evening we would battle halfway up the steep icy track that served the cove, to catch a mobile signal and phone Rosie. '*Are you OK?*

Yes, we're OK.' None of us were OK, but the words were immaterial. It was contact.

After we got back to Dorset there was nothing for it – I had to go back to work. The work itself didn't daunt me, but I dreaded having to mix with so many people who would have no insight into my emotional state. I was right to be uneasy; within two hours of my return one colleague, Phil, told me that he was finding my talk of grief depressing. I solved this in part by (a) never troubling myself to speak to Phil again; and (b) spending most of the day in the deserted basement, from where I could still make calls and send emails.

A survey by the stillbirth and neonatal death (SANDS) charity found that nearly half of 2,700 people reported that no one talked to them about the death of their baby when they returned to work. My experience was very close to this, but my loss was acknowledged by a handful of kind workmates. To physically express their sympathy two colleagues actually hugged me: Eamonn, an Irishman, and Kamlesh, an English Asian. My entire being drank in their sympathy. The Anglo Saxons didn't touch me. Not that they were all unfeeling; Mike Trace, someone I rarely saw eye-to-eye with, went out of his way to offer words of kindness.

For the next two years I acted as a living cliché, burying myself in work. I dived deep into it, like some obsessive submariner, but as soon as I resurfaced, the sorrows of loss would crowd in on me. Being at home was becoming less bearable for Debbie and me, and unbearable for Rosie; she couldn't bring herself to come there and so we had to meet her on common ground, usually her Auntie Denny's. By springtime Deb and I decided enough was enough, and out of instinct and desperation we bought a two-room tent, a gas stove and some pots, and drove off to Cornwall to live by the beach. We'd return to Dorset for a bit, then head off for the coast again: Devon or Norfolk, wherever the map showed a big sandy bay. We kept mainly to ourselves, living like emotional refugees. I'd commute from the tent to wherever I had to get to for work. Being by the sea soothed us. We shed our tears and absorbed our seismic waves of grief without going under. The tent was a fitting home for two people beset by a storm – a canvas-thin barricade against roaring winds and freezing night air. A shelter as temporary and vulnerable as existence itself.

It's August 2010 and we drive with Rosie to Brecon. The weather's unreliable, but we set off anyway to walk up one of the peaks. As we approach the summit the clouds come down, shrinking visibility to a couple of meters. We are on a narrow ridge with a steep escarpment - a lethal drop - immediately to our right. The fog thickens, and both the huge drop and the way ahead vanish from sight. We are in danger. '*We need to stop,*' I say. Panic grows in me that only nine months after Jack's death, a second family disaster is about to strike. Rosie is unfazed. She's a rock-climber and an experienced sky-diver, and easy with risk. Debbie, on the other hand, has a lifelong dread of heights. She can't bring herself to look down from a third-storey window. But today, raging with grief, she embraces altitude. '*This is great!*' she laughs, walking on into the invisible. Tormented and amused, she goads the grim reaper: '*With any luck, we'll die.*' The cloud lifts for just a moment, revealing the horrible precipice beside us, and then all is white mist again. Debbie, indifferent, strides on. Even Rosie is moving more cautiously than her mum. Finally, we make safer ground. I'm furious with Deb for having put herself in jeopardy. '*Anything could have happened!*' I rant. '*Good. I wish it had. Why should I care if I live or die?*' I can't offer an answer. The matchless grief of a mother gives her the right to Russian roulette.

A new life is marked by a clutch of anniversaries: first tooth, first smile, first word, first steps, first haircut, first birthday. Equally, with a new death comes a sequence of milestones, each a sickening appointment with pain: first birthday after death, first Christmas, first anniversary of being last seen alive. Some of these dates fall so close they merge and entwine into a poisoned arbour, a gauntlet that every bereft parent must force themselves through every year. Horror began to build as we approached each first anniversary: 13th September marked the day we'd said goodbye to Jack at the airport, the 16th September was Jack's birthday. By now we'd packed the tent away for the year and moved back home. In a panic, we drove off to South Wales. It was the weekend and all but the most depressing places were booked up. We drove around Glamorgan for hours, in search of a room, fuelled by our own frenzied disturbance. In the end we pointed the car home, getting back around midnight. We were bleak and distraught. More anniversaries followed. 30th October was Debbie's birthday and one year, to the day, from her last phone conversation with Jack. December 5th was the day his life support was switched off, the 21st marked the anniversary of his funeral. Christmas, Jack's absolute favourite day, was horrible. I don't drink, so to escape all the ghosts of Christmas past, I downed several cups of high-octane Javan coffee for breakfast. I felt no different, just more nauseated.

January, usually a depressing month, arrived like a life raft, and to this day it stands as my favourite month of year. I spend it and the rest of the new year reading any and every book I can find on death. I'm desperate to know how others, across the years, have coped with grief.

Grief over the Centuries

Top 5 Movies of All Time: Citizen Kane (1941)
I'm looking into making a sequel called Citizen Dane about '90s heartthrob Dane Bowers, but thus far I've only been told that I'm 'out of my mind'.

Jack Marteau, Student Direct Magazine 2008

On September 15th 1833, a young man called Arthur died suddenly from a stroke while on a touring holiday with his father. He was 22. Arthur's death was the spark for one of the most significant pieces of English art of the 19th Century, *In Memoriam A.H.H.,* a poem by Alfred Tennyson. It ensured that the name Arthur Henry Hallam would live on for two centuries or more.

Tennyson and Arthur Hallam became friends at University. Everyone loved Arthur. He had some magic about him. Gladstone, who was at school with him said, *'Arthur Henry Hallam was a spirit so exceptional that...he resembled a passing emanation from some other and less darkly chequered world.'* When Tennyson's sister Emily met Arthur she quickly fell in love, and they had become engaged by the time Arthur set off on his fateful holiday. Arthur's death pulverised the Tennysons and moved Alfred to write *In Memorium.* It's a 160-page investigation of loss and sorrow, the high-water mark of the Victorian obsession with death. At times it's impossible to fathom, like a 5,000-piece jigsaw of blurred colours and forms, but its emotion is simple to follow. Right from the first line we can see that Tennyson is going to give death a thorough going over. He tells the *'Son of God'* that He (the Son of God) created us all, but Tennyson can't help noticing where Jesus was resting his foot:

> *Thou madest Death; and lo, thy foot*
> *Is on the skull which thou hast made.*

We're off to a flying gothic start.

Tennyson sees three personalities involved in Arthur's early death, Nature, God and Death. Of the three, Tennyson seems to be angriest with Nature, who he pictures as a heartless female untroubled by the ending of any life. He imagines her saying, '*I care for nothing. All must go*'. Death then steps in to do the dirty work. As far as Tennyson is concerned, this lets God off the hook; Nature and Death are to blame for tragedies like Arthur Hallam's. Although Tennyson believes that God created Death, Death seems to have gone freelance, and is, unfortunately, very hard-working. As a nervous defence, Tennyson chooses to believe that we are basically tiny fragments ('*broken lights*') of the Creator, and so we'll probably be OK when our last days come. He's not too worried about that: he's just broken-hearted that Arthur is gone:

> *Beneath all fancied hopes and fears*
> *Ay me, the sorrow deepens down.*

At one point, Tennyson is so bereft that he leaves his own body:

> *And circle moaning in the air:*
> *'Is this the end? Is this the end?'*

Tennyson's not an idiot; he knows that people will think that he's indulging himself by going on and on about his own misery while so many others face massive problems in the world. He even wonders if he is guilty of '*half a sin*' for writing the poem in the first place. If there is half a sin, it's not that there's too much emotion in the poem (although there is a metric tonne of it) or that it's too long (it is). No, if there is a fault with *In Memoriam AHH*, it's that Tennyson stows away something as messy and hollow as grief so neatly in the final verse by saying that Arthur is now with God,

> *That God, which ever lives and loves,*
> *One God, one law, one element*

It's nice to believe, but can the believer believe completely, all the time, especially when tragedy leaves them in desolation? And what comfort is this for the unbeliever?

Fairly late in the poem Tennyson mentions a mysterious experience he had when standing alone in a garden at night. He believes he hears Arthur's voice and feels his presence:

> And all at once it seem'd at last
> The living soul was flash'd on mine

Tennyson feels that Arthur takes him out of his own body, and they travel together until they,

> came on that which is, and caught
> The deep pulsations of the world

It was brave of Tennyson to put this in, giving readers the chance to mark him down as a crank as well as a wimp. He doesn't say what '*that which is*' actually is. He says that he doesn't have the words for it, which is fair enough but frankly disappointing from a professional poet. But he does have a stab at it twenty years later, when he writes about this and other strange experiences he'd had in his life:

> *individuality itself seemed to resolve and fade away into boundless being, and this not a confused state, but the clearest of the clearest, the surest of the surest, utterly beyond words, where death was an almost laughable impossibility, the loss of personality (if so it were) seeming no extinction, but the only true life*

But if the personality does melt away, how does Tennyson think that Arthur could get in touch with him from beyond the grave? He provides an explanation in the poem, saying that when Arthur died, he merged again with '*the general Soul*,' but this general or eternal soul can re-divide itself at any time it likes, leaving Tennyson confident that Arthur can show up, and '*I shall know him when we meet*'. I hope he did. But of all the words of comfort or insights than can be drawn from this gothic skyscraper of a poem, two short and bitter-sweet lines have taken on a life of their own:

> *Tis better to have loved and lost*
> *Than never to have loved at all.*

23

In 1999 the poet Michael Rosen's son Eddie went to bed a vigorous young man but died in the night from acute meningitis. Powerless to do anything, Rosen did the thing he could; he wrote poetry. He recalled bringing Eddie back home from the mortuary following post-mortem:

> *It wasn't a good idea to leave him in the morgue.*
> *He came back to the house and people went in to see him.*

Rosen remembers a telling sign Eddie had gone upstairs and never came back down

> *His shoes were where he left them.*

With the next and final line, Rosen reveals the continuing present tense of grief

> *His shoes are where he left them.*

Following the sudden death of her son Jacob, the English writer Denise Riley published the poem *A Part Song* in 2012.
In her heartbreak, Denise takes her anger inward, calling herself:

> *A fat-lot-of-good mother with a pointless alibi:*
> *I didn't know*

She didn't know Jacob had a heart condition. She couldn't know. Nobody knew, including Jacob. Still, Denise feels that in a genuine way she has now failed as a parent:

> *What is the first duty of a mother to a child?*
> *At least to keep the wretched thing alive?'*

Tortured by grief, Denise takes herself to the edge of a high cliff, watching seabirds dive into the creased waters below. She has only to jump and all her pain is at an end. She resists the urge, mainly to spare her daughters further suffering, but also because she fears that as punishment for her suicide, she and Jacob might be kept apart for eternity,

One crying, Where are you my child
The other calling Mother

In another poem, *A Gramophone on the Subject*, Denise shuts out to those who avoided her after Jacob's death, '*It isn't catching, you know*'. We can't catch it; we're born with it. Death is congenital. But Denise's experience chimes with mine – people avoided me like the plague because at an unconscious level they feared I might just have the plague. In a primeval sense both Denise and I are wrong, and almost everyone else is right: Death can be catching.

Two weeks after Jacob has died Denise is barely able to write, but she does manage to put down this brief note:

> *You sense that a part of you, too, died instantly. At the same time, you feel that the spirit of the child has leaped into you. So you are both partly dead, and yet more alive. You are cut down, and yet you burn with life.*

In this electrified state, generated by the shock of tragedy, Denise loses sense of time. She is, she says, '*pulled right outside of time*'. In the grip of grief, she is no longer certain the sun will rise tomorrow. She finds herself in a timeless, empty world, '*wandering around in an endless plain.*'

The earliest insights into grief and the English come from the fireside folk tales they used to tell one another. One of the first features an old widow who, knowing the route that grief must take, is overwhelmed at the funeral of Beowulf:

> *Wailing her woe, the widow old...*
> *sung in her sorrow, and said full oft*
> *she dreaded the doleful days to come*

Although we can picture the widow's pain, we can also imagine she survived the '*doleful days*' that followed Beowulf's death. A thousand years on, we get a real-life account of a woman so devastated by grief that it becomes the death of her. In 1714, Roger Wrightson and Martha Railton from Bowes in Yorkshire were young and in love, due to be married. Roger then fell seriously ill. For much of what happened next, we must turn to a ballad, written by their former schoolmaster.

According to the song, Roger's family prevent Martha from spending time alone with her fiancé as he lay dying. Roger's sister Hannah is portrayed as particularly hostile. So Martha is at home when she hears the death bell ring for Roger. She collapses. Her mother and a local man, Thomas Petty, try to calm and revive her, but Martha knows that her life is ebbing away:

> *My heart is burst,*
> *My span of life is near an end;*
> *My love from me by death is forced,*
> *My grief no soul can comprehend.*

Martha lives for another twelve hours, but,

> *Then her poor heart being sadly broke,*
> *Submitted to the fatal stroke.*

Neighbours and friends want Roger and Martha to share a grave, but Roger's sister Hannah, swearing worse than a fish-wife ('*In words not fit for Billingsgate*'), won't agree. True love, however, conquers all, and Roger and Martha are buried together in Bowes church, where they lie to this day. The church register bears this entry:

> *Roger Wrightson, Jun., and Martha Railton, both of Bowes, Buried in one grave: He Died in a Fever, and upon tolling his passing Bell, she cry'd out My heart is broke, and in a Few hours expir'd, purely (or supposed) thro' Love.*

Death from a broken heart isn't some romantic fantasy: in 2014 Iain Carey and Sunil Shah of the University of London discovered that in the month that follows their bereavement, people who lose a partner are twice as likely to suffer a heart attack or stroke than other members of the public of the same age.

The writer Patrick Harpur sums up the physical assault of grief:

> *We lose parts of ourselves, our physical selves, when we are bereaved: 'I'm all in pieces...gutted...my heart has been ripped out...it's surreal...like a terrible dream.... I seem to be in another world'.*

Chaucer gives us a clear sense that grief was every mile as deep to the people of the 14th Century. One of his characters, a knight, is in total despair at the loss of his love. Even surviving for half a day is too tall an order. He just wants to be dead:

> *Nothing can make my sorrows slide away...Woe is me that I should live even another twelve hours!*

But for all the Knight's tortured suffering, Chaucer is certain that no grief can be deeper than that of a mother who loses a child. Quoting the Roman poet Ovid, Chaucer writes: '*He is a fool that disturbeth the mother to weep at the death of her child, till she has wept her fill'*.

In her poem *Remembrance*, Emily Bronte visits the grave of her childhood sweetheart, who has been dead 15 years. She tells him that even after all this time, thinking of his dying for too long will cause her to give up on life:

> *And even yet I dare not let it languish,*
> *Dare not indulge in Memory's rapturous pain;*
> *Once drinking deep of that divinest anguish,*
> *How could I seek the empty world again?*

Emily didn't have to suffer anguish much longer: she died two years after the poem was published.

Grief can well up in an instant, triggered by a sight, a random memory, an old song, or by apparently no cause at all. It breaks over the bereaved and for a while loss is all there is. Eventually, that attack of grief passes its peak and draws back, allowing the everyday world to reappear. Echoing a similar observation by C S Lewis, the writer Vicki Harrison says, '*Grief is like the ocean, it comes in waves, ebbing and flowing.*' But as Lewis knew, whether grief comes or goes, it cannot alter the plain fact of loss: '*So many roads once; now so many culs de sac.*' Death builds dead ends.

With its combined toll of sorrow, pain and despair, grief is like the deepest depression, with one surprising exception: while the truly depressed person never laughs, the bereaved's sense of humour remains intact. I'll give a personal example: my sweet sister Elizabeth took her own life by jumping from a cliff. On the day we got the terrible news, neighbours from two doors down knocked at my parents' door to offer condolences. This couple had never had any conversation with my mum and dad that went further than, '*Nice day again,*' or '*Cold for the time of year*', but they were very keen to come in. They sat on the sofa while we sat looking at our hands, our feet, the floor. No-one had a word to say. What was there to say? Time crawled on, and still the neighbours sat there, uninvited and all but invisible to us. Eventually, the husband, Mr Neighbour, could contain himself no longer: '*So, she just flung herself off, did she?*', he asked, with sham casualness, as if referring to a third type of weather. This cack-handed attempt to conceal naked prurience was, to me, hilarious black-humour theatre. Convulsed by suppressed laughter, I could just about stagger out the room.

There's black humour aplenty when poet Michael Rosen's next-door London neighbour Rob offers him micro-sympathy and crass small talk following the death of his second son Eddie:

> – *Rather you than me, he said.*
> *We went on standing*
> – *And best of luck Saturday, he said.*

I thought, but the funeral isn't on Sunday
– And, he said, Arsenal playing Spurs.

On 14ᵗʰ December 1861 Queen Victoria's husband Albert died suddenly at the age of 42. On that day began a period of widow's grieving so protracted that even the Victorians considered it over the top. Talking about herself in the third person 15 months after Albert's death, Victoria said, '*She can only hope never to live to old age but be allowed to re-join her beloved great and loyal husband before many years elapse.*' She was out of luck, as she lived for another 38 years, dressing in black every morning until her last.

Victoria seemed to lose all interest in her regal duties. It wasn't until October 1863, two years after her husband's death, that Victoria felt able to make a first public appearance, and that was to unveil a statue of Albert. By 1867 the public were becoming impatient: she was booed on her way to the State Opening of Parliament. There were calls from politicians and trade unionists for the Queen to be removed from the throne, and numerous republican clubs were established around the country. By 1871, Victoria's own children began to worry that their mother's neglectful attitude would finish the monarchy. Vicky junior, her eldest daughter, wrote a letter to her mum which her siblings co-signed, telling the Queen '*something must be done…to avert a frightful calamity.*' Events overtook them all, as later that year Prince Edward picked up typhoid and almost died. His near-miss brought the royal family back into England's good books.

The people's loss of patience with Victoria was unsurprising; the English could put up with a year or two of dysfunction from their bereaved queen, but six years felt like self-indulgence. Some of these attitudes no doubt sprung from straight-up envy (the queen had several palaces while the poorest lived several to a room and had to put their children to work down mines or up chimneys), but there was also residual sentiment from a century or three before when, as the writer Clare Gittings points out, excessive grief was considered to be an insult to God, since it was God's will that everyone must die. To complain about the burden of your suffering, to allow yourself to fall into deep despair over the death of a loved one, was close to blasphemy. The 18th century preacher Zachary Taylor, for instance, warned against excessive grieving in a sermon titled *The Decency and Moderation of Christian Mourning*. There was also the great worry, common in Tudor times, that excessive grief might lead to insanity. Young Lucius in Shakespeare's super-brutal *Titus Andronicus* says that his granddad had often warned him that, *'extremity of griefs would make men mad.'* In *Hamlet*, Ophelia loses her mind when her dad dies, and ends up drowned; King Lear goes completely mad when he learns that his one likeable daughter has died.

Shakespeare learnt first-hand about tragedy when his only son, Hamnet, died aged eleven. In that same year, 1596, he wrote *King John*, a play that contains some of the most painful insights into grief in the English language. One of its central characters, Constance, is in utter despair at losing a son:

> *…O Lord! my boy, my Arthur, my fair son!*
> *My life, my joy, my food, my all the world!*

She is so beside herself with anguish that she pulls out handfuls of her hair and calls on death to come and take her. Two men, Cardinal Pandulph and King Philip, shocked and perhaps embarrassed by this show of raw emotion, try to close her down. The Cardinal, believing it would be of help, tells Constance she is losing her mind:

> *Lady, you utter madness, and not sorrow.*

King Philip makes an equally clumsy attempt. He somehow calculates that the best way to help Constance is to have a go at her: *'You are as fond of grief as of your child.'* Constance puts the blundering buffoons straight:

> *Grief fills the room up of my absent child,*
> *Lies in his bed, walks up and down with me,*
> *Puts on his pretty looks, repeats his words,*

> *Remembers me of all his gracious parts,*
> *Stuffs out his vacant garments with his form*

In looking down on his empty bed and 'vacant' clothes, Constance's (and/or Shakespeare's) grief is so vivid it almost makes Arthur/Hamnet materialise.

There have long been limits to male grief in England. Shakespeare gives us a clue as to how much emotion Tudor men were permitted to show in the face of loss when, in *Anthony & Cleopatra*, two of the characters gossip about Anthony's tendency to be a bit of a cry baby.

Agrippa:
> *When Antony found Julius Caesar dead,*
> *He cried almost to roaring;*
> *and he wept*
> *When at Philippi he found Brutus slain.*

His colleague Enobarbus adds sarcastically that Anthony did seem to suffer from particularly watery eyes that year. But in an unguarded moment of honesty, Enobarbus admits that Anthony's wailing had set him off too.

The Stiff Upper Lip

Three Crowns 2-4 Tisbury Dynamites
Dynamites Complete the Triple Crown
Dynamites Rob the Crown Jewels
Dynamites Crowned Comeback Kings
Dynamites Win Match

The sun was blazing like Shaun Paul on the morning of Sunday February 4th, with the explosive baker's dozen of feisty young go-getters attempting to shake off three consecutive defeats, and climb out of what can only be dubbed 'Shit creek'.

Jack Marteau Tisbury Dynamites FC match report 2007

The English unwillingness to let their emotions flow is a relatively recent trait. Although they set limits, the Tudors were freer than the modern English at showing their sorrow, believing it was unhealthy and even dangerous to do otherwise. When MacDuff learns that his wife and children have been murdered, his friend Malcolm advises him to: '*Give sorrow words; the grief that does not speak whispers the o-er fraught heart and bids it break.*' Grief must be expressed. The Tudor poet Edmund Spenser, felt that those who hide and deny their grief risk doubling the pain they attempt to avoid:

> *He oft finds med'cine, who his grief imparts;*
> *But double griefs afflict concealing hearts,*
> *As raging flames who striveth to supress.*

Upon visiting London at the end of the 15th century, the Rotterdam scholar Erasmus was shocked by the frequency with which the English kissed each other. '*Wherever you move there is nothing but kisses,*' he wrote to the folks back home. The Tudors were as liberal with their tears. On 6th July 1535, the daughter and grandson of Thomas More arrived at the Tower of

London to witness his execution for treason. More's grandson described what happened next.

> *His best-loved child, my aunt Roper...ran hastily unto him, and without consideration or care for herself, passing through the midst of the throng and guard of men, who with bills and halberts compassed him around, there openly in the sight of them all embraced him, and not able to say any word but, 'Oh my father! Oh my father!'*

As he was being led away, she again threw her arms around More and sobbed,

> *whereat he spoke not a word, but carrying still his gravity, tears fell also from his eyes; yea, there were very few in all the troop who could refrain hereat from weeping, no, not the guard themselves.*

When, in March 1664, his brother Tom lay dying of TB, Samuel Pepys stayed beside him up until his last few moments but was too upset to be with him as he died. He left the room and came back fifteen minutes later to find Tom dead: *'a most sad sight, and that which put me into a present very great transport of grief and cries.'* That night, Pepys wrote, *'I lay close to my wife, being full of disorder and grief for my brother that I could not sleep nor wake with satisfaction.'* Pepys went to work the next day, *'but God knows my heart and head is so full of my brother's death, and the consequences of it, that I can do very little or understand it'*.

Pepys's diary suggests that Englishmen were relatively emotional in the 17th century. As well as crying when his brother died, news of his mother's death set Pepys *'a-weeping heartily.'* He wasn't alone in letting his feelings show. As he approached the funeral of a naval commander, Christopher Mings, Pepys tells us that, *'About a dozen able, lusty, proper men come to the coach-side with tears in their eyes.'* Pepys adds that he himself, *'could hardly abstain from weeping.'* Emotionality continued into the 18th century: the

33

novels of Laurence Sterne and – as we shall see – Henry Mackenzie are almost waterlogged with tears. Change came towards the end of the century, at the time of the French Revolution. Some argue that this was no coincidence: the blood-letting chaos in France caused alarm this side of the Channel, and the English, especially the richer ones, were terrified. Loss of reason and a primacy of passions were blamed for the havoc. Emotion had become undesirable, and high emotion positively dangerous. But it seems from letters written from France immediately after the Revolution by an Englishwoman, Helen Maria Williams, that our upper lips must have been thoroughly starched before the Bastille was stormed. Following a visit to the theatre, Helen wrote:

> *You will see Frenchmen bathed in tears at a tragedy. An Englishman has quite as much sensibility to a generous or tender sentiment; but he thinks it would be unmanly to weep; and, though half choked with emotion, he scorns to be overcome, contrives to gain the victory over his feelings, and throws into his countenance as much apathy as he can well wish.*

She added, '*We seem to have strange dread in England of indulging any kind of enthusiasm*'. But it would take until the second half of the 19th century for the stiff upper lip to assume supreme national authority.

The shift from Henry Mackenzie's tear-soaked tales to the self-repressed England of the late 19th century is evidenced by an 1888 edition of Mackenzie's 1771 sob-athon *The Man of Feeling*, whose hero, a Mr Harley, weeps buckets upon hearing successive melodramatic tales of woe: the death of a girl's fiancé from fever, an unmarried daughter losing her honour to a blackguard, a dog called Trusty dying of old age. To warn readers that they were about to enter a world of naked emotion, the book's Victorian editor inserted an *Index to Tears*, a listing of 38 separate incidents of weeping, bewailing and sobbing.

If it wasn't the French Revolution, what had caused such a huge shift in the national attitude to feelings? According to the writer John Raymond de Symons Honey, whose name suggests he'd been in a position to judge, it was the English public school. Honey argued that in order to produce citizens capable of building the British Empire, boarding schools needed to separate their pupils from their feelings, inoculating them against the paralysing effects of grief when their fellow soldiers were killed, and of pity and guilt for any peoples that imperialism was bound to conquer and supress. Eton, Harrow and the other major public schools began to emphasise the value of emotional restraint and fortitude, along the lines of the stoic philosophers of ancient Greece. Any display of upset was frowned upon and even punished. Incidents of overt emotion were stamped out like outbreaks of wild fires. Public schools became emotional decontamination units.

Open demonstrations of distress were also discouraged outside of elite schools. When in 1888 a Sergeant Holmes broke down when having to testify against a fellow officer at a fraud trial, his lack of restraint was ridiculed in a short story published in a satirical magazine of the day, *Funny Folks*. The tale, titled *Robert Emotional*, featured a policeman who breaks down in the witness box while giving evidence in the trial of a street beggar. When the beggar is handed a seven-day prison sentence, Robert *'goes into screaming hysterics'* and loses consciousness. The story ends with everyone in the court, presumably all good Englishmen and true, forming *'a tableau of disgust'*.

Darwin, a Victorian as much as he was a genius, regarded adult weeping as a perversion of what he theorised to be its true function, the safeguarding of babies' eyes during screaming fits, tears being forced out by the ocular muscles during hysterical infant outbursts. These tear drops would lubricate and bathe the child's eyeballs, protecting them from damage or infection. As soon as we leave infancy, we should, according to Darwin, grow out of crying. Adult weeping was, *'purposeless,'* said the great man, adding (perhaps in an unconscious reference to the true origin of the stiff upper lip) that, '*Savages weep copiously from very slight cause.*' And, to Darwin's supremely dry eyes, our fellow Europeans often let the side down: '*Englishmen rarely cry, except under the pressure of the acutest grief; whereas in some parts of the continent the men shed tears much more readily and freely.*'

The *Gentlemen's Book of Etiquette*, written in 1860 by Cecil B Hartley, utilising '*the best French, English and American authorities,*' gives man-to-man advice on how best to respond to someone recently bereaved.

> *If they speak of their departed relative, join them. Speak of the talents or virtues of the deceased, and your sympathy with their loss. If, on the other hand, they avoid the subject, then it is best for you to avoid it too. They may feel their inability to sustain a conversation upon the subject of their recent affliction, and it would then be cruel to force it upon them.*

Say nothing unless they do.

The cultural imperative to show no sorrow was tested most by the industrialised destruction of young English life in the First World War. One event in particular pushed national self-repression to the edge: on an October morning in 1915, the English nurse Edith Cavell was shot by a German firing squad for helping prisoners of war escape from Belgium. Back home there was outrage over Edith's execution and a fortnight of national grief ensued. At least one periodical, *The Academy*, was deeply affronted by this display of public sympathy:

> *The hysterical outburst which followed the execution of Miss Edith Cavell is one among many signs of the flabbiness of certain people's minds...that England should be kept rocking on its base, as it were, for a whole fortnight over such a tragedy is, in our opinion, to be deplored; and probably nobody would have been more startled or*

distressed by the public attitude in the matter than Miss Cavell herself, who...was a firm woman and insisted on the stiff upper lip.

The nation was told to stop snivelling and carry on.

World War One and the Spanish flu that followed killed one million British citizens. By 1920 we had seen enough of death to last several lifetimes. The upper lip was set rigid.

A 1926 etiquette manual, uncovered by historians Peter Jupp and Tony Walter, offers advice to the English on how best to deal with grief:

> *The ladies of a bereaved family should not see callers, even intimate friends unless they are able to control their grief.... solitude is often the greatest solace for grief.*

Is it? Grief had become, like lust or rage, a shameful emotion, a sickness that demands sufferers go into quarantine, less they contaminate the rest of us. If you're grieving, you're not functioning like a good modern citizen, not progressing. Why sit by a grave every weekend? You should widen your interests, make new friends.

This self and mutual emotional repression saw the country through the entirety of two world wars and deep into the rest of the 20th century. In February 1958, for instance, there was a brutal press reaction when stage actress Anna Neagle broke down during the live transmission of the biographical TV show *This is your Life*. Having been shown a clip of her great friend and fellow actor Jack Buchanan, who had died only four months earlier, Anna Neagle lowered her head and wept. The Daily Mail ranted:

> *Anna Neagle broke down in floods of tears the night before last during the BBC programme entitled This is Your Life. Of all the television programmes this is the most revolting. It was a non-stop exercise in embarrassment wrapped up in unbearable sentiment.*
> *It is about time this maudlin mush was broken up. Then they can all go and have a good cry - in private.*

Another national paper, the Daily Sketch, described the scene as '*shameful*,' declaring that the show, '*has nothing to do with decency, or with human dignity.*'

The first cracks in the dam appeared in the 1960s, when counter-cultural types started reading the works of R D Laing and decided that emotional repression had been driving the nation to mental instability. But it is the death of Diana in 1997 and the eruption of public grief that followed that did most damage to the stiff upper lip. As the flowers piled up and the tears multiplied outside Kensington Palace, I even felt a tear come into my eye, much to my own confusion, as I'd never met Diana and couldn't guess whether she was likeable or not. Suddenly, emotion's time had come again. Reality TV stars could break down because they had been on some sort of 'journey'; sportspeople were free to weep copiously when they won, when they lost, or when they couldn't do either because they had a bad foot.

And yet our new age of hugging and sobbing has proved a false dawn for grieving: no public figure has been mourned so overtly in the two decades that have passed since Diana's death, and other than at the graveside, the English still hardly ever shed tears of grief in public. Death remains best ignored in England. Before 1860 most deaths happened at home. Today fewer than one in four deaths occur there. We've cleared away the evidence of death; let's not blow it by getting all sorrowful in public places.

London Psychiatrist Colin Murray Parkes is worried that people these days grieve too little. He thinks that some of this is due to the idea that grief should come to a neat and timely end, with the sufferer reaching a kind of *closure*. He really doesn't like that word: '*It reflects a feeling that people ought to 'get over it'...you will allow people to open the box of grief for a while, but if they go on too long something's gone wrong and you've got to close it*'. As we've seen, it used to be believed that too much grieving drives us mad, but from his own research Colin is convinced that delayed or restricted grieving is worse for our mental health: '*almost the first thing a mother says to a child is 'stop crying'; we're taught from an early age to control our feeling. In point of fact, you're much more likely to have a nervous breakdown if you don't grieve than if you do.'* Colin, who has made bereavement his life's work, has a simple explanation for why we must suffer when someone dear to us dies. *'Grief,'* he says, *'is the price we pay for love.'*

And as we are about to see, there can be no greater love than a mother for her child.

Modern Grief

Julie

In November 2015, Julie Thomas lost her eldest son, Jonathan. She told me about the grief she has suffered:

Initially I could talk about Jonathan all the time, but now I find it far more painful. Jonathan was 34 when we lost him, our first-born son. Everybody's son is wonderful, aren't they?

A policeman knocked the door. I was on my own in the house. It was on a Sunday; we were having friends for Sunday lunch. They didn't actually say the words, I just guessed from the wording they used, what it was they'd come to tell me. They just kept saying that there'd been 'an incident'. I kept saying to them, 'What's he done? What's he done?' and they said, 'Well, there has been an incident.' And then they said, 'Are you on your own? Would you like to sit down?' Once they'd said that, I knew. And then I screamed, I screamed around the house. They then asked me did I want them to ring anybody to tell them. I said no, I would tell them myself. So I rang my husband, which was a really stupid thing to do, because he could have crashed the car, on the way back from the shops. And then I rang my two closest friends.

He always drank a little bit too much...I always thought it was to mask his insecurities...he was very highly thought of, but he had this wild streak. We lost him on the first of November [2015]. About sixteen months before he had met his latest girlfriend [Sid]. He really fell for her...he went to live with her in London. He came home for the weekend. He hadn't lived at home since he was 18...He went out to a nightclub in Swansea, he got into an altercation with a boy, he was very drunk...There was pushing and shoving and he turned to walk away from the boy, and as he walked away the boy punched him into the back of the head and severed his carotid artery so..[Julie takes a deep breath]..hopefully he died instantly. It's us that suffered. Are suffering. And I think we'll always suffer, won't we?

I don't think I believed it, and I don't know if I believe it now. I couldn't do anything, I could not do anything, I couldn't make a cup of tea. I couldn't do anything at all. And in those first few days I hardly slept; I hardly ate. I don't really think I cried a lot, but I had people with me all the time, and I drank a lot of wine…. I would have thought I'd have been permanently crying, but I wasn't. I was very numb. I was very numb in the first few days, I was very numb in the first few weeks. I think I'm still a bit numb now.

I asked Julie how others had responded to her grief.

I think I have realised now that sometimes I was let down because people can't deal with it. I think people were afraid to see me, because they didn't know how I would be, or how we would be, or how they would cope. I felt a couple of people let me down, and yet others really stepped up to the mark that you wouldn't have thought so. People's reactions are one of the biggest things; I think you learn so much about people. What I've noticed….is that nobody really wants to be around a miserable grieving person all the time, do they?

At first, the grief is nowhere near as intense. I remember one Compassionate Friends [the bereavement charity] leaflet saying that at times you're going to feel as if you're going out of your mind, and I remember thinking, 'No, I don't feel like that at all.' Well, within two weeks I knew exactly what it meant.

In first six months I read constant books about grief, mediums, dying. Constantly. I couldn't download enough onto my Kindle. I think you have intense, intense, intense; you can't describe the pain. In those early days they're with you constantly, they're in your thoughts constantly, but if I felt I wasn't grieving, if only for a minute or so, I felt so, so guilty. You can't allow yourself to laugh. I do laugh now. I feel I have to laugh, otherwise I

41

will go mad. I can't explain the pain we've been through and are going through and will go through.

I didn't go to see Jonathan in the mortuary, and I don't regret that either. Nicky [Jonathan's brother] sleeps in his bed. I slept it in it one night, and it was too distressing for me to walk past it. He's had all the clothes. It's helped Nicky, and it's helped me as well. Things like his iPad and his phone are in the drawer. I don't think I will ever be able to look at them again. At first I could look at his WhatsApp messages and I also have voice recordings and in those first few weeks I could listen to them. I could never do that now.

I was a very outgoing gregarious person before, and I think I've become even more outgoing now, if that makes sense. Obviously, we don't go to many places, but wherever we go, people are totally aware of our situation and have been wonderfully kind. I find it's a struggle sitting down of a night and watching television, as if nothing's happened. I can't do that. So, what I tend to do is surround myself with people, either here in the house with me, or I tend to go out, to be with people as much as I can. I said to my counsellor last time I went to counselling, the night before we'd had four friends around and we'd had a couple of bottles of wine and nibbles, and we'd had a bit of a laugh, and I said I felt terrible. You have a high, and then you plummet lower.

I've met people who have lost children, and they don't get out of bed for two years. That is not me. My grief I can tell you is unbearable. But to try to deal with it, I try to surround myself with people. That is my way. Jonathan's friends have set up the Jonathan Thomas Memorial Fund. We've raised an awful lot of money for charity and I've become part of that.

I asked Julie if she had been changed by Jonathan's death.

I have changed. For the first three months I didn't function at all, I didn't drive a car, I didn't do <u>anything</u>. I think for the first six months I was just a shell of myself. I did think after that I could feel myself getting a bit stronger, and I felt I've also got Nicky, and he couldn't cope with seeing me

42

like that, together with his own grief, so I feel from about six months on I got a bit stronger, I probably laughed a few more times, and I think I learned how to wear a mask. I have changed. I think my husband has changed more than me. He is having a terrible day today. I don't think I'll ever be the person I was.

I am far more sensitive. Although I surround myself with people, I feel very lonely...I feel very, very lonely at times, because one of the biggest things is watching people get on with their lives; and you want to tell them, 'Hang on a minute.'

Steve

In cases of incurable illness, grief can begin before death. Twenty-two years ago, Steve and Val Harrison were living a normal family life with their three young children, Lakshmi, Raph and Charissa. In the spring of 1996, Lakshmi began to feel ill. Steve, an NHS Specialist, recalls what followed:

She'd fainted at school, and it was unusual for her: she was a healthy kid. So there were little disconcerting things that wound up with us having an appointment for a chest X-ray.

She had her chest X-ray, and the lady in the X-Ray department, the radiographer or whatever, came back. She looked very shocked, and said, 'We need to have her in, her X-ray's not right.' She couldn't see her lung very clearly. So, she went through to the paediatric day unit and Val came up, and they said there's a lot of fluid on her lung and they wanted to drain it off. So they took her down, and I think they drained about a litre of fluid off her lung.

And then they were saying they wanted her to be transferred to Newcastle...we went to Newcastle and we saw some more doctors and I think they wanted to drain some more fluid off her lung and go for an x-ray. And then she went and said, 'Am I brave Dad?' or Daddy, something like that, and we kind of reassured her, and she went. The doctor who we saw came in twenty minutes later and was as white as a sheet. He said, 'Something's gone wrong; I've got some bad news.' And I felt me knees...I remember just the lower halves of me legs just ceased to hold me up. And they were saying whilst they were draining the fluid from her lung, she went into an arrest. They started to resuscitate her – doing CPR – but it wasn't working, and then they did an internal: squeezed the heart from the inside. And he said words to the effect, 'It didn't feel like a normal heart.' That was when he figured out that it had tumour around it. They got her heart going again, but there'd been a big lapse, so there was a big risk of brain damage.

We were just in some kind of void, I think, trying to make sense of it; just reeling from it and clinging to each other. One thing we noticed during those days was that our senses were so much sharper, and I was on edge with everything. I remember being in a little coffee shop with Val, and there was a couple having a conversation a long way away, and I could hear it as clear as if they were next to us. I just remember me and Val clinging to each other in this tiny bed. I think we stayed for the night. Over the weekend it became clear that when she woke up, she was in – a 'lovely' phrase – a 'vegetative state'.

Once, she would wake up, but she couldn't speak; it was hard to say whether she could hear or not. She couldn't move very easily; she certainly had no coordination or anything. I guess we started to have conversations about what we were going to do about the cancer. I don't think we thought too long about, 'Well, if we put her through a lot of punitive chemotherapy and radiotherapy, what would she be like at the end of that? And what would she have had to go through to get to the end of that?' So I think we figured out fairly quickly that this was about trying to make a good end for her, rather than prolonging...

Steve doesn't compete the sentence.

We were living from minute to minute. Life got stripped away: work just went somewhere else, any arrangements or plans went somewhere else, we spoke to only people we needed to let know. We came home and told Raph and Charissa, which was a big, a big moment for us. We tried to tell it in as simple, as succinct way and as straightforward a way as possible, and we needed to tell them the hard bit, that we knew that she wasn't going to get better. . . . We ended up with a belief, (and I don't know when this came into a sentence, but it was during this time), that if you're going to be on the edge of a precipice, you're better off in the light than in the dark. If you are in a dangerous place, knowing where you are is better than being in a dangerous place and not knowing where you are.

The kids were tearful, and we comforted them, and we just went from moment to moment; one thing to the next thing. The shocks had stopped, but I guess we were all coming to terms with where we'd wound up in a very short space of time, from the Friday, when the shock kind of hit us, to the Monday when she was on a ventilator and God knows what. It was a colossal change of our life.

I remember screaming, like the painting 'The Scream', at some god-knows-what time, two o'clock in the morning or something, in James Cook car park, a massive car park with only me in the middle of it, and the moon. Just, you know, a primal scream. I would have bursts of that, and then you would just blow your nose and drive home, or wherever. I think we all had moments of real sobbing. I remember proper physical heartache; it wasn't something in songs. Your heart ached. It just felt wrong, the grief of it really. There were times when I was shrieking and Val was quiet, and there were times when Val would be crying and I was quieter, and we probably did a bit together. It came in waves. It went in for a bit, and then it was very intense when it came out, and you would just get on with the Next Minute. . . .this was the loss of our daughter. This was loss of the sparky kid who was lively and friendly and cheeky, and a sweet kid. I think we were going through all sorts of losses, that I think made sense to us as grief. I'm

45

sure I did the bargaining thing that I'd cheerfully go up if a miracle could happen, change places and all that. We were in the process of lots of losses. The loss of hearing her chattering, the loss of playing together, the loss of just normality, the loss of a kid who could move, the loss of our family as we'd had it.... I think we were going through it over a protracted period of time.

So we moved into the final phase while she was alive, of having her back in her bedroom. We lived at home, we set up medicines, and the kids would sometimes give the medicines through her NG [nasogastric] tube; we would set it up in syringes. And that was, bizarrely, a really lovey time. It felt like life was very distilled.

She slept with us in our room. We moved the beds about to make that happen, and she died on the morning of Val's birthday, the 30th November. It was quite early in the morning; she was struggling to breathe, she was getting laboured. I think we said, 'This is it,' and me and Val were there, and she died. And I'm sure we wept and I'm sure we felt the impact of it, but I think we'd been through a lot of the really turbulent stuff at the beginning. As it went on, it was more stable. I mean, it was painful, but it wasn't that absolutely shaking your fist and screaming, despondent; I think we'd had time to prepare ourselves for the end.

The social worker knew a funeral firm that refused to charge families for children being buried. They were saying, 'It's bad enough for you having to deal with the loss of a child, without having to deal with all that,' and so we knew the funeral people we were using, and this being Middlesbrough, a guy a couple of doors down, he was one of them that was doing it, and he came with a white van, and I insisted on carrying her out. I was saying, 'We carried her in to the house, I'll carry her out.,' and kind of put her in a blanket and put her in the back of this van. They were very perturbed about that, saying you could get noises and that, air going over vocal cords or whatever, but I was solid on it, and did it.

I asked Steve what or who had helped with the grieving.

We all leaned on each other. The kids helped us, and we helped them. We stayed solid, and if anything, it made us closer. So you didn't feel isolated with it, and I think the paediatrician, the social worker and the nurse were the next layer, telling us what we needed to know, and helping us get from one stage of care to the next. But I think the relationships between me, Val and the kids were the main thing. There were people who would come around and spend time with us, so I don't think we excluded people. I think people quite enjoyed coming and spending a bit of time with us; Val's brother, of course, was a big help, but then my cousin would come, and our friends would come.

And what, I asked Steve, didn't help?

We could have done without the existence of non-Hodgkin's lymphoma. I think the thing Val had to contend with more than me was that some people who hadn't been particularly close beforehand, kind of gathered around the tragedy, and Val was saying it was like, 'Why suddenly am I having to deal with you, whereas prior to this, we weren't close?' I think that was something Val had to contend with, more than me: 'Why have we got some professional mourners?' Which was weird. I call them 'professional', but we weren't paying them!

Afterwards was all the series of losses. Because she was physically gone, and what do you do with her room? And what do you do with her things? When you start to change things in the house, you take away something that she would have recognised, taking away the bed...so there were all those series of losses. It was difficult but not unhelpful. Just hard.

We could be forgiven for thinking of grief as essentially a problem of later life and looking upon childhood as a time when most of us are spared any bereavement. But this is not the case: Lucy Harrison and Richard

Harrington from the Royal Manchester Children's Hospital found that more than three-quarters of eleven to sixteen-year-old school children had experienced at least one significant loss in their lives. Teenager Neville, taking about the death of his mum, had this to say:

> *when it's really hard, it's like losing part of yourself ... it's like learning to walk again ... Maybe the rest of them are just coping with it or looking as if they're coping with it but I'm not. There's times when I really don't cope at all.*

Jane Ribbens McCarthy and Julie Jessop spoke with another young person, Brian, whose sorrow on losing his father is painfully clear:

> *[I] still replay it back in my mind, even now, nearly two years ago, wonder what would happen if... [father] wouldn't have got the cancer.*

I don't know where Neville or Brian are now (they'll be young men), but I hope they have found some peace of mind.

Hedei

Bereavement during childhood can reverberate throughout life. Looking back across thirty years, Hedei Frost told me about the devastation that had unfolded in her life.

I lost my brother when he was 9 years old. I was 13. Dwayne's been gone 30-odd years. It was a Wednesday, a Wednesday evening. Dwayne came home, and he'd got a headache and he went straight to bed. It got progressively worse as the night went on. I remember waiting for the ambulance and it took three and a half minutes, but it felt like thirty-three and a half minutes. It felt like it took forever.

I went to school the next day…I remember going home that day and I walked in to look at my dad, and I said, 'He's gone, hasn't he?' and dad just said, 'Yes,' and burst into tears…he'd gone about quarter to four time.

It was still very raw with my parents, but from that moment on I had to grow up rapidly. [I recall] a constant flow of people, some of who I didn't even know, neighbours we hadn't met; we hadn't lived there [in Kettering] very long. A lot of waking up to find mum or dad or both of them up, a lot of talking. I spent a lot of time sleeping on the sofa. That's what I remember of the day of the funeral – I fell asleep on the sofa. There were cat-naps, but not an awful lot of sleep.

I asked Hedei if she had been concerned for her parents.

Very, very concerned. When you're thirteen years old you think you have to be both people, and that's what I tried to do. I suddenly developed this fear of the dark, which I'd never, ever had in my life. But because Dwayne had had a fear of the dark, I thought I should have a fear of the dark. I tried to take on characteristics that were his not mine; I basically tried to replace him. It was definitely unconscious: only in looking back I realised what I was doing. It took until five years ago, when I finally got proper counselling, to stop blaming myself, stop thinking it was my fault. I mean I wasn't even at the same school as him, so there is no way I could have done anything. You want to find out why. Dwayne was killed at school…he was punched behind his ear. His skull was as thin as an eggshell and it burst a blood vessel that flooded the brain.

I wondered if, in the years that followed Dwayne's death, Hedei had noticed any significant change in her parents.

Oh, definitely. It was the start of the breakdown of my parents' marriage. My mum tried to kill herself…My dad refused to talk to her…I watched her beg him for forgiveness; there was no compassion in my dad anymore. He lost his faith, he started to drink heavily: completely different to the dad that I'd ever known. I basically became persona non grata; he's actually told

49

me to my face that it should have been me that died and not my brother, all sorts of things. We don't even talk now. He speaks to my children, but he doesn't speak to me and my mum anymore.

When you talk to other people who have lost brothers and sisters, every family goes through the same stages. There's this stage where the person who has gone is put on a pedestal, they're put on a pedestal and they never did anything wrong. And then there's a stage where you yourself as a child are angry because they've left you behind, and you've got to deal with all this stuff and it's not your place to deal with it and why should you have to deal with it?! And then there's the calm acceptance: it can take a few months, it can take a few years, but it eventually comes. Once I suddenly realised that Dwayne's death was nothing to do me and there was nothing I could have done to stop it, once I accepted that, the whole situation became calmer.

I had two children by the time I went [for counselling]. I'd had very severe post-natal depression after the birth of my son, and that's when they decided that I needed counselling, because it had gone past the point of post-natal depression and had turned into proper depression. Within three months of going into this counselling everything had come out and I felt so much better. I would say to anybody, if they asked, 'Do you think counselling could help me?' I would say, 'Yes, go, talk,' because you can talk to a stranger. It's so easy. But you see, sometimes children get left behind: people ask how your mum is, and how your dad is; they don't say, 'How are you?' They forget that you're part of it too. You just kind of get on with it when you're a sibling left behind. You have to be there for everybody, that's how you feel anyway.

People say to kids, 'Oh, you know, it's up to you to be the brave one now, you've got to be a grown-up.' Don't ever tell a child they've got to be a grown-up because they'll grow up far too quickly, cos I had to. It doesn't help, and it doesn't work. I had lots and lots of grown-ups say to me, 'Now, you've got to be the brave one, you've got to be there for Mum and Dad,' you know, 'You've got to be the strong one,' and I'd think, 'Ohhh Kayyy.' I can remember walking along to school some mornings and just sobbing because I've got to be strong enough, but I thought I couldn't be strong enough for everybody. At school at that time there was no particular pastoral care.

My mum and I are very, very close; my mum and I have a wonderful relationship, and I think my relationship with my children is far better because of what I went through; we talk about everything constantly. My house is never quiet!

I asked Hedei if she could describe the range of emotions she felt when Dwayne died.

I think it was empty, I felt empty. Because he and I were each other's friends when we lived abroad, I think we were so close anyway, but I just felt like I'd lost my best friend. He'd just gone. He just wasn't there anymore. And I felt empty. Empty and alone.

I still suffer from the depression; I don't think I'll ever get over that, but I'm a much, much stronger person now. I'm in such a good place at the moment...I have a fantastic husband, fantastic family, I would say about four or five very good friends. My daughter is definitely my best friend, without a doubt. I can deal with my dad much, much better now.

It doesn't get better, it gets easier. There's still that missing person at the dinner table, Christmas and birthdays. It's still there, but you learn to deal with it in different ways.

Carrying On

Top 5 Movies that Star Bald Guys: The Transporter

Rarely does a bald delivery boy ever look cool, but British ultra-hunk Jason Statham pulls it off with considerable aplomb in this action masterclass. I used to work as a paperboy and the most exciting thing I ever did was ride into a bin and cry about it for 10 minutes. Have a bit of that Statho.

Jack Marteau, Student Direct Magazine, 2008

Work

Some months after returning to work, developments there began to trouble me. I was employed by the government as a clinical advisor on the treatment of drug and alcohol addiction. In 2010 a new government had formed, and among its concerns was the fact that some patients were spending years in drug treatment. To people who don't work in the field, this certainly looks like a problem. Surely it can't take years to help someone get better. Unfortunately, it can, as addiction is a tenacious affliction, often persisting for decades. Research had found repeatedly that the longer a person spends in drug treatment, the longer they are likely to live. Conversely, as a rule of thumb, the shorter someone's drug treatment, the sooner they are likely to die. Nevertheless, David Cameron's coalition government was convinced that not enough was being done to get people out of treatment, fully recovered from drug addiction. To remedy this, they decided that English NHS organisations should complete drug treatments in a timely fashion or suffer financial penalty. Those NHS areas that kept people in treatment for longer than the government liked stood to lose up to 20% of their funding.

Livelihoods were on the line, and patients soon found themselves being nudged towards the exit door. I used research data to make a general calculation on the impact of this policy; I worked out that two hundred

52

extra people would die from drug overdose during the first year of this new system. These would be somebody's mother, father, daughter or son. The very last thing I wanted was for any additional family to suffer the anguish that we had experienced. Alarmed at what was about to happen, I raised the issue at every government policy meeting I attended. I got nowhere. I wrote to the Minister for Public Health, telling her that this policy was highly likely to result in additional deaths. My letter was intercepted and kept from her by one of her civil servants, and I was warned not to try anything similar again. I knew that I would be sacked if I did so, but for Jack's sake I had to try to stop any avoidable tragedy. One month later I sent an email to twenty senior health figures in Whitehall, attaching some advice I had secured from the government's own lawyers that the new policy was illogical and potentially unlawful.

Five minutes later the Deputy Director from my department called me to say that I was suspended. As soon as the call was over the screen on my government-issue BlackBerry turned completely black, but for the single white word '*Wiping*'. A bar appeared on the left side of the screen and quickly stretched its way eastward. I tore out the battery, but the thing had been destroyed. Several text messages from Jack were lost forever.

In the morning a letter arrived telling me that I was suspended from duty on the grounds of Gross Misconduct. The letter instructed me I was not to leave my home between Monday to Friday. Effectively under weekday house arrest, I used Debbie's personal laptop to go on the www.gov.uk website to keep up to date on the new policy. The laptop began behaving strangely, with a Google notice telling me that the site was unavailable. I quickly realised that the same people who had immobilised my smartphone from 100 miles away had been tampering with my personal ISP address. I had managed to make myself an enemy of the state. It felt like I was in a low-budget Jason Bourne film. What, I wondered, if they invalidated my passport? Debbie and I locked up the house and left the country. We moved through southern Europe for four months, and then rented a flat for a while on the Costa del Sol. I earned a bit of money along the way, working for the European Union.

Walking

In August 2011, as a tribute to her brother Jack, Rosie had walked a pilgrimage route from the French Pyrenees to Santiago de Compostela in Northwest Spain. Called el Camino, or The Way, the long-distance walk to the purported bones of the Christian disciple Saint James had been gaining popularity since its rediscovery in the 1970s. We told a local woman we had a half-formed idea to follow in our daughter's footsteps. '*It's not necessary to go from France,*' she said, '*You can walk to Santiago from here in Andalusia.*' We checked it out, and she was right. With the mountains of Morocco at our backs, we headed north from the Straits of Gibraltar, walking up the Atlantic coast. At Cadiz we caught a train to Seville, and from there set out on a barren 1,000 km path to Santiago de Compostela.

The weather was fine for the first three weeks, but then clouds gathered, and rain beat down for days on end. As the temperature dropped, the rain would turn to hail, sleet and even snow. We walked on, often soaked to the skin. We waded across swollen rivers, sometimes up to our waists, as rain or snow fell from above. Our bodies ached, and our feet were blistered. When we reached a small refuge for the night, it was often unheated and at times there was nowhere to buy food. I lost so much weight my trousers wouldn't stay on. I bought a smaller pair. A week or so later they too started falling off. I was as thin as a medieval pilgrim. For once we had bodies as distressed as our souls. Our physical miseries mirrored but in no way exceeded our heart-pain; we were almost indifferent to our bodily suffering. After a month or so of walking, a bone in Debbie's foot broke. She carried on. My right shin developed a strange red bulge. It turned into a stress fracture of the tibia. I carried on. On 19th March, after walking for seven weeks and 1,100 km, we at last reached the cathedral of Santiago de

Compostela. As a symbolic climax to an effort that is itself metaphor for the hard road of life, we dropped a heart-shaped stone we had carried from a beach on the Costa Del Sol behind one of statues of saints that stand sentinel around the internal walls of the building. The stone lodged itself in a narrow gap between Saint Jude's back and the wall behind. I imagine it will stay there for a century or more. Later, I learnt that Jude is revered as the patron saint of lost causes, or, as I prefer to see him, the champion of hope in times of desperation.

In addition to showing us that we could take weeks of physical assault, the pilgrimage taught us that throughout hours of walking, the mind becomes strangely empty. This second lesson was a helpful surprise. We'd anticipated thinking about a mountain of things along the route, our minds busy and rich with new ideas. Instead, we found that beyond pedestrian concerns about food, shelter or losing our way, for long stretches of the day we had thought about almost nothing. After months of ruminating and fixating on our loss, we had found a means to respite, a route to some tiny islands of calm and quiet.

Following Jack's death, I had done a prodigious amount of thinking. Thinking about what to do now, what to do next, what I should have done, what Jack might have done. Now, after three hard years of thinking, I'd come to conclude that thinking is overrated. Too often it turns in on itself, twisting into a closed loop of fret. I had started with a problem, 'We feel utterly bereft', moved onto a febrile sequence of thoughts (*Maybe we should: stay here, leave here, set up a restaurant, work for a charity, open a restaurant for a charity*) which prompted internal responses (*Maybe not, Maybe but when? Why exactly?*) which in turn lead to the almost universal thought: *That wouldn't work*. Thinking had served me badly: instead of just feeling desolate, I was now desolate and burdened with a bundle of rejected ideas. But thinking had finally come up trumps. We had been thinking that a long-distance walk might help us, and it had. Thinking had given us a method to stop thinking.

We decided that as soon as we could walk some distance again, we'd do just that. It wasn't until the following year that we were in the right shape to set out on the Hadrian's Wall path, a hilly slog across the country, from the North to the Irish Sea. On the seventh day Debbie started to limp, and on the final stretch along the Solway Firth the pain was so bad she spent as much time sat on the ground as walking. Once home she found out she had a foot injury called plantar fasciitis. Walking any distance was out of the question for a year or so. Cycling, however, caused her no pain, so three months on, dwarfed by its immensity, we pedalled onto a giant car ferry in Harwich. For the next six weeks we rode across Holland and Germany, zig-zagging between various cities to see friends. I'd packed an iPad, so I could work while we were on the road.

We got back to England on 29th October. I sent my dad an email to say that I would be down to see him the following week. I was just getting into bed when my mum rang. Dad was dead, aged eighty-nine.

My Dad

Piet was as much a paradox as any of us. A peace-loving man who had gone to war to fight, he rarely showed any anger and his body language was almost apologetic, despite being physically very strong. Although no more than a middleweight, during his time in the army he would hire himself out as sparring partner at sixpence a round, holding his own against far bigger opponents. He loved to sing but had no aptitude, hitting a correct note by chance alone. Yet he was a good jazz pianist and accordion player.

Born in 1925, Piet was a child of the Victorians, a people with straightforward values: worship God, serve your country, respect your elders. This last ethic proved problematic for Piet. He had always done as his parents wished, even abandoning his ambition to be a mechanic to take a desk job at their insistence. He accepted this as part of the natural order; when he became the head of his own family, he would hold the authority his seniority warranted; it would be his turn. But to his confusion, the 1960s ratted on the deal. Suddenly the young felt they had the right to do whatever they wished, regardless of the orders or opinion of any parent. A naturally energetic and upbeat man, Piet went with this brave new world initially, learning a couple of Beatles tunes to knock out on the piano to please us kids, but the permissive society, with its pre-marital sex, eastern mysticism, communal living and drugs, was to Piet's mind Not a Good Thing: the world had taken a wrong turn. He didn't dwell on this development. Instead, he kept to ways he favoured: providing for the family, attending the local church and helping charitable causes; and he never fully surrendered the value, core to his upbringing, that elders have ultimate authority over the family. In the days that followed Jack's death, the volcanic anger erupting from my ruptured heart had collided with Piet's sense of entitlement to direct his family as he saw fit.

I miss his cheery appetite for life, but as he'd been very unwell for the last two years of his life, this part of my dad had eroded. Some days I feel guilty that he and I had fallen out so drastically after Jack's death. On other days I feel no regret: I was a different me in the weeks and months that followed Jack's death. I didn't stop loving Piet, I just couldn't face being around my parents. I felt that if we had remained in contact, something bad might happen. Perhaps, like Elizabeth, I would kill myself. I'm not sure I was wrong.

Back to the Start

From: Jack Marteau <Jack.Marteau@student.manchester.ac.uk
Sent: 10 November 2008
To: Debbie Marteau

Sorry deb it's been a rather crazy weekend. Bloody good to see you too, always nice to have the four of us back in action...Cheers for the words deb, I love you big time.

Me

I was born in London. My dad worked for a bank and my mum, who had been a secretary when they met, was a fulltime housewife. I was the only boy and I had four sisters. We were a middleclass family and we lived in an Edwardian redbrick semi in Southgate, a standard suburb at the upper reaches of the Piccadilly line. I was brought up a Catholic. Life as an English Catholic is like drawing a bad hand at Scrabble: the pieces won't quite come together. Catholicism is a technicolour religion, filled with flaming reds hearts, glowing gold haloes and priestly costumes of emerald green, yellow and purple. This carnival palate is better located under the sun-brilliant skies of Rio, Seville or Rome rather than the flat grey canopy of the UK. And Catholicism's fantastical tales of wine being turned into blood or saints levitating into the heavens sit easier in the magic-realist imagination of South America than the let's-be-sensible English mind. Not that any of this occurred to me during my formative years. Catholicism was normal to me: we went to the church every Sunday (why not, didn't everyone?); I was sent to a Catholic primary school (naturally – my three elder sisters were there) and on to a Catholic grammar school (of course – all my friends and even my cousins were headed there too). The world, as far as I knew, was Catholic.

Fairly early on I got told about Original Sin, a thing that meant I was in big trouble and could go to hell. The sin wasn't mine, it was Adam and Eve's. They'd stolen an apple from the Garden of Eden. God was furious and for reasons unclear decided it was not only those two who were guilty of the crime, but every one of their descendants, me included. I was therefore an offender against God, on parole from birth. If I ever strayed from the straight and narrow, I was certain to end up somewhere terrible. I didn't know exactly what hell was like, but our weekly trip to our local church gave an alarming clue: a giant statue of Jesus nailed to a cross towered over me, his eyes rolled upwards in agony as rivulets of blood ran crimson-fresh from his head, hands, feet and ribs. Me and my best friend Larry had nicked a couple of apples (not just one, as in the primary offence) from some garden, and this only compounded the dread in my six-year-old mind. I was plainly a very bad person, bad as Adam…the future was looking black, and blood-red.

But don't worry Dave, help is at hand. The teacher, or the priest, or whoever was kind enough to let me know that God blamed me for everything, also mentioned another invisible being: my Guardian Angel. This angel (I never found out his or her name) hovered a bit just above and behind me, keeping watch and helping me to stay out of harm's way. This was a good thing. Unfortunately, as well as always knowing what I was doing, this guardian angel also knew exactly what I was thinking, all the time. And so, I was assured, did God! So, if ever I had a bad thought about how much I hated one of my sisters, or some kid in class, or indeed the authority figure who'd told me about this unsolicited mind-reading, then I was definitely going to hell where I'd definitely be nailed to a giant cross and definitely left to hang forever. This frightened the living daylights out of me. I was a nervy child anyway, and I had become an established bedwetter and prone to nightmares. I don't know if any of these things are really connected – I subsequently found out that some kids are such heavy sleepers that not even their bladders wake them up.

As a child I had some behavioural problems. Or, a problem behaving. I could be disruptive in class, and a bit light-fingered with school property, albeit for fun rather than profit. These days they'd have a diagnosis and professional help for me, but back in the Sixties the system was perfectly happy to judge me a Bad Boy and give me good hiding. My primary school teacher, Miss Borrot, an ardent smoker, would grab hold of me and slap the back of my leg quite hard, while clamping a burning cigarette tight between her lips. Like every boy back then, I wore short trousers until I was 11, so the whacks were painful. When the slaps failed, she sent me to the headmaster, a fat mirthless man with a purple face. Mr Moffat hit me across my upturned hands with a purpose-made bamboo cane. That hurt really bad; welts came up across both palms, forcing me to keep my hands hidden when I got home. For much of the remainder of my school career I had teachers beat me with hands, sticks, shoes and strips of leather. I reasoned that as school and I couldn't get along, it was wise not to go there too often; truancy became my number one behavioural problem. By the time I was 15 years old all my close friends had already been expelled and I was on my final warning. Thankfully I beat the axe as my dad got a change of job and we moved out to the countryside. I stumbled through the rest of my school career then left home for a new life in London.

My childhood now feels nearer than it has at any time since I became an adult. While it grows and reanimates in my memory, I find it increasingly difficult to recall my twenties, thirties or forties. Conversely, while I was living those younger adult decades, my formative years were remote and indistinct. I had, I believed, left them behind forever. But now it seems my life has followed an elliptical course, burning the fuel of adult desires and ambitions to rocket away from boyhood, before rounding and heading straight back to where I began. Jack's death marked the outer limit of my journey; pulled into the orbit of that black hole, I was slung-shot back towards my start. I feel it getting ever closer, and when I reach it, my birth day and death day will become one and the same. I don't fancy it much, but

I fancy even less losing one more person I love. No, for purely selfish reasons, I want to be next.

I apologise for going on about myself. My reason for doing so is to help you understand that my upbringing formed two elements of my personality that still influence how I view death: a troubled relationship with religion, and an overdeveloped sense of the supernatural. So much for my beginnings; what of England's?

Prehistory and then the Romans

People have been living and dying in England for around a million years. The earliest evidence we have of any human life on these shores are the 800,000-year-old footprints of a small group of early humans, found in tidal mud in Norfolk. Their owners appear to have been walking in tight circles, as if trying to keep warm. We can't know what this barefoot family thought about death, but it seems that it has always mattered to us. We are a fairly long-lived species, but in comparison to other life-forms we have been short-changed. It's hard to accept that a tortoise lives longer than us, even some fish, and just about every tree. Some sponges live for over two thousand years. Looking around at the generous hand dealt to many other creatures, it didn't take us long to come up with the idea that this life must just Part I, and we will be given the remainder of the existence we are owed after a short, dark intermission.

The earliest evidence of any English beliefs around death comes from excavations of earth tombs in Wiltshire. Disturbances made in the soil around 5,000 years ago suggest that on occasions people would take bones of their dead ancestors from earth tombs. It seems they would then perform rituals with these skulls or femurs, in the hope that the dead owners would put in a good word with the gods to keep sickness or crop failure at bay. It's likely this practice went on for several hundred years before suddenly coming to an end. By this time the climate had cooled, and the bad harvests that resulted may have triggered a loss of faith in the power of long-gone tribe members. The tombs were closed off, and people turned to a bigger idea: build large stone circles and start dealing with heaven direct. These stone circles —most famously Stonehenge – remain, but because they developed no written language, quite what the people who built them believed about any afterlife remains a closed book to us.

We can, however, have some confidence that both the earth and the sky were regarded as sacred; jewellery and pots of seeds would be buried together, presumably as an offering to the gods in exchange for a good harvest. And water was magical: knives, brooches, helmets and other high-value objects were thrown into rivers and lakes of England by the tribespeople of the Bronze and Iron Ages, to please and appease the water gods. Animals too had spiritual significance: a giant white horse was carved into the chalk uplands at Uffington, Oxfordshire over 3,000 years ago. It remains there to this day, modern as a Picasso. As we shall see, there is strong evidence that the earlier inhabitants of England believed that horses lead us from the grave to a next, new life. The special affection the English still hold for horses created a near-spiritual crisis in the 2013 horsemeat scandal. The names of any ancient horse-gods are lost, but in parts of the country they may have become transmuted into the pagan goddess Epona, who protected horses and looked after crops.

When the Romans invaded, they brought with them the written word, and suddenly the light comes on. We get to read numerous contemporary facts and several first-hand misconceptions about the inhabitants of England 2,000 years ago, including the Druids. These were a special class of citizen who could recite box-set length poems from memory, settle disputes between neighbours, sit as judges in trials of wrong-doers, and – crucially – use their pointy hats and long sticks to pick up signals from the gods themselves. This specific talent meant that Druids were exempt from taxes and excused military service. Things were going nicely for the them until the Romans turned up. It may just have been racist propaganda, but the Roman Tacitus alleged that the Druids made human sacrifices to their water gods on '*blood-soaked altars*'. Tacitus had in fact never been north of Calais, and by contrast the Greek writer Diodorus Siculus described the Druids as peace-makers: '*Often when the combatants are ranged face to face, and swords are drawn and spears are bristling, these men come between the armies and stay the battle.*' Pacifists who make human sacrifices sound like an unlikely group, but I once met a born-again Christian who became, when necessary, an armed robber.

Although Druids didn't normally approve of violence, Julius Caesar pointed out that their belief in reincarnation gave them the courage to fight when their backs were against the wall: '*the most important Druid belief was that after death the soul passes from one to another – hence the Celts' bravery in battle.*' In a poem addressed to the Druids, the Roman Lucan says, '*If we understand you right, death is only a pause in a long life.*' The Druids were wiped out before they could give a proper response. Even if they were reincarnated, any history or evidence of human sacrifice in the UK died with them in their last stand on Anglesey.

The standard Roman belief was that after death the soul would migrate to the underworld, where Pluto was in charge. By virtue of their demi-god status, emperors and great military heroes were given an automatic upgrade to the Elysian Fields, which were just perfect. It's possible that the average Brit didn't love this two-tier afterlife arrangement, but just managing to get by in this life was probably enough to occupy much of her or his thoughts. Not that they didn't consider the spiritual world: it was common to believe there were spirits everywhere, with the gods controlling the weather, sickness, luck and even, in the view of Cambridge-born writer Jonathan Black, the thoughts inside one's own head. So it was as well to give gifts to the gods, sometimes very valuable ones. Scratch their backs and who knows, perhaps they'll scratch yours when your time is up.

One Roman god that was said to offer true believers a safe and luxurious afterlife was Mithras. He was particularly attractive to Romans soldiers, who were assured a relatively dangerous and uncomfortable earthly life, scrapping with almost anyone from Baghdad to Berwick on Tweed. Mithras was celebrated for slaying a bull and then enjoying some nice roast beef with the sun god Sol. The religion featured some very close parallels with Christianity, including a miraculous birth (Mithras emerges from a large rock) witnessed by a group of shepherds on December 25th, a baptism ritual, and a supper shared between followers.

After almost 400 years of moaning about the weather, the Romans had to leave Britain in a hurry. To find out what happened next, we must turn to two people to: an outstandingly grumpy monk called Gildas and the great Northumbrian scholar Bede.

Gildas begins his book, written around 550 AD, by giving us a quick and fairly accurate geography lesson:

> *The island of Britain, situated on almost the utmost border of the earth and is eight hundred miles long and two hundred broad, except where the headlands of sundry promontories stretch farther into the sea.*

Sounds nice enough, but the title of his work, *On the Ruin of Britain*, gives a solid clue where Gildas is headed next. Britain is, in his opinion, a disgrace:

> *This island, stiff-necked and stubborn-minded, from the time of its being first inhabited, ungratefully rebels, sometimes against God, sometimes against her own citizens, and frequently also, against foreign kings and their subjects.*

It's already sounding like home.

We can guess from his mention of just one god, with a capital G, that Gildas is a Christian. He shudders at the thought of the dozens of gods and goddesses worshipped by the pagans as, '*those diabolical idols of my country, which almost surpassed in number those of Egypt.*'

Shivering in his damp stone monastery, Gildas recalls the arrival of Christianity in Britain: '*these islands, stiff with cold and frost, and in a distant region of the world, remote from the visible sun, received the beams of light, that is, the holy precepts of Christ, the true Sun.*' Not everyone, however, was instantly won over: '*These rays of light were received with lukewarm minds by the inhabitants, but they nevertheless took root among some of them in a greater or less degree.*' And some of those who did see the light were, to Gildas' mind, no better than the pagans. Many British priests were, in his words, '*lustful*', '*deceitful*', '*impudent*' and '*dumb*', motivated by the love of '*filthy lucre,*' and prone to '*indecently entertaining strange women.*' Finally coming off the fence, Gildas sums up these vicars as '*unworthy wretches, wallowing, after the fashion of swine, in their old and unhappy puddle of intolerable wickedness.*'

Death is a constant theme in Gildas' history: The Romans turn up and kill loads of locals; warriors from Germany, Ireland and Scotland turn up and kill loads more locals. Attacked on all sides, the people send a desperate message to Rome: '*The barbarians drive us to the sea; the sea throws us back on the barbarians: thus two modes of death await us, we are either slain or drowned.*' No reinforcements come. Unable to beat away invaders, the locals turn on each other. Gildas rolls his eyes: '*it has always been a custom with our nation, as it is at present, to be impotent in repelling foreign foes, but bold and invincible in raising civil war.*'

Even when things go well, they go badly. After some success pushing the Picts back into Scotland, there is a bumper harvest, '*the island was deluged with a most extraordinary plenty of all things, greater than was before known.*' But instead of living in peaceful harmony, Gildas reports that people took to a life of lying, laziness and sex, developing a '*hatred of the truth*' and electing kings on the principle of meanest available candidate, 'and soon after, they were put to death by those who had elected them....because others still more cruel were chosen to succeed them.'

As they continue what Gildas calls a 'downward path of vice', the people are set upon by the plague, a disease that killed, 'so large a number of persons, that the living were not able to bury them.' Soon the Picts are streaming down from Scotland again. Severely weakened by the plague, the locals do a deal with the Saxons, offering them goods and money in exchange for protection. Gildas is beside himself, saying the plan made as much sense as inviting 'wolves into the sheep-fold'. To his mind the Saxons are, 'a race hateful both to God and men'. Naturally the Saxons welch on the deal and are still busy killing locals as Gildas sits quill in hand, scribbling out his rage.

The Saxons

With the Roman Empire disintegrating, the Saxons and their pagan North European neighbours the Jutes and the Angles were quick to to invade and grab different parts of the country. They brought a whole bunch of useful gods within them, including Tiu (god of war), Woden (god of war) and Thor (god of war). We can't say we weren't warned. Together these gods live on in the names of the days of midweek, and perhaps in an English warrior spirit (more of which later).

In 595 AD, a few years after moany old Gildas has tutted off to his grave, the big push came from the Pope in Rome to convert England fully to Christianity. The great Bede, writing in his monastery one hundred years on, thought the man had done the country a huge spiritual favour: 'Pope Gregory...by his zeal converted our nation, the English, from the power of Satan to the faith of Christ.' In fact, it was Augustine who put in the legwork, travelling to Kent to convert the local king. There were teething problems: when prince Eadbald, the king's son came to the throne, he rejected Christianity and began a scandalous affair with his mother-in-law.

But Christianity in England got a tremendous boost with the conversion of a northern king, Edwin of Northumbria. Bede tells us that Edwin was on the run from an enemy with little hope of survival when a vision of Jesus appeared to him and gave a promise that everything would work out fine if only he (Edwin) would become a Christian. Edwin agreed, and very soon he found himself the most powerful king in England. Bede's story may have been accurate, but it's best not to overlook the fact that Edwin had married the Christian princess Aethelburh from Kent (the sister of Eadbald, the one who got on so famously with his mother-in-law), so perhaps Edwin merely took up Christianity at Aethelburh's suggestion.

Anyway, king Edwin starts looking to convert his chiefs, one of whom (Bede doesn't give us their name), gives one of the most poetic responses in the history of early England:

> *The present life of man, O king, seems to me, in comparison of that time which is unknown to us, like to the swift flight of a sparrow through the room wherein you sit at supper in winter, with your commanders and ministers, and a good fire in the midst, whilst the storms of rain and snow prevail abroad; the sparrow, I say, flying in at one door, and immediately out at another, whilst he is within, is safe from the wintry storm; but after a short space of fair weather, he immediately vanishes out of your sight, into the dark winter from which he had emerged. So this life of man appears for a short space, but of what went before, or what is to follow, we are utterly ignorant. If, therefore, this new doctrine contains something more certain, it seems justly to deserve to be followed.*

With stories and reasoning as good as this, it wasn't going to take long for Christianity to catch on. Even now I worry a bit about that sparrow.

Christian England and Death

By around 700 AD Christianity was firmly established as the religion of England. With the debate settled as to whether several gods existed or just the one, there seemed no reason for further dispute over religion. But precisely what this one god thought, said and wanted would fuel a series of arguments that ran on for the next thousand years. Whoever won these disputes could satisfy themselves that a good death and an even better after-death awaited them. For the losers, a bad death was as certain as rain on a Bank Holiday. The primary weapon in this war was the charge of heresy.

Not that heresy was a Christian invention. Any insult to the pagan gods could result in a death sentence. This left the early Christians in a dangerous position, and the first of them to fall foul of a charge may have been Alban, a man from Hertfordshire. According to Bede, writing more than 400 years after the event, Alban had been arrested by the Roman authorities for promoting Christianity. Alban told the judge that it was pagans who were the real heretics, and they were certain to 'receive the everlasting pains of hell.'

This was a bold but undiplomatic move: the judge, like almost everyone else in the country at the time, was a pagan. And he was the judge. He promptly ordered that Alban should have his head cut off. It could be argued that Alban had the last laugh, because as the axe came down, both of the executioner's eyes fell out and dropped to the ground next to Alban's severed head. Served him right (the executioner, not Alban). Bede adds that at the site of the execution, 'there ceases not to this day the cure of sick persons, and the frequent working of wonders.'

There's some confusion even now among believers about whether people who, like Alban's pagan adversaries, are sent to hell are obliged to live there eternally, or if they just get burnt to nothing and that's the end of them forever. Either way, hell is to be avoided. It certainly was in the Dark Ages. At a time when almost no one could read or write, images were the most effective way to communicate an idea. And the idea of hell was depicted in terrifying detail by gigantic church murals of the doomed being perpetually slow-roasted or tortured by an army of hideous scaly-skinned demons. Some of these larger monsters were shown eating men alive and shitting out others as they chewed. The excreted folk had barely a second to get their bearings before they were grabbed by giant claws and swallowed again. The roasted, tortured and recycled souls were to have no final release from their suffering, but instead remain in hell for the full duration of eternity. The message of this cartoonish horror show was clear: a terrible fate awaited anyone who hadn't led the life of a saint.

The Anglo-Saxons' word for body was bone house ('banhaus'), suggesting that a body was some kind of shelter for the soul. Or even a cage. Much as he hated the pagan Saxons, the medieval monk Bede seems to have been influenced by their bone house idea. When he mentions the death in 690 of Theodore, the Archbishop of Canterbury, Bede says that, *'his spirit went forth from the prison-bars of the flesh.'* And to Bede, it wasn't necessary to die in order to escape from the cage of the body. He reported that Pope Gregory had kept his mind so concentrated on heavenly matters that, even while still alive, Gregory *'broke through the bonds of the flesh.'* The Saxon banhaus concept was still going strong in the 18th Century, when William Blake wrote, *'I am wrapped in mortality, my flesh is a prison, my bones the bars of death'.*

For Bede the next world is more real than this one. Describing the last days of Cuthbert, Bede says he entered, *'into that life which alone can be called life.'* Another of the early English Christian saints, Abbess Hilda of Whitby, passed, according to Bede, *'from death unto life.'* He goes on to describe the unusual circumstances of Hilda's death:

> *In a monastery called Hacanos* [Hackness, near Whitby], *there was in that monastery, a nun called Begu. Opening her eyes, as she thought, she saw the roof of the house open, and a light shed from*

above filling all the place. Looking earnestly upon that light, she saw the soul of the aforesaid handmaid of God [Hilda] *in that same light, being carried to heaven attended and guided by angels.*

It's a tall tale, but as Bede and Hilda were from the same part of the country, and their lives overlapped by eight years, it's conceivable he may have spoken to witnesses to validate the story.

Medieval Times

By the middle ages there was an established English belief in one Christian god, one heaven and – on the downside – one hell. The fiery tortures of the nether world lay in wait for some of the highest in the land as well as the commonest thief. In 1170 King Henry II had personally ordered the murder of god's own representative in England, the Archbishop of Canterbury. Four years passed, and a panic-stricken Henry became convinced that in setting up the hit on Archbishop Thomas Becket he had booked himself an everlasting residence in hell. To escape this terrible fate, he travelled to Canterbury cathedral where he asked to be beaten for his crime. The brethren of the church were happy to oblige, taking it in turns to give the king a good hiding.

Heaven was equally real to the medieval kings of England. If his faith had been weakened by the death of his daughter Joan in the 1348 plague, Edward III gave no sign when he wrote that, '*We give thanks to* [God] *that one of our own family…has been sent ahead to heaven to reign among the choirs of virgins.*'

Heaven and Hell

You are really, really, really, really good looking.
Congratulations.

Love poem? by Jack Marteau 10th September 2009

Because, as Paul McCartney and Stevie Wonder noticed, there's good and bad in everyone, the permanent heaven or eternal hell system appears ill-matched to the averagely behaved person. You might, for instance, be lying on your medieval deathbed, having on balance done just enough good deeds in your life to have earned a golden ticket to paradise, when a nurse drops a scalding cup of soup on your exposed stomach. In shock, you swear at her, and before you have a chance to apologise, collapse back onto your pillow, stone dead. Consequently, rather than loafing on Cloud 9 for eternity, your 90th minute own-goal results in your being tortured without pause or mercy until the very end of time. This seems unreasonably harsh. To address such borderline cases, the Christian afterlife was expanded to include Purgatory, a temporary hell, with every chance of parole once you've been tormented long enough to pay for the soup incident.

Purgatory and hell were equally grim. Sinners were frequently burnt by the constant fires, other souls were drowned repeatedly, brought back to life, and then drowned all over again. Gluttons were swallowed by serpents or hideous giant toads, hot-blooded lecherous types were frozen, and lazy individuals were nailed to the ground so even if they could be motivated to move, they couldn't. Spiteful gossips were strung up by their malicious tongues, money lenders were forced to drink molten gold, murderers were butchered, the proud took a succession of fatal falls into a burning pit, and the rich and vain had their fine clothes set on fire. How long all this would go on for was anyone's guess, but as a rule of thumb, the worse your in-life behaviour, the more protracted your after-death maltreatment.

But where exactly were heaven, hell and purgatory? St Patrick, (who according to the historian Simon Schama may have been English), had been shown the entrance to purgatory; it was located in a cave on Station Island in Lough Derg, Donegal. Heaven was somewhere in the northern sector of the empty sky, and hell was thought to be either under the earth or in the skies above, but still — of course — below heaven.

One thing no citizen wanted to do was leave this life with a serious black mark against themselves. If someone had a major misdemeanour chalked-up on their spiritual slate as they lay on their death bed, the one way to wipe it clear would be to make a full confession to a priest and plead for divine forgiveness. As death approached the priest would be summoned to hear this confession and to say some specific prayers that ensured the dying person made their peace with god. As they always had to be on call to provide this emergency service, (known as *Extreme Unction*), these priests were forbidden to ever leave the parish.

The stakes were high for any medieval citizen suffering a worrying dip in health; death had to be approached with great care. Fortunately, someone had put together a guidebook on the subject. *The Book of the Craft of Dying*, written sometime in the 1300s, is an instruction manual for the dying, their relatives and for members of the clergy on how to prepare for your own or another's death. No-one knows who wrote *the Craft of Dying*; it's possible that several people had a hand in it. The book is a fascinating mixture of straight talking (*'the dying person's feelings should not be spared. They should be told plainly that they are going to die,'*) and medieval superstition (*'Our last days can be the most dangerous, the devil with all his might is busy to avert fully a man from the faith in his last end.'*)

For premium anti-demon protection, the book recommends that a dying person should, *'pray devoutly within himself, with his heart and his desire, as he can and may, and so yield the ghost up to God; and he shall be safe.'* For further insurance, the book suggests Holy Water is sprinkled *'oftentimes upon him, and the others that be about him,* [so] *that fiends may be voided from him.'* Returning to more practical advice, the *Craft of Dying* gives a solid recommendation that, *'religious people and women...should not run, but to a man that is a-dying and for fire,'* which is quite a decent joke.

The unnamed author or authors explain that their work is intended to help the many of us who find death *'right fearful and horrible'*. The reassuring news is that, so long as we live a decent life and are genuinely sorry for the times we've failed to do that, we shall find ourselves spending the next life in *'a place of refreshing'* in a state of *'bliss and joy'*. Heaven awaits! The book stays upbeat with an assertion that, *'Death is nothing else but a going* [out] *of prison, and an ending of exile.'*

The book warns us all, however, of the price to paid for living a *'sinful'* life; we will experience *'spiritual death,'* which is *'much more horrible and detestable'* than physical death. The soul, it explains, is *'more worthy and more precious'* than *'ye body.'* To the author(s), the soul is as real as the knee or elbow, and infinitely longer-lasting. So spiritual death is a problem that never dies. For the sinful, Hell will always find some room.

It should be no surprise that the *Craft of Dying* provides several prayers that a priest can recite when they attend a dying person. The words of one of these are a touching blend of humility and beauty, with a light garnish of desperation: *'We cry to the root of Thy most benign heart that Thou forgive the soul of Thy servant all his sins.'*

The book was much in demand: the 1300s was the great century of death in England. Two terrible famines and the bubonic plague swept away vast numbers of the population, giving people a multitude of causes to think on what might lie beyond the grave. As we shall see, two of England's greatest female mystics, Julian of Norwich and Margery Kempe, lived through these times, as did another big name of the 14th century, East Midlander Walter Hilton. Although not a visionary like Julian or Margery, Walter spent a lot of his life following a religious path and thinking about the bigger picture. His work *Ladder of Perfection* was a spiritual hit across Europe.

In the *Ladder of Perfection* Walter, comes across as a very humble bloke. He describes himself as a '*wretch*', but the book is the work of someone dedicated to learning and living the right way. He stresses the need for an internal life, based on prayer and meditation, which Walter says is even more valuable than doing '*external works of charity to thy neighbour.*' This is almost an Eastern approach.

Walter concentrates on love as a central part of spiritual development: '*Love, and Jesus and God...all is one, and nought but one; Jesus is love.*' He has no time for hypocrites who make a show of their religious faith. He much prefers honesty. '*God is truth,*' he says. Unlike most other medieval preachers, Walter's not so fixed on the devil, or '*the fiend*'; he regards him as just so much harmless hot air to those who have their heads on right: '*The soul feareth no more the blusterings of the fiend than the stirring of a mouse.*'

To scale the ladder to perfection, Walter recommends, '*A loathing of all this worldly bliss,*' and, '*a forsaking of all fleshly or sensual love.*' It's a tough ask: without worldly bliss and fleshy or sensual love, weekends are largely a non-event. But Walter is realistic about his spiritual recipe, saying that some of his readers will choose to lead a '*mixed life,*' spending time in the real world while still doing some meditation and praying. If we were alive back then, this is the sort of path many of us might have decided to take, and we can feel a bit self-satisfied when Hilton refers to people like us as, '*worldly men and women.*' He spoils it though by adding that such folk are basically '*gross and ignorant.*' He is a bit of a wretch after all.

Walter makes it clear that the stakes are high for those who fail to live according to the Bible. The sinful can expect to find themselves in hell for all eternity. Not that Walter wants his readers to panic, particularly those who have behaved badly on a number of occasions. No, he is at pains to

74

point out that provided we keep trying to climb the steps up his ladder of perfection, all is not lost:

> *Though thou shouldst fall another time into the same defect, yea, an hundred times, yea, a thousand, yet still do as I have said, and all will be well*

Even if all the devils in hell, or every living person on earth and the very angels of heaven tell us we can't be saved, we should not believe any of them, counsels Walter. Every one of us can make it to the '*bliss of heaven.*'

Although wonderful throughout, Walter's heaven is split in two. Perfect souls (including apostles and martyrs from the very early days of Christianity) get to stay in the better part as they are, as Walter puts it, '*God's darlings.*' The other half is occupied by the more regular '*God's friends*' who receive a '*lower reward in the bliss of Heaven.*' Seems fair enough. Far less reasonable is the ban on Jews and Turks, who must all go to hell instead, along with every bad Christian. The Christians receive harsher treatment down there because unlike members of other faiths or heathens in general, they had known '*the truth*' but had failed to live by it.

Most of us try but fail to be a really good person, and we can be confident our medieval friends were no different. But while we might respond to our own personal screw-ups by feeling guilty for a day or two then shrugging our shoulders, the medieval English had to take their own misdemeanours far more seriously: to their minds such slip-ups meant they could expect to fry for months, years or even forever. Someone who had struggled to live a life of virtue might find trouble sleeping at night as they approached the end of their days. And when they did drop off, the chances were high their dreams would be a mire of flames, screaming and pitch-forks. Is there nothing that could save them from their terrible fate? The *Art of Dying* and *Ladder of Perfection* offered reassurance about the effectiveness of deathbed confessions, but what if the authors had got it badly wrong? Or if the sub-saintly individual dies without warning, before they can confess all? In a jam, people's minds turned quickly to where they might find a Get out of Hell Free card.

Thankfully, as in every domain of human activity, where there's a market, there's a seller. As it turned out, anti-damnation nectar points could be earned by buying and lighting candles, giving to the poor, and going on a pilgrimage to Rome, Santiago in Spain, or, (like Geoffrey Chaucer's characters), to Canterbury. Another option was to pay hard cash to have your worst behaviour deleted from the afterlife database. Believers would give a senior church figure, a Pardoner, an amount of money to have their sins officially forgiven. Sometimes, the Pardoner would charge the anxious punter extra to touch bits of old bone or cloth, '*holy relics*', on the shared understanding that contact with these remains of a long-dead saint provided a divine guarantee of forgiveness.

Pardoning was little more than a method of swindling the superstitious. Geoffrey Chaucer, writing in 1392, called time on the scam. A Pardoner joins the group of Chaucer's pilgrims headed to Canterbury and offers their tour guide, Harry Bailey, a selection of holy relics to kiss, to smooth Harry's path to heaven for the bargain price of one silver piece. Harry is having none of it:

> *Even if Christ sends me to hell, I'll give you nothing.*
> *You'd make me kiss your old trousers,*
> *And swear they'd belonged to a saint,*
> *Even though they were soiled by your arse!*
> *But by the true cross that St Helena found,*
> *I wish I had your balls in my hand*
> *Instead of your fake relics;*
> *I'd then cut them off and enshrine them*
> *In a pig's turd!*

All the other pilgrims have a good laugh at the Pardoner's expense. Humiliated, he can find nothing to say as a comeback.

As a final hell-evasion strategy, you could always leave money to the church in your will, so that some bespoke prayers are offered up to save your soul, or a full religious ceremony, a mass, is performed in your name. This system was a terrific earner for some churches. Taking no chances William Courtney, the Archbishop of Canterbury, paid for a ludicrous 15,000 masses to be said for him following his death in 1496.

Eventually, nuns and monks were so busy praying and singing for thousands of dead countrymen that their vocal cords had an equal or greater need of salvation. Common sense took over and a cover-all prayer was introduced across many abbeys and monasteries for everyone that had died and paid money.

By the 1500s, people in England were becoming bold enough to speak out against the selling of these two supernatural cleansing products, pardoning and masses for the dead. In 1529, before Martin Luther had risked his neck in Germany, a man called Simon Fish from Kent defied the authorities and booked himself a guaranteed incineration at the stake. He printed a leaflet that decried all pardons and masses for the dead as a complete waste of money, cash which would be far better spent, he asserted, relieving the suffering of the poor. The courageous Mr Fish was arrested on a charge of heresy but avoided his inevitable execution by dying shortly afterwards from the plague.

But in less than 20 years the game was up anyway: in 1547 a new law signed by the Protestant boy king Edward VI made it clear that faith in Christ was the one and only thing needed to book a place in heaven; no amount of purchased pardons or masses could make an inch of difference to whether a newly dead person ascends to everlasting heaven or plunges to eternal hell. The Protestants were certain that everyone's fate was sealed at the moment of death. No need then for loads of chanting, singing and praying for the soul of the departed. Every chapel that had been wholly funded by donations from individuals wishing to secure their own salvation was demolished, on the order of the king; every chapel that is except his own at Windsor castle, which was extended. When it came to his eternal fate, the boy king privately reasoned it was better to be safe than sorry. At this same time England also backed away from the notion of Purgatory. In Protestant England, afterlife options were now down to two: eternal bliss or everlasting misery.

When I said that everyone came to agree there was just one Christian god, this was not absolutely the case. Some early Christians believed in a female as well as a male god. There was a religious group living in Israel around the same time of Jesus, the Essenes, who had their own gospel, which was excluded from the Bible. In it they talk repeatedly about a heavenly father and an earthly mother. The earthly mother seems to have equal status with the heavenly male; they both have a team of angels. The Essenes gospel, for instance, quotes Jesus as saying to his followers, '*your Earthly Mother and Heavenly Father will send you their angels to teach, to love, and to serve you.*' It's unlikely that early English Christians had any information about this belief, but medieval images of Jesus' mother Mary, such as the Wilton Diptych in the National Gallery, portray her as a near-goddess, perhaps serving a lingering need for a sacred female figure.

We can't know what Shakespeare believed about any after-world: he was far too cautious to provide us with any definite statement. The nearest to a clue comes in the Merchant of Venice, when Lorenzo talks to his lover Jessica about music that is said to come from the stars and planets:

> *Such harmony is in immortal souls;*
> *But whilst this muddy vesture of decay*
> *Doth grossly close it in, we cannot hear it.*

To Lorenzo, heaven may be calling sweetly to us from up there, but since we are encased in human form, we are deaf to its song. Shakespeare also brought the whole idea of immortality down to earth, by taking eternal life to mean never being forgotten in this world. He predicts that the lines to his Sonnet 81 will be read and spoken aloud by generations to come, ensuring that his lover will live forever in the minds of those yet to be born:

Your name from hence immortal life shall have...

Your monument shall be my gentle verse,
Which eyes not yet created shall o'er-read,
And tongues to be, your being shall rehearse,
When all the breathers of this world are dead

Shakespeare boasts that he's so brilliant a writer (*'such virtue hath my pen'*) that no-one will forget his lover. Maybe not if he had only troubled himself to include their name in the poem. So as things turn out, we all know Will, but we haven't a clue to the identity of Ms/Mr 81.

The Coming of Science

From: Jack Marteau <Jack.Marteau@student.manchester.ac.uk
Sent: 11 November 2009 21:21
To: Dave Marteau

I lost my phone, I borrowed a shite phone, I got fed up and bought a new phone, my old phone arrived in the post the next day. A quick mental calculation tells me I've owned over 11,000 phones in my short lifetime.

Magic, Experimentation and the Other Side

In the play Henry VI Part 2, Shakespeare has Eleanor Cobham employ black magic to help her become queen of England. A magician called Roger Bolingbroke conjures up a spirit on her behalf, but their illegal seance is busted by the Duke of York. Eleanor is thrown in gaol and her husband is put under arrest. Eleanor decides she will be far better off dead:

my joy is death – Death, at whose name I oft have been afeard.

When Eleanor is told that rather than being executed, she's to be exiled to the Isle of Man, her response is, '*That's bad enough*', which is a bit Manxist, but funny all the same. But who was the inspiration for the magician Roger Bolingbroke? Most likely a remarkable scholar called John Dee.

Dee was perhaps the greatest scientist of Elizabethan England. Particularly brilliant in mathematics and astrology, he was employed as scientific adviser to the queen herself. His position and reputation throughout Europe was secure, but Dee found himself increasingly drawn to the practice of magic. This obsession led Dee to abandon conventional studies to pursue the paranormal, '*to*,' in the words of historian I R F Calder, '*the ruin of his mind and fortunes*'.

For the rest of his days Dee searched in vain for the philosopher's stone, the fabled substance that turns base metal into gold, and for the elixir of life, the potion that gives its drinker immortality. According to some reports, Dee believed he'd found the elixir in the ruins of Glastonbury Abbey, but as he eventually died, we have to mark this down as an error on his part. Above any other mystery, Dee was most desperate to find a way to penetrate the spirit world. He recorded one of his early attempts to communicate with angels using a *scryer*, a person who gazes into a crystal ball to see into the unknown:

> *I willed the scryer named Saul to look into my great Crystal Globe, if God had sent his holy angel Annael...Saul, looking into my aforesaid stone (or Crystal Globe) for to espy Annael, he saw there one which answered [to] the name...Another did appear, very beautiful with yellow apparel, glittering like gold; and his head had beams like star beams, blazing and spreading from it, his eyes [were] fiery. He wrote in the stone very much in Hebrew letters...there appeared also a white dog with a long head.*

Unfortunately, Saul couldn't read Hebrew and the dog couldn't talk. Saul did, however, pass on some verbal messages from the angels. These words went into Dee's *First Book of Mystical Exercises*. Dee would write a further four of these with the help of a medium called Edward Kelley. Dee and Kelley used a range of other devices to contact the other side, including a black stone mirror made by the Aztecs or Mayans of Central America, and a table edged with strange symbols that Dee believed, for some reason, represented an angels' alphabet.

Kelley and Dee took their mystical methods and messages on tour to Europe. They found themselves accused of necromancy (using magic to speak with the dead) in Poland and were lucky to escape with their lives. Once they'd made their escape, Kelley told Dee the angels had been in touch again and had said they wanted the two men to swap wives. Dee was none too happy, but believing the message to be genuine, he agreed. His wife subsequently became pregnant with Kelley's child, and Dee (as loyal as he was naïve) raised the lad as his own.

As well as the fictional magician Roger Bolingbroke, Dee was probably the inspiration for Christopher Marlowe's character Doctor Faustus, Ben Jonson's The Alchemist and Shakespeare's Prospero. In *The Tempest*, Prospero practises magic, using a supernatural assistant, Ariel, to shipwreck his enemies and deceive the surviving mariners via a combination of invisibility and flight. Marlowe's play is considerably darker: a respectable scholar called Faustus decides to summon up a demon called Mephistopheles and goes on to sell his soul to Lucifer for superpowers that include invisibility and the capacity to turn his enemies into animals. Tremendous fun at first for Faustus, but the Breaking Bad doctor ends up with his soul carted off to hell by a team of demons.

While Prospero and Faustus have genuine magical powers, Ben Johnson's Doctor Subtle is an out-and-out fraud, bereft of any supernatural talent. Subtle poses as an alchemist and separates gullible fools from their money by promising to turn base metal into gold, or to make them unbeatable at gambling. Blending all three characters, Prospero, Faustus and Subtle, we gain a window into the different ways Elizabethan society came to think of Dee: as a harmless magician, a complete phoney, or an agent of the devil (you could still stand trial for the practice of magic in Tudor England; Dee's house was once ransacked by a mob that believed he was a sorcerer).

Dee's appearance in three separate plays demonstrates a considerable contemporary hunger to understand the forces that operate beyond or behind the everyday world. Disease and natural disaster could strike at any time, and without the insights of modern science, the Tudors turned to superstition for explanation. Dreadful events had to be the work of malevolent spirits. The air hummed with invisible life. Talk of ghosts was commonplace and it was so widely accepted that demons and angels could be summoned from other worlds that parliament passed laws against witchcraft in 1542, 1562 and 1604. In 1553 Dee himself was accused of employing magic in an attempt to kill the newly crowned Queen Mary and was briefly imprisoned.

With Columbus's discovery of the Americas, and translations of ancient books entering Europe from Istanbul, the Elizabethan period was alive with the possibility that arcane knowledge had become available from remote cultures. Columbus's discovery of an entirely new world was enough to convince many that there were deeper supernatural realms out there, ready to be revealed. Caught up in this excitement, Dee abandoned himself in search of something he would never find. Once a wealthy man, Dee died a pauper in 1608.

The Puritans

Puritans took hold of England in the 1650s, following the Civil War. A bunch of spiritual killjoys, the Puritans delighted in telling anyone who seemed pleased with life that they were headed straight for hell. Among these miseries was Jeremy Taylor. who we find at home in Cambridge in 1651, putting the finishing touches to his dour book, *the Rule and Exercises of Holy Dying*. Taylor's message is simple: we'd better be careful: '*Every vice of our own managing in the matter of carnality, of lust or rage, ambition or revenge, is a sword of Satan put into the hands of a man.*' If things end badly for us, Jeremy warns, the outcome will be nobody's fault but our own: '*we hug the poison, and twist willingly with the vipers, till they bring us into the regions of an irrecoverable sorrow.*' If we keep to our greedy, over-sexed or ill-tempered ways, there's only one place he can see us ending up, and we'll be sorry, as '*the torments of hell are so horrid, so insupportable a calamity*'.

Taylor is not without his own faults. He comes across as a racist bigot who failed GCSE Geography when he writes, '*Most of the men that are now alive, or that have been living for many ages, are Jews, heathens, or Turks*'. The problem for these non-Christian *men* (add 'sexism' to Jeremy's list of defects) is they're all going to hell, regardless of whether they've been naughty or nice. Taylor feels that this fate of non-Christians is '*extremely sad*,' but like Walter Hilton, he doesn't worry his head too long over this. Instead, he reverts to telling his Christian readers how to save their own skins. His method is simple: be an obedient kid, grow to be a young adult free of '*lust and other passions*', mature to become '*modest and industrious*', and go on to live a '*prudent and sober*' life, remaining religious right up to the end. It hardly seems worth all the effort, but Jeremy reminds us that if we mess up, we are likely to roast in the '*eternal never-dying flames of hell*'. To be fair to him, Jeremy sees hell as a sort of divine last resort. Taylor's god has reasonable expectations of us: he knows we're going to slip from time to time, and provided we've made a solid effort to behave ourselves and be kind to others, he'll probably let us squeeze through the gates of heaven. Unless we're Jewish, a Heathen or a Turk, in which case we're screwed.

Let's leave happy Jeremy now, and move onward a few years and westward a few miles to a cell in Bedford prison where we find another Puritan, John Bunyan, scribbling away. Published in 1678 and a huge global hit, Bunyan's *Pilgrim's Progress (Part I)* describes a hazardous journey made by a man called Christian to the Celestial City (heaven), from the City of Destruction (his, and our, home address.)

Just about everyone in the City of Destruction, including his wife and kids, think Christian is crazy to go on a quest to the Celestial City, but he is determined and sets out alone. Along the way he is persuaded by the apparently friendly Mr Worldly Wiseman, Mr Legality and his son Civility to abandon the '*narrow way*' he is following and take a short cut. The message is clear here: charming people can tempt us from the path of righteousness. In the nick of time Christian is put right by a man calling himself the Evangelist: '*Mr. Worldly Wiseman is an alien, and Mr. Legality is a cheat; and for his son Civility, notwithstanding his simpering looks, he is but a hypocrite, and cannot help thee.*'

Christian hooks up with Faithful, who has also quit the City of Destruction, and for a very reasonable reason: *'I did believe, and do still, that the end of our city will be with fire and brimstone from above; and therefore I have made my escape.'* The everyday world is a modern Sodom and Gomorrah, damned to get its due.

Christian and Faithful's route takes them through Vanity Fair, a shameless town where anything goes. When he condemns the local godless ways, Faithful is put on trial there and executed. Thankfully, as a martyr to Christianity, Faithful is given direct promotion to the Celestial City.

Bunyan wants to make it clear there's no such hope for those who don't live a religious life. Calling in at the house of a stern moralist called the Interpreter, Christian is introduced to a man imprisoned in an iron cage. The man tells Christian that he has been locked up, *'For the lusts, pleasures, and profits of this world; in the enjoyment of which I did then promise myself much delight.'* He is certain he'll never get out, as it was God himself who locked him in the cage for all eternity. It's hard to believe this is a kids' book. As if further comment were needed, the Interpreter says to Christian: *'Let this man's misery be remembered by thee, and be an everlasting caution to thee.'* Christian swallows hard, makes his excuses and heads straight back onto the road. Our hero faces many more tests, including a fight with a hideous monster, but by keeping his head and his faith, he is welcomed into the Celestial City.

In Part II of the book Christian's wife Christiana, their four children and their servant Mercy all set off for the Celestial City. Again, there are bad people to avoid and demons to fight, but the women show just as much courage as Christian in facing down these dangers. Eventually Christiana and her family reach the enchanted ground, a place, *'where the sun shineth night and day.'* As they rest beside the river that separates them from the Celestial City, a letter arrives from *the Master*, summoning Christiana to join him in the city within the next ten days. With the letter comes an arrow, *'with a point sharpened with love'* which is designed to pass easily into her heart. The gift's meaning is clear: to reach the heavens we must die. Christiana again shows no fear, and calmly says her goodbyes to family and fellow pilgrims.

Its strict Christian morality, which viewed almost every human behaviour as a sin (Bunyan himself listed two of the worst things he'd ever done as dancing and ringing church bells too loudly) makes Pilgrim's Progress a sanctimonious read today, but like *Wizard of Oz, Lord of the Rings*, or *Zelda and the Ocarina of Time*, it is at heart a tremendous quest. And at a time when women were still being burned at the stake on suspicion of witchcraft, Bunyan's female characters are a modern equal of any man.

Jeremy Taylor and John Bunyan's convictions about the existence of heaven and hell (they were both preachers, although Bunyan's unofficial status caused his imprisonment) were still widely held in mid-17th century England. With his executioner standing in wait on a winter's morning in 1649, King Charles I made the confident afterlife prediction: '*I go from a corruptible to an incorruptible Crown.*' To Charles, heaven was not only a reality, it was founded on a divine class system that guaranteed him a seat at its top table. The fact that so many people were willing to see him killed meant that a fair number had moved away from the idea that kings were selected by a god, or even that there was a heaven at all. When Samuel Pepys' brother Tom lay dying in London in March 1664, Samuel asked him straight where he imagined he might end up after death:

> *He in distracted manner answered me – 'Why, whither should I go? there are but two ways: If I go, to the bad way I must give God thanks for it, and if I go the other way I must give God the more thanks for it; and I hope I have not been so undutiful and unthankful in my life but I hope I shall go that way.' This was all the sense, good or bad, that I could get of him this day.*

Although it's plain from this exchange that Tom Pepys held to a conventional view on the afterlife, Samuel's own beliefs seem less solid.

The great majority of 17th century citizens of England had only to gaze up at the vast night sky, with its numberless stars lighting the way to infinity, to find all the proof they needed that the heavens were the work and home of God. Isaac Newton believed this as strongly as anyone, (he had thirty versions of the Bible and even learned Hebrew to deepen his understanding of the earliest scriptures). But instead of achieving his intention to reveal the glory of his god, Isaac's work picked away at the foundations of religion. In a letter in 1692, Newton set out how he thought galaxies were formed: some parts of matter, he believed, would come together *'into one mass and some into another so as to make an infinite number of great masses scattered at great distances from one to another throughout all that infinite space'*. He felt that this explained the birth of stars as well as planets. It was a brilliant piece of deduction that still explains much of the known universe. It highlighted the huge power of natural forces, an evolution of the heavens that did not necessarily depend on the sculpting hand of any god.

With the emergence of science and reasoning, people began to lose fear of hell. No longer symbols of personal terror, red horns and pitchforks became fun items of fancy dress. The afterlife turned from a place where 50% of residents lived in constant torture to a nice sunny location where people met up with dead friends and relations. In with this new optimism came the Graveyard Poets, a bunch of radical young artists set on meeting death head on. Among them was Philip Doddridge. Philip grew up steeped in death. He was one of 20 children born to Monica Doddridge, 18 of whom died in infancy! Monica herself died when Philip was eight years old, and he grew to be a serious-minded, excitable and very religious adult. He wrote gleeful hymns, one of which, *O Happy Day*, won a Grammy 200 years after Doddridge's death:

> *Happy day, happy day,*
> *When Jesus washed my sins away!*

Philip became a Christian spiritual leader, attracting a number of followers. His rigorous devotional approach involved several hours of prayer each day, frequent giving to the poor, a near-starvation diet, precious little sleep and unlimited bible study. Some of those who chose to live exactly like Philip lost their health, their minds, and even their lives. The graveyard poet James Hervey was never the same after following the Doddridge plan, dying at the age of forty-four. Doddridge himself didn't fare much better, checking out at forty-nine. He seems to have been OK with it though; as he lay on his deathbed he is reported to have said: *'Such transporting views of the heavenly world is my Father now indulging me with, no words can express.'*

In 1743 the poet Robert Blair wrote the anthem of the Graveyard poems. It was called, of course, The Grave. The poem states its purpose right from the off: *'the task be mine'*, says Robert, *'To paint the gloomy horrors of the tomb'*
'Death's thousand doors stand open', adds Bob, cheerily.

Blair goes on to consider the effect dying might have on a man who has spent his life indulging himself in wealth and luxury:

> *How shocking must thy summons be, O Death,*
> *To him that is at ease in his possessions*

Likewise, Blair asks how a materialist woman might take the news that her number is up. The answer is not too well:

> *Her very eyes weep blood, and every groan*
> *She heaves is big with horror!*

In case it had slipped our minds, Bob reminds us:

> *Sure 'tis a serious thing to die.*

Blair lightens the mood significantly by promising us that the moment of dying is just the crossing of an *'inoffensive stream.'* The opposite bank – the next world – is a beautiful land carpeted in flowers. It is, in fact, *'our home.'* Instead of diving for cover when we see him coming, he suggests we embrace the grim reaper. Blair channels the future poet Lionel Ritchie, to say he's not just once, twice, but '*Thrice welcome Death!*

The poem is full of melodrama, like a train crash in a soap opera, but what could be more melodramatic than death? Young, old, healthy and sick, they all must go.

Things work out nicely in the end: come Judgment Day, body and soul are reunited forever. Reaching for the exclamation mark on his heavenly keypad, Blair is once again triply delighted:

> *Thrice happy meeting!*
> *Nor time, nor death, shall ever part them more!*

The poem was a big seller, and deservedly so. It took death down a peg or two. From a flaming torture chamber of eternal agonies, Blair turned the afterlife into a Tellytubbieland, easing death from the grip of religion by barely mentioning any god and whittling the ten commandments down to one: Don't be a Selfish Git. To Blair, death is really the person we should be dealing with, rather than any gods or demons. The modern world had arrived! Three years after the publication of The Grave, Blair died. With a smile on his face, perhaps.

But not everyone was convinced that the next world would be all hunky dory. The 18th century poet John Newton covered religious subjects in a straight-laced style; (he wrote that dreary standard *Amazing Grace*). In another hymn, *Judgment Day*, John warned us of all of what might happen when God arrives to weighs us all up:

> *By his looks prepare to flee:*
> *Careless sinner, what will then become of thee?*

Newton had his own reason to fret about Judgment Day; he used to captain slave ships from Africa to the Americas, something that caused him deep regret in his later years.

Virginia Woolf, like Robert Blair dared to peer into the grave. In the 1929 short story *Three Pictures*, Woolf imagines herself in some perfect English village:

> *Death is cheerful here, one felt. Indeed, look at that picture! A man was digging a grave, and children were picnicking at the side of it while he worked.*

Virginia innocently asks the digger's wife if the grave is for some old villager who has recently passed away. '*Oh! no. It's for young Rogers, the sailor...He died two nights ago, of some foreign fever. Didn't you hear his wife?* Virginia had indeed heard a loud screech in the middle of the night. The picture-perfect world disintegrates.

Religion Today

How do the two main religions of England, Christianity and Islam, regard death today? I met with John Pares, a Church of England priest who has worked in rural Norfolk and Bournemouth. What experience, I wondered, had John of working with dying and death.

I've not been a lifetime priest; I was ordained in 2010. I haven't that much experience in accompanying people on that last part of the journey. In a sense, I think, that's almost a reflection on the way society is going. That process is medicalised a lot of the time: the end of lifetime equals hospital. There isn't that cultural thing of someone's near the end, we'll call the vicar.

Most of my experience is around funerals and helping people through funerals. It is an enormous privilege to be involved at that time of life, when people are open to some big questions. I personally don't have a huge 'This is an evangelical opportunity;' I'm there for the family and for the next of kin.

John is aware of the rise in atheist funerals that 'celebrate' the life that has ended. He is uneasy about this trend.

More people are choosing secular people, humanists. There also is this move towards a celebration of life and not dwelling on the death, the sadness, the grief and the mourning, and I think that's a profound mistake because you have to deal with those things. There's always mourning, there's always shame – I'm speaking perhaps more as a psychologist now! – there's always emotion to deal with. And the Anglican funeral service has wonderful words that help people through those stages; they confront the fact that we are only here for a short time, but they offer the love of God and the hope of eternity with him. We can't prove that, but we talk about it with faith and with joy, but also talk about the grief that people must feel, how bereft and completely shocked and stunned they must feel, depending on the circumstances of the death.

Having done funerals for people who have gone in very shocking circumstances, I think the Anglican service, the words, they bring up the hairs on the back of your neck: 'For He knows of what we are made, he remembers that we are but dust, our days are like the grass. We flourish like a flower in the field, when the wind goes over it, it is gone, and its place remembers it no more, but the merciful goodness endures forever.' Every time I read that I think that we are loved, we have a place, we've done things – we've had an impact on the world – but now our time, or the time for this person has gone. I think the words of the service are almost enough to help people through those feelings and through that door. It's a liminal period a funeral, it's like a doorway: you've lived a life with this person, they've always been around, you are looking forward to a time in the future without them, and the funeral, the grieving, dealing with all that is like going through a doorway, and it's very disorientating and frightening.

In funerals people confront their own mortality….it's as much about that as it is about grief and paying respect…people don't think about their own death or even the death of a close relative until it confronts them.

One of the most rewarding funerals was somebody from church, a pillar of our church society. He had planned it with me beforehand….he was one of these, 'I don't want people to be sad.' I say, if we want to be sad, we are going to be, but we'll also celebrate. Because it's not real, not to. And I think profound unhappiness comes from denying that you're grieving.

I asked John if the church funeral service is designed to be cathartic.

Oh absolutely, yes. You have to go through death. Think of the Christian faith; it's founded on the festival that is the most important for us, which is when Jesus died on a cross. God came to earth and died. What could be more horrible, dramatic, terrible than that? But he rose again. What is human experience? Human experience is suffering and misery, but hope! Hope comes from that, and you can't have one without the other.

I don't really like the word 'Religion'. If you're religious, you do all these things to get to God. But God loves you, and it's having faith, faith is a better way of describing it. I'm a person of faith, and I would say aspiring to be a spiritual person. I think being a Christian is being hopeful, always thinking and being open to the good possibilities of a creative loving god, and that's in personal relationships, how you live your life, how you approach your work, how you are, and how you approach your death....God created you in his own image, he knew you by name before you were born, and he is waiting for you to come back, and then he will rejoice.

Paul Salahuddin Armstrong is Co-Director of the Association of British Muslims. Paul told me that he was brought up by agnostic parents and religion was never a part of his childhood:

When I was a child I was very much into science. If you'd have spoken to me when I was 12 or 13 and said, 'You know, one day you're probably going to become religious,' I'd be laughing, I'd be like, 'You're kidding me!' It's the last thing I would have considered doing. But I read the Qur'an.

Paul went to university but dropped out during a personal existential crisis:

I didn't have a spiritual or a sort of philosophical framework. 'What am I here for? What's it all for?' These questions kept bugging me. 'What if I die and there's something there, and I've wasted my life?'

Paul laughed as he recounted his first approaches to Islam:

I went to a couple of mosques in Wolverhampton; one of them was quite welcoming, but at the other one I was basically told to get lost! 'White kid: what's he doing?!'

Perhaps as a response to the way Islam is frequently misperceived in the west, Paul was at pains to emphasise the inclusivity of its scripture.

There's an acceptance in the Qur'an that there are believers in other faiths, people who give to charity, who pray, and these are good people. There's a verse that says of the Jews and Christians, 'no fear need they have, neither shall they grieve.' The interesting thing about Islam when you read the Qur'an is that it's not a religion that claims to be exclusive. It sees itself as the way of all the prophets, that includes the Jewish prophets, includes Jesus, and it could include the Buddha and Krishna. Certainly, in my interpretation it does, that these are all messengers of God. This really appealed to me about Islam, it's really open, and eventually when I realised that this is Islam, and not necessarily what some Muslims do, something clicked.

That was eighteen years ago. I was twenty. I decided to embrace Islam. I didn't want to do it in front of a mosque or anything, I just wanted it to be between me and God. I asked a few friends who were Muslims to witness, and I actually embraced Islam at the back of a chemist's shop. We recite, Ashadu an la ilaha illa illa-ilah, wa ashadu anna muhammadan rasul ullah, which in English is, 'There is no god except God, and Mohammed is the messenger of God' It's a simple declaration of faith.

I am a student of two Naqshbandi sheikhs. Naqshbandi is a Sufi order. Some of the teachers I follow are Malaki. Malaki is a school within the Sunni tradition. I am Sunni, but I wouldn't turn around and say because someone followed a different school of thought, they weren't a Muslim.

Within every religion you get people who understand things literally, and those who understand things esoterically. I understand things a bit more esoterically. I personally do not believe that sacred scriptures need to be taken so literally – there are certain things in them that are understood at different levels. If you're talking to quite simple folk who are quite violent, the scriptures tell them if you live your life like that [and] don't change your ways, then you're going to go somewhere that's not nice. My understanding now of these passages is that God's primary characteristics, as far as we can explain in human language – because human language is always flawed when talking about the divine – are benevolence, kindness, compassion.

94

This is why a Muslim, before we read the Qur'an, have food, or so many other things, we say *bi-smi llāhi r-raḥmāni r-raḥīm*, which means 'In the name of God, the most compassionate, the most kind.' The reason we keep repeating this is because God's primary characteristic in Islam is understood to be compassion. So, how can a compassionate god after we die grab us and put us into a fire? It doesn't make sense. We also understand that God is a god of justice, and that wouldn't be just either. We can't say God's unjust. How can God not be just? So, when we reflect on these things we come to a slightly different understanding.

My understanding now is that when a person passes away, they face themselves. In life, when some people are doing a lot of bad things, they tend to drink a lot or abuse drugs, something that dulls their senses and allows them to escape from facing what they're doing. When the soul passes from the physical body into another realm, I believe we can no longer do that. We have to face what we have done. So, a person who has lived their life compassionately – we know everyone makes mistakes, but they don't harbour ill intent towards other people, they haven't gone out of their way to be unkind to others or enrich themselves – when that person passes, no matter what religion they are, they don't really have anything to worry about. They've got nothing attached to their soul that they're going to have to face when they die. They are free. For them, it's going to be bliss. And the same applies to children, because children haven't done anything wrong: they're innocent. Even in the most conservative Islamic schools of thought they say this, children below a certain age, before puberty, are pure; they just go to heaven.

Paul has an interesting take on hellfire

It will be very painful for someone who has lived a bad life and committed a lot of crimes against other people. You already see it in this life: if you do the right thing you feel good about yourself, your conscience isn't biting away at you. You know when you're doing wrong, and if we do really bad things and we haven't tried to change or make amends, then my sense is that

that would be like a burning, which is why it's depicted in this imagery in the Qur'an and the Bible. It's not that God is going to burn us. No, it's us; we have to face ourselves.

We believe spirit is actually real, thought is actually real. Although in this life we tend to focus on physical things, because of the nature of this realm, in the next life these things, spirit and thought, are much more real.

Among the most striking aspects of John and Paul's statements of belief is the emphasis they place on a positive life after death. Both their gods are fair and compassionate; they're on our side. Hell has largely evaporated as a realistic divine threat. Paul's faith retains the possibility of after-life suffering, but it's us and not punitive gods that are meting out the pain. With hip celebrities such as Stormzy to Zayn Malik declaring themselves believers, mainstream religion has come through a drought of unfashionability and now holds appeal for a new generation. If believers in England grow in number in the coming years, their interpretation of and consequent actions upon scripture will shape future social and political events. Whether their gods are vengeful or benign will depend on the persuasions of the new faithful. History suggests that divine diktat will be evoked to justify a full spectrum of behaviours, from marvellous to maniacal. As nations compete for diminishing global resources, clerics may once again be blessing bullets; or perhaps a school of eco-preachers will emerge, advocating self-denial and peace to save an overheating planet. Or maybe we will have a new intersex god, like the Hindu deity Ardhanarishvara, to suit our age of gender politics and inclusion.

Atheism and Satanism

Top 5 Unnecessary Sequels. Speed 2: Cruise Control

The tension caused by having to avoid traffic and pedestrians is replaced by the tension caused by having to avoid mackerel.

Jack Marteau Student Direct Magazine 2009

It's 1970 and twelve-year-old me is sat at a sloping-topped school desk. It has been gouged by years of compass points; the inkwell (biros are banned!) and the area around it are stained blue-black with *Quink*. There are 35 other boys crammed in the classroom. Built in the Thirties, it has steel-framed windows and parquet wood flooring. Twin rows of enamel-shaded light bulbs run from the back of the class to the front, where Mr Farrell, the Religious Education teacher, is writing on a blackboard. The chalk clacks and squeaks as the words *Israelites* and *Canaanites* materialise. He is saying something, but I'm not really listening; my mind is far outside the room, nowhere near Israel, Canaan or the school.

Paul Wiltshire has a question. He usually does. '*Sir, I heard that even if you've been really bad, say a murderer, and you don't feel at all sorry, as long as someone has prayers said for you in church when you die, you won't go to hell. Is that right sir?*' He's got that wrong. '*That's right,*' says Mr Farrell. What? '*How can that be right?!,*' demands almost all the class. '*It's correct because,*' and at this point Mr Farrell quotes some obscure bit in The Bible: *Yea, though thou might be the most wanton and wretched of God's sinners and verily the keenest servant of Satan upon this great Earth, yet should but one...* something along those lines. I've stopped listening again. It doesn't occur to me that Mr Farrell might be talking cobblers and Paul Wiltshire's hypothetical bad ass is bound for hell notwithstanding any number of good words said on his behalf, but in a sense that doesn't really matter – the whole heaven and hell thing has become just too implausible for me. My drift to atheism begins.

In 1782 Matthew Turner, a Liverpool doctor, published what is probably the earliest atheist document printed in England. In his pamphlet Turner mocked belief in any god as a fantasy of the weak-minded. According to Turner, citizens were simply dreaming the whole god thing up: '*They reason themselves into imaginary Beings with more imaginary properties, and then fall down and worship them.*'

As the first to go into print against Christianity, Turner took the sensible precaution of using a false name, William Hammon, but he had not invented English atheism: there has long been a significant amount of scepticism within these shores. Peter of Cornwall, for instance, writing in 1200 complained that some of the locals had no belief in life after death. But Turner's idea was still extreme for the late 1700s, and it marked a turning point, with an increasing number coming to share his non-beliefs. By the 21st century, atheism had become mainstream. In 2016 Jenny Diski, dying from lung cancer, wrote her own atheist headstone: '*Gone nowhere. No where to go. No she to go to it.*' In agreement, punk mortician Caitlin Doughty says, '*We are all just future corpses.*' So that's us then: the pre-dead.

If Matthew Turner rattled the temple doors, Thomas Paine, born in Thetford, Norfolk in 1737, kicked them off their hinges. In 1797 Paine wrote, '*Of all the tyrannies that affect mankind, tyranny in religion is the worst.*' He highlighted the Bible's many references to God striking people blind, sending plagues their way, or casting them into an inferno: '*It is not a God, just and good, but a devil, under the name of God, that the Bible describes.*' This was revolutionary stuff, but as he had already helped inspire the American War of Independence and risked his life a second time in joining the French revolution, Paine was neither low on courage nor light in appetite for insurrection. He now felt sufficiently emboldened to take on the ultimate adversary: God himself, or at least his holy text. He denounced the Bible's Book of Jeremiah as '*false,*' and '*put together by some stupid book-maker*,' but Thomas saved his heaviest ammunition for the Biblical hero Moses, who is reported in the Bible as ordering murder and child rape:

> *Among the detestable villains that in any period of the world have disgraced the name of man, it is impossible to find a greater than Moses, if this account be true.*

Paine's writing was banned in England, and scandalised almost every reader in America, but unlike Matthew Turner, Paine believed in God, albeit not the vengeful one depicted in parts of the Bible.

As we came to learn that the world wasn't six thousand years old, but had in fact been home to dinosaurs many millions of years ago, and as growing numbers were persuaded by Darwin's theory that we were descended from apes rather than a pair of gullible nudists, the Bible began to look wrong in a number of key areas: a prophet living in a whale's stomach, a talking donkey and a man more than 900 years of age. In Germany, Friedrich Nietzsche put the scientific cat even deeper among the pigeons by declaring that God had existed but, unfortunately, he has since dead. It's one thing to deny the existence of the almighty, but to say he was as mortal as a human or even a centipede was really putting the atheist boot in. It was a low blow that had Christianity staggering back towards the ropes; for a growing number of the English, there was now no god, no heaven, no hell, no nothing.

In 1891, Thomas Hardy reflected this shift in his novel *Tess of the D'Urbervilles*. After years of brutal mistreatment, Tess stabs and kills her abusive husband Alec. She goes on the run with her lover Angel Clare. Exhausted and fully aware that her capture and execution are inevitable, Tess turns her thoughts to an afterlife:

> *'Tell me now, Angel, do you think we shall meet again after we are dead? I want to know.'*
> *He kissed her to avoid a reply at such a time.*

'Oh, Angel- I fear that means no! What- not even you and I, Angel, who love each other so well?'

Angel never answers her question.

Strident hellfire preaching, broadcast in weekly instalments from church pulpits over and into the heads of uneasy congregations, sputtered and all but died out during Hardy's lifetime. Charles Spurgeon was the last noted preacher of the 19th century still playing the obey-the-lord-or-go-directly-to-hell card. Absolute adherence to the teachings of the church was, according to Spurgeon, obligatory. Thinking for oneself, he declared, was the devil's own work: *'Free will carried many a soul to hell, but never a soul to heaven.'* But that line couldn't work anymore: Spurgeon complained that at times the faithful responded to his sermons with hisses and even verbal abuse...the world had moved on, and it felt obliged to give Charles a shove to help him catch up.

And he had some catching up to do, because all pagan hell was about to break loose. Born in Warwickshire in 1875, Aleister Crowley was a drug-taking sex addict and practitioner of black magic. 'The Beast', as Crowley's own mother called him, blended Egyptian mythology, the thoughts of the hedonistic 16th Century monk François Rabelais, a supply of mind-altering drugs and a decent amount of sex magic to produce a wholesome belief system that was fun for all the family. He called this new religion Thelema, after Rabelais' fictional Abbey of Thélème.

The basis for Thelema was revealed to Crowley in April 1904 in the form of a book, *Liber Legis*, dictated to him by a servant to the Egyptian god Horus while Crowley lay in a three-day trance. It may not be the deepest shock to us that parts of Liber Legis read like mumbo-jumbo. For instance, *'The Khabs is in the Khu, not the Khu in the Khabs.'* Of course not; and, *'Nothing is a secret key of this law. Sixty-one the Jews call it; I call it eight, eighty, four hundred & eighteen'*....and the bonus ball is...

But in other ways Thelema's good book is very straightforward. It has just two rules:

1. *'Do what thou wilt shall be the whole of the Law'*
2. *'Love is the law, love under will.'*

Rule number one is very much the number one rule. Made a nice break from the Puritans. Rule two sounds friendly enough, but in Thelemic creed and practice, wilfulness predominates. Naturally, the book gives Crowley a decent mention, declaring that, *'the chosen priest & apostle of infinite space is the prince-priest the Beast'*. Liber Legis ends with a fearful curse on the casual reader: *'The study of this Book is forbidden. It is wise to destroy this copy after the first reading. Whosoever disregards this does so at his own risk and peril. These are most dire.'* Since the book is now on the internet, destruction is unfeasible. A reader could try deleting their browsing history but shouldn't be surprised if she/he breaks out in hives and has their car fail its next MOT miserably.

Crowley's new religion attracted some followers, but with a belief system that asserted everyone should do whatever they wanted, some conflict was inevitable. In reality, Thelema seemed to mean that everyone did whatever Crowley wanted (sex, drugs, the washing up). It was fun while it lasted, even if it did leave some people penniless, psychologically dismantled and even, in the case of one follower, dead from drinking contaminated water or, as the writer Nina Hamnett claims, the blood of a sacrificed cat. Remarkably, Thelema has resurfaced and is now a legally recognised religion in the UK. Perhaps the Khabs were in the Khu after all.

Christopher Hitchens, who died in 2011, was 21st century England's most severe and eloquent critic of religion. Among Hitchens' refutations of the truth of religion is that, *'It wholly misrepresents the origins of man and the cosmos'* and *'is ultimately grounded on wish-thinking.'* We made it all up because we can't face our future non-existence.

In his 2007 book *God is not Great*, Hitchens notes that the Jewish, Christian and Muslim faiths are strongly related to one another, all featuring the prophets Moses and Abraham, and each sharing the creation tale of Adam and Eve. Hitchens sees the survival of these religions to the present day as a result of parochial chance rather than divine fate:

> *of the thousands of possible desert religions there were, one branch happened to take root...one or two military victories the other way and we in the West would not be the hostages to village disputes that took place in Judea and Arabia.*

The local setting of the stories told by these religions is important to Hitchens. He points out that the sacred books of the three major desert faiths (the Hebrew Torah, the Christian Bible, and the Islamic Qur'an) never mention parts of the world any distance from the Middle East or North Africa. No Americas, no Asia, no Oceania, no Scandinavia, no jungle, no tundra. And no England! This despite the claim of each book that it is the word of the one true god who made the entire planet.

And if God is great and God is kind, how, wonders Hitchens, does anyone explain the vicious things that happen in the holy books? In the Bible's Book of Numbers, God instructs Moses and the Children of Israel to attack the Midianites. The Children of Israel obey and go on to kill every surviving Midian adult male and take captive every woman and child. Hitchens quotes Moses's instruction to his troops:

> '*Now therefore kill every male among the little ones, and kill every woman that hath known man by lying with him. But all the women children that have not known a man by lying with him, keep alive for yourselves.*'

Hitchens doesn't believe that any god would promote total genocide, incorporating the wholesale murder of women and children, and supplemented by the rape of young girls. In fact, Hitchens doesn't believe in any god at all. As he puts it when considering all the brutal acts described or recommended in the three holy books, '*God did not create man in his own image. Evidently, it was the other way about.*'

Hitchens knew the risks he was running by declaring himself an infidel and attacking rather than ignoring religion. He commented: '*All religions take care to silence or to execute those who question them.*' That didn't keep him from saying, when asked at a public meeting about the religion of Islam, '*Don't waste my time: it's bullshit.*' Not that Hitchens only deplored Christianity, Islam and Judaism; he had very limited time for Eastern faiths either. He believed that the Asian religious notion that this life is an illusion caused followers, '*to put their reason to sleep, and to discard their minds.*' Most people have a soft spot for Buddhist Dalai Llamas. Not Hitchens:

> *The first foreign visitors to Tibet were downright appalled at the feudal domination and hideous punishments that kept the population in permanent serfdom to a parasitic monastic elite.*

He notes that during the second world war Japanese Buddhists proclaimed the Emperor Hirohito a 'tathāgata', a fully enlightened being, despite the bloke having the spiritual charisma of a retired dentist from Bromley. At that time, according to Hitchens, Buddhist and Shinto priests were actively recruiting kamikaze suicide bombers. In the interest of fairness, Hitchens also accused Christianity of dealing with blood-handed dictators, alleging that, '*The Catholic Church was generally sympathetic to fascism as an idea,*' forming a '*working alliance*' through treaties between the Pope of the day (Pius XI) and Mussolini in 1929, and Hitler in July 1933.

Satanists aside, every religion aims to build its churches on the moral high ground, but Hitchens is having none of it. Crusades, Witch-hunts, Inquisitions and the Slave Trade, all done in the name of a god, are evidence enough to Hitchens of religion's historical injustice and brutality. Much of this bloodshed was founded on an argument that is impervious to reason or fact: '*To be accused of demonic possession, or contact with the Evil One, was to be convicted of it.*' It would be of no benefit to say, 'Look, there is no Evil One': such a statement would be taken as absolute proof the defendant was under Satan's spell. Hitchens neatly hijacks this crazy logic by saying that any present-day believers who criticise him for his anti-religious views are, in fact, criticising their own god, since it must have been that god that made Hitchens such a died-in-the-wool atheist.

It was cancer and not a religious fanatic that got Hitch in the end. Typically unflinching, he kept a record of his last few months. In writing that he had woken up, *'feeling as if I were actually shackled to my own corpse,'* he describes a sensation that only the very nearly dead can share. As he absorbs the reality that his time is up, Hitchens turns to English understatement and humour: *'in whatever kind of 'race' life might be, I have reluctantly become a finalist.'*

As his health implodes (*'the runs, vomiting, dripping nose, hair loss'*), Christopher Hitchens, a clear-minded atheist to the last, sees that when his body goes, so too does he: *'I don't have a body, I am a body.'* When he collapses at the airport in Boston, Hitch gives us a world of black humour in just three words: *'At Logan - can't breathe! Next stop, terminal.'*

Writing about Hitch shortly after his death, his editor Graydon Carter said of his fearless friend, *'To those who knew him well, he was a gift from, dare I say it, God.'* Hitch was too dead to be offended.

Facing Death

Top 5 Unnecessary Sequels: Home Alone 2: Lost in New York
Someone call social services because this is getting ridiculous.

Jack Marteau, Student Direct Magazine 2008

England has enjoyed a pleasing run of successes over death. Disease epidemics and starvation, once huge threats, are now nicely under our control. But it hasn't been this way for long. As recently as 1851, the life expectancy for people living in central Liverpool was just 26 years of age. Throughout much of the 19th century, fifteen of every 100 babies born did not make it to their first birthday. Today, 199 of 200 babies born in England will survive beyond twelve months, and 198 will make it to adulthood. Advances in medicine really took off in the early 19th century with Edward Jenner's development of the smallpox vaccine. It's hard for us to imagine the terrible threat that disease represented; prior to Jenner's pioneering work, smallpox killed one in ten of the population, and as many as one in five town and city dwellers.

Improved sanitation coupled with further medical breakthroughs almost halved the national death rate between 1870 and 1928. As 20th century medicine advanced, diseases such as diphtheria, scarlet fever, TB, cholera and typhoid lost almost all their power.

The historian Pat Jalland sees these victories as provoking a revolution in the way the English view death: '*Within half a century death began to be perceived as the monopoly of the elderly and society's preoccupation with death receded.*' Out went the Victorian obsession with death, and in came a nervous silence. When death had stalked us all, young and old, we knew that some of us would escape. We had hope as well as fear. Now the Grim Reaper has been pushed into a far corner, with usually just the old within the radius of his scythe. But not just some of the old. All. Ironically, in winning so many victories against death, citizens of the 21ˢᵗ century now find themselves with no prospect of survival. As Gordon Morse, a doctor from Wiltshire puts it, *'No medical treatment is life-saving; it can only be death-deferring.'* Gulp. No matter how healthy our lifestyle, eventually the numbers stop adding up. If we put this fact together with a decreasing national belief in Mr God, (between 2001 and 2011 the number of UK adults declaring they had no religion almost doubled), it should be small surprise that death is a touchy subject in 21ˢᵗ Century England. More than 'touchy', it is all but taboo.

A conspiracy of coy talk and silence became the default English response to this hard truth. TV ads for pension plans show snow-haired couples wandering off into a sunny but soft-focused future. Destination nice but nowhere. A ninety-three-year-old is admitted to hospital with multiple health problems, and family members ask the staff, *'He is going to be alright, isn't he?'* Jesus. We've somehow convinced ourselves that if we don't mention death, death won't notice us. We'll let the sleeping dog lie.

Like everyone else the English have rarely shown an appetite for death. Bede saw it as, *'a terror to almost all men'*, and when death is in town, things can turn desperate. One way of facing death is simply to deny it. This isn't necessarily a conscious response: for many months after my sister Elizabeth had died, I would 'see' her among a crowd of people, on the street or in a shop or pub. A part of me had refused to accept she was gone. And when I stood at Jack's bedside as he lay in a coma, I 'failed' to recognise him. I knew he had to be Jack, but the young man in the bed didn't look much like my son at all. I realised immediately that the same mechanism that had superimposed Elizabeth's features onto passers-by – denial – was at work in my brain again, this time substituting a stranger's features for those of my priceless son. I accepted he was truly Jack to avoid the agony of 'seeing' him again in the months ahead; I dreaded the knife to the heart that always followed my mistaken sightings of Elizabeth.

In the early Nineties I worked briefly with Jason, a young guy who was in the advanced stages of HIV/AIDS. Treatments were very ineffective back then, and his condition worsened. As death neared, Jason became more and more agitated. At one point he declared, '*It's a scientific fact that there's no such thing as AIDS!*' In a desperate attempt to avoid his deadly condition, Jason simply denied its existence. When, in *Wuthering Heights*, the doctor tells Hindley Earnshaw that his wife Frances is so sick with TB that there's no point in his making any more home visits, Hindley completely denies that his wife is dying: '*she's well—she does not want any more attendance from you! She never was in a consumption. It was a fever; and it is gone: her pulse is as slow as mine now, and her cheek as cool.*' He's wrong of course, and Frances only lasts a couple more pages.

In *Jane Eyre*, Jane's best friend at school Helen Burns is young and terminally ill. Although she claims to be very happy to die, it seems Helen is simply unhappy to live:

> '*I am very happy, Jane.…. I shall escape great sufferings. I had not qualities or talents to make my way very well in the world: I should have been continually at fault.*'

Her solid belief in a heavenly afterlife keeps Helen's spirits high, but Jane has doubts about the existence of paradise. She asks Helen if she is certain there is such a place as heaven:

> '*I am sure there is a future state; I believe God is good; I can resign my immortal part to Him without any misgiving. God is my father; God is my friend: I love Him; I believe He loves me.*'

> '*And shall I see you again, Helen, when I die?*'

> '*You will come to the same region of happiness: be received by the same mighty, universal Parent, no doubt, dear Jane.*'

> *Again I questioned, but this time only in thought. '*Where is that region? Does it exist?*'*

If Jane Eyre's creator Charlotte Bronte had doubts herself about the existence of any afterlife, her private letters suggest these were only momentary interruptions in faith. In December 1836 she wrote to a friend, Ellen Nussey,

> *I go on constantly seeking my own pleasure...I forget God and will not God forget me? And meantime I know the greatness of Jehovah. I acknowledge the truth, the perfection of his word.*

In Shakespeare's Henry VI part I, Talbot rationalises rather than denies the dangers he faces just before he goes into battle:

> *If I today die not with Frenchmen's rage,*
> *Tomorrow I shall die with mickle* [old] *age*

It's a plucky attitude that glosses over decades of healthy living he might still enjoy if he turns and runs. Although not a soldier, this is exactly what the cowardly Jos Sedley does at the Battle of Waterloo in Thackery's *Vanity Fair*. Having pledged to stay and protect his sister Amelia, Jos panics at the first cannon shot and orders a horse and carriage to flee the battle zone. He demands that Amelia come with him, but Peggy O'Dowd, a Major's wife, is having nothing to do with Jos Sedley's pathetic plan. *'Is it her mother you're going to take her to?'* asks Peggy, *'or do you want to go to Mamma yourself, Mr. Sedley?'* she sneers. Back in England Jos constructs every tall tale of a heroic involvement in the battle, but he is believed by no-one and is doomed to be known as *Waterloo Sedley*, a figure of chronic ridicule.

A decent joke can be of help on a final day. Shakespeare's Posthumus, mixes courage and gallows humour, saying to the gloomy prison warder who has come to take him to the scaffold, *'I am merrier to die than thou art to live.'* In real life – and death – Oscar Wilde delivered his final one-liner as he laid on his death bed: *'This wallpaper and I are fighting a duel to the death. Either it goes, or I do.'* He did.

Death's not always so bad. Shakespeare's Edmund Mortimer is not young, stuck in prison, and sees death not as an enemy, but as someone who can do him the ultimate favour of bringing his innings to a close: *'Death, kind umpire of men's miseries'*. Edmund Spenser, another Tudor writer, failed to understand why plainly miserable people cling to their joyless lives:

> *O why do wretched men so much desire,*
> *To draw their days unto the utmost date,*
> *And do not rather wish them soon expire*

Like Shakespeare, Dickens thought that death can do some good. In *a Tale of Two Cities*, Sydney Carton, who is nice enough but a bit of a prat, transforms himself to a hero when he surrenders his life so that Lucie, the woman he idolises, can go on to a happy life with his love rival Darney. *'It is a far, far better thing that I do, than I have ever done,'* says Sydney as he faces the guillotine; *'it is a far, far better rest that I go to than I have ever known'*.

In Bleak House Dickens provides a less romantic reason why death might be, on balance, a Good Thing. Liz and her baby are lodging in a hellish slum near the Thames. She wonders out loud if it would be such a tragedy if the baby were to die. Police Inspector Bucket is appalled, and challenges Liz: *'Why, you an't such an unnatural woman, I hope…as to wish your own child dead?'* Of course she isn't, *'But look around you at this place. Look at them,'* she tells the Inspector, nodding at drunken men, unconscious on the floor. Bucket chokes on the room's foul air. We can all but smell Liz's despairing point of view.

Moving out from the darkness of Dickens' imagination, William Blake offers us a brighter reason why death might be no catastrophe: *'I cannot consider death as anything but a removing from one room to another.'* Death isn't an end to life, simply a relocation of self, a drift into the non-living room. In *Wuthering Heights,* Emily Bronte imagines such a transition, with Frances Earnshaw dying with ease in her husband's arms:

a fit of coughing took her—a very slight one—he raised her in his
arms; she put her two hands about his neck, her face changed, and
she was dead.

It's small wonder Emily Bronte depicts death as a natural event: none of her four sisters nor her brother reached the age of 40. Emily herself was dead at thirty.

Hamlet's mum is equally matter-of-fact about what's to come:

> *All that lives must die,*
> *Passing through nature to eternity.*

As if to prove the point, she fails to make it to the end of the play.

Some of Shakespeare's characters are in such despair they are prepared to take their own lives, but in the case of Corialanus's good friend Menenius, this despair is a source of defiance. When soldiers attempt to intimidate him, Menenius makes it clear that won't wash, as he quite fancies dying anyway: '*He that hath a will to die by himself fears it not from another.*' Or, as John Lennon said to the Phil Spector when the brilliant but unhinged producer fired a gun right by Lennon's head: '*Phil, if you're going to kill me, kill me.*' Lennon's indifference to survival was probably related to childhood trauma: his dad walked out of his life when John was five, and his mum was killed when he was seventeen.

If the prospect of death appeals, it's likely that living does not. Life has come to mean nothing. Macbeth's habit of murdering others suggests he is not the spiritual type. He summarises his beliefs in a speech low on uplift:

> *Life's but a walking shadow, a poor player*
> *That struts and frets his hour upon the stage*
> *And then is heard no more. It is a tale*
> *Told by an idiot, full of sound and fury*

There are no gods or goddesses in Macbeth's world, no reason, no harmony, no point. Life is just random noise and violence, a meaningless activity, a deeply unfunny joke. Which is why most of the audience feel like cheering when big Mac is finally put out of his misery.

When Lear's daughter Cordelia dies, the old King despairs, wondering how she can have died while a common rodent lives on:

> *Why should a dog, a horse, a rat, have life,*
> *And thou no breath at all?*

Maybe it's just down to chance. Geoffrey Chaucer played with this idea, having one of his characters (Arcite) complain that the time and nature of his death were predestined:

'*Shapen was my death erst than my shert*' ('My death was set before my baby clothes were made.') Another of Chaucer's characters, a grief-struck knight, complains that fortune has killed the love of his life:

> '*She* [fortune] *began to play with me at chess; and with her various little cheating moves, she tricked me and stole away my queen*'

Meanwhile, the ghost of Chaucer's King Ceyx complains, '*Our bliss lasts for so short a time!* But before allowing ourselves to get too glum, we should take comfort in the thought that when his own time finally came, Chaucer was untroubled by fate. In what's believed to be his last poem, the great man suggests we follow our hearts, and everything will be alright:

> *Hold the high way, thy soul the pioneer,*
> *And Truth shall make thee free, there is no fear!*

For John Milton too, death can be good news for the dead: '*to the faithful Death* [is] *the Gate of Life.*' John was willing to put his theory to a premature test by publishing anti-monarch pamphlets. Enough of his comrades were sentenced to be hanged, drawn and quartered for this level of sedition, but by chance Milton survived and lived into his sixties.

Chaucer offers us the simplest reason why death is good news for the departed: living tends to be crap:

Death is the end of every worldly pain.

Fine for the one that goes, but what good can death do to those of us left behind? According to Shakespeare, one potential benefit is improvement of character. Speaking of Henry V, who had been a useless prince in his early years, the Archbishop of Canterbury recalls how Henry had shaped up after his father died:

> *The breath no sooner left his father's body*
> *But that his wildness...seemed to die too.*

But Shakespeare knew this character-building effect of tragedy is no golden rule: Hamlet turns into a genuine liability and eventually a killer after his father is murdered.

The politician Horace Walpole, writing just before his death in 1797, reflected, '*Nor will* [Death] *I think see me very unwilling to go with him...I came into the world so early, and have seen so much that I am satisfied.*' He'd got to eighty and wasn't going to grumble. Easy for an old man like Walpole to accept death, far harder if you're 27 and about to leave behind two children and a partner. In 2009 reality TV star Jade Goody sent a last message: '*I'm happy. I could bitch about dying young, but at the end of the day, I can look back on my life and be proud of what I have done.*' Jade even felt free enough for a last laugh, suggesting a mourner, '*send me a wreath in the shape of a Marmite bottle with the words written underneath: 'You either loved or hated her'.*'

In the late 1980s I had the privilege of working in a hospice in Gloucestershire. Leckhampton Court is a medieval manor house, set in emerald countryside and run by the Sue Ryder charity. The staff there were extraordinarily calm and caring, and the place reverberated with tranquillity. In part this was because all the great struggles of life were now at an end — no more school bullies, faithless lovers, money worries, personal insecurities or stressful jobs. And outside of the self, no further losses.

Perhaps the greatest English example of good coming from death is the short life of Stephen Sutton from Burntwood in Staffordshire. Stephen raised more than £3million pounds for the Teenage Cancer Trust before his own death from bowel cancer, aged just 19. Stephen had been diagnosed at 15, and two years later learned the terrible truth that his cancer was incurable. He devoted the little time he had left to raising money for the charity. Showing a level of courage that would humble almost all of us, Stephen posted a smiling selfie in April 2014, saying, '*It's a final thumbs-up from me! I've done well to blag things as well as I have up till now, but unfortunately I think this is just one hurdle too far.*' He lived for three more weeks, fund-raising to the end from his hospital bed. On 14th May Stephen's mum made a noble and heart-wrenching announcement: '*My heart is bursting with pride but breaking with pain for my courageous, selfless, inspirational son who passed away peacefully in his sleep in the early hours of this morning......We all know he will never be forgotten, his spirit will live on, in all that he achieved and shared with so many.*'

Mixed Feelings

The message of the old poem *The Life and Age of Man* is simple: Death comes to us all, so we may as well get our heads around it. The poem traces the life of its anonymous author from boyhood to grave, in steps of seven years, with the writer going to school, then partying for seven years, getting married, having kids, working hard, and at the age of seventy admitting to himself that his race is run:

> *I looked up, and saw the sun*
> *Had overcome the crystal sky.*
> *So now I must this world forsake,*
> *Another man my place must take.*

He's not whinging that he has to die, but he's not too chuffed either. With stock English matter-of-factness, the poet concludes that all '*mortal men...must leave off as they begun.'* The unnamed poet and the rest of us may believe we'll be sanguine about dying, but when our moment comes, we may be far from easy about the event. David Bowie, aware he had advanced liver and lung cancer, put his mixed and powerful feelings about impending death into his final work, *Black Star.* In one of its tracks, *Dollar Days*, New York resident Bowie is in defiant mood:

> *If I never see the English evergreens I'm running to,*
> *it's nothing to me.*

Not that he is giving up; Bowie ends the song by singing four times:

> *I'm Trying to,*
> *I'm Dying to.*

He's trying to survive, dying to live. Or just trying and dying. In the video to another track, David is already gone. Lying on a death bed, eyes bandaged, Bowie cries out:

> *Look up here, I'm in heaven...*
> *Look up here, man, I'm in danger*
> *I've got nothing left to lose*

A second, healthier Bowie sits beside the bed, scribbling delightedly: ever the artist, he will exploit anything for inspiration, including his own imminent death. Yet even this late in the game, Bowie holds a hope of giving mortality the slip: the song's title is *Lazarus.*

In the last song of the album, Bowie again indicates he is in no mood to go. Pointing out his shoes are decorated with skulls, he sings, '*I know something is very wrong.'* The final words of a man who loved both mystery and life tie the two together in a riddle and a refusal: '*I can't give everything away.'* Does he mean he can't give away all his feelings about dying? Or is he simply saying he can't accept that he absolutely must go? It seems that Bowie, an enigma from his boots up, really wants us not to know.

Tennyson, when still a long way further back from the grave than Bowie, pondered the reality of death in two contrasting poems. The first has the optimistic title, *Nothing Will Die*:

> *The stream flows,*
> *The wind blows,*
> *The cloud fleets,*
> *The heart beats,*
> *Nothing will die*

The second is called, more realistically, *All Things Will Die*

> *The stream will cease to flow;*
> *The wind will cease to blow;*
> *The clouds will cease to fleet;*
> *The heart will cease to beat;*
> *For all things must die.*

He appears to be in two minds as to whether we go on or come to nothing. As we shall see, it's perfectly normal to be in at least two minds.

To Shakespeare's Edgar in *King Lear*, even a terrible life is preferable to death. He is on the run, living the life of a mentally ill tramp. Each day, in fact each new hour, takes him to a new level of hell. Edgar regards his life as no better than death, but clings to it all the same.

> *O, our life's sweetness,*
> *That we the pain of death would hourly die*
> *Rather than die at once*

Shakespeare gives us a clue to his own spiritual beliefs in Sonnet 146. In the poem he chides himself to stop wasting time and money on fancy clothes, and instead concentrate on feeding his inner self. '*Within be fed, without be rich no more*'. By ignoring physical pleasures (such as clothes and, most likely, gluttony, sex and alcohol), he will starve the only thing that death can take from him: his body. Death will then have nothing to feed on, and will itself be starved to death

And death once dead, there's no more dying then

Meanwhile the rest of him, what Shakespeare names his *soul*, will escape and achieve immortality. Fine intentions, but from his very next sonnet it's plain that Shakespeare is a million miles from putting his spiritual plan into action. Instead, he is '*frantic mad*' in love and lust with someone, and when he's already in too deep he sees that his beloved is, '*black as hell, as dark as night*'.

John Keats

The poet John Keats formulated his own neat belief about death. He reckoned that we come to this world as an '*Intelligence*', a spark of life that builds itself into a unique identity through all the pain and setbacks it endures. He called this process '*Soulmaking*'. If we die in childhood, then we just go back to where we came, having lost nothing. If we live long enough, we become an individual soul and survive after death.

Keats thought a lot about death, and at times had consoling fantasies about leaving this world:

I have been half in love with easeful Death,
Call'd him soft names in many a mused rhyme,
To take into the air my quiet breath;
Now more than ever seems it rich to die

They say be careful what you wish for. We can join Keats on 27th July 1819 on the Isle of Wight, where he is staying at a friend's house, trying to work and recover from a mystery illness. John is twenty-three and madly in love with Fanny Brawne, his neighbour back in Hampstead. He doesn't know it, but he will be dead within two years. He has TB, the disease that killed his younger brother Tom the previous summer. He is writing a love letter to Fanny, filled with passion and morbid obsession, fed perhaps by an unconscious sense of his premature demise:

> *I have two luxuries to brood over in my walks, your Loveliness and the hour of my death. O that I could have possession of them both in the same minute. I hate the world…I could take a sweet poison from your lips to send me out of it.*

Two months later they are engaged. If anything, John's love for Fanny has become more intense. In his letter to her dated October 1819, love and death entwine themselves in John's sick and troubled mind:

> *I have been astonished that Men could die Martyrs for religion — I have shuddered at it. I shudder no more — I could be martyred for my Religion —Love is my religion — I could die for that. I could die for you…I cannot breathe without you.*
> *Yours for ever John Keats.*

Keats had medical training, and when four months later he coughs up a large quantity of bright crimson blood, he turns to his friend Charles Brown and says, *'I know the colour of that blood; it is arterial blood. I cannot be deceived in that colour. That drop of blood is my death warrant. I must die.'* No-one recovered from advanced TB. He forces himself to write to Fanny with the fatal news:

> *My dear Fanny—*
> *On the night I was taken ill— when so violent a rush of blood came to my Lungs that I felt nearly suffocated—I assure you I felt it possible I might not survive, and at that moment thought of nothing but you. When I said to Brown 'this is unfortunate', I thought of you. I wish I had even a little hope. I cannot say forget me —but I would mention that there are impossibilities in the world.*

In another letter that week, written to his friend James Rice, Keats describes the impact knowing he will soon die has had on the way he sees nature:

*How astonishingly does the chance of leaving the world impress a
sense of its natural beauties upon us!....I muse with the greatest
affection on every flower I have known from my infancy — their
shapes and colours are as new to me as if I had just created them
with a superhuman fancy.*

But in addition to wonder, John's diagnosis pushes him towards panic and
despair, which combine and curdle into possessive jealousy. He writes to
Fanny in May 1820:

*If you would really what is called enjoy yourself at a Party — if
you can smile in people's faces, and wish them to admire you
now— you never have nor ever will love me....you must be mine
to die upon the rack if I want*

This isn't exactly love talking, and later in the same letter John tries (and
largely fails) to retract his unhinged rant.

*No— my sweet Fanny — I am wrong— I do not wish you to be
unhappy — and yet I do...O the torments!*

In July 1820, in a moment of inner calm, he finds words to put things right
between Fanny and himself:

*If I have been cruel and unjust I swear my love has ever been greater
than my cruelty which lasts but a minute whereas my Love, come
what will, shall last for ever.*

But the heart rarely goes where the mind thinks it should, and come August
John is drowning again in his own anguish:

*I should like to die. I am sickened at the brute world which you are
smiling with. I hate men, and women more.... I am glad there is
such a thing as the grave —I am sure I shall never have any rest till
I get there...I wish I was either in your arms full of faith or that a
Thunder bolt would strike me.*
God bless you, J.K.

These are the last words we have from John to Fanny. In September, with a vain hope the warmer climate will save him, John's friends club together and buy him a ticket to Italy. In a final letter to his good friend Charles Brown, dated 30ᵗʰ November 1820 and sent from Rome, Keats knows that he has drifted beyond life, and he must now say farewell:

> *I am leading a posthumous existence...I can scarcely bid you good-bye, even in a letter. I always made an awkward bow.*
> *God bless you!*
> *John Keats*

In a way John had been preparing for the end throughout his adult life. As a teenager he wrote a short poem about mortality in which he wonders how others can view dying as falling asleep, since this world is no more real than a dream. He goes on to say that worse than a dream, existence is a nightmare, ('*a life of woe*'), and we should be fairly pleased about death, because it's the moment we finally wake up. Sounds great.

As a doom-soaked teenager, Steven Morrissey would ride out to graveyards to read the tombstones of the people buried there. Like Keats, at times Morrissey is half in love with death, and this on-off romance finds its greatest expression in 1986 and his lyric for the Smith's *There is a Light that Never Goes Out*:

> *And if a double-decker bus*
> *Crashes into us*
> *To die by your side*
> *Is such a heavenly way to die*
> *And if a ten-ton truck*
> *Kills the both of us*
> *To die by your side*
> *Well, the pleasure - the privilege is mine*

But, in a flatter mood, Morrissey finds cause to think twice:

And when I'm lying in my bed
I think about life and I think about death
And neither one particularly appeals to me
[Nowhere Fast, 1985]

It's OK to be miserable, but to be miserable and hilarious is a genuine gift. In revealing to the press in October 2014 that he had cancer, Morrissey was his standard bleak and frank self: '*If I die, then I die. And if I don't, then I don't.*' He'd probably agree with Gerry O'Driscoll, a staff member at Abbey Road studios who gives a recorded opinion at the opening of Pink Floyd and Clare Torry's 1973 Great Gig in the Sky: '*I'm not frightened of dying, any time will do, I don't mind. Why should I be frightened of dying? There's no reason for it, you've gotta go sometime.*'

It is one thing to look upon death as OK, quite another to see it as funny. As England moved into the 18ᵗʰ Century, it shook off the last lingering influence of those spiritual Nazis the Puritans. Thinking was freer now. Clergyman and writer Jonathan Swift took advantage to laugh at death itself, becoming the first champion of black humour. On hearing that the body of a young woman executed in Taiwan had been sold to senior politicians for them to eat as a delicacy, Swift imagined that, '*if the same use were made of several plump young girls in this town, who without one single groat to their fortunes…appear at a play-house and assemblies in foreign fineries which they never will pay for; the kingdom would not be the worse.*' And in writing about the funeral of the footman of the amusing but penniless Dr William King, Swift noted that the servant '*died of a consumption, a fit death for a poor starving wit's footman.*'

When a man by the name of Dr William Pratt (an open goal for Swift) died in 1721, Swift wrote, '*He had schemes of long life. . .. What a ridiculous thing is man!*' To Swift, too many of us have the Pratt delusion that death will only call when we reach a goodly age. What's more, there is

no goodly age: *'Every man desires to live long, but no man wishes to be old.'*
Swift, outrageous two hundred years back and still near the mark today,
doesn't appear quite so callous in the light of his positive take on death: *'It
is impossible that anything so natural, so necessary, and so universal as
death, should ever have been designed by providence as an evil to mankind.'*

Philosophical reflections are all good and well, but did Swift feel as easy
about mortality when it came his way? When Stella, the love of his life, died
in 1728, Swift was devastated. Being a writer, Swift wrote. But being Swift,
he couldn't resist a gag, describing how Stella had grown to become *'one of
the most beautiful, graceful, and agreeable young women in London, only a
little too fat.'* Becoming more serious, Swift listed all of Stella's personal
qualities in a series of touching recollections: her sincerity, her kindness, her
courage. What Swift never mentions is his personal sense of loss. He won't
allow himself to grieve. To find its voice, his sorrow translates itself into
physical illness.

> *'January 29th, My head aches, and I can write no more.'*

> *'January 30th, Tuesday. This is the night of the funeral, which my
> sickness will not suffer me to attend. It is now nine at night, and I
> am removed into another apartment, that I may not see the light in
> the church, which is just over against the window of my
> bedchamber.'*

He's not laughing now.

In *The Importance of Being Earnest*, Oscar Wilde's fictional character Lady
Bracknell jokes about orphan Jack Worthing's lot:

> *To lose one parent, Mr Worthing, may be regarded as a misfortune;
> to lose both looks like carelessness.*

In clumsier hands this would be a cruel line, but really it is the emotionally
void Lady Bracknell and death itself that Oscar is targeting, not Jack
Worthing's losses and pains.

In the 20th century, other writers took up Swift and Wilde's campaign of black humour. In her novel *The Voyage Out*, completed in 1912, Virginia Woolf writes about a death on a cruise ship. Susan Warrington tells her ageing aunt Emma Paley, who is pretty deaf, that one of their fellow passengers, a 24-year-old called Rachel Vinrace, has died:

> *'You heard, Aunt Emma, that poor Miss Vinrace has died of the fever,' Susan informed her gently. She could not speak of death loudly or even in her usual voice, so that Mrs. Paley did not catch a word. Arthur came to the rescue.*
>
> *'Miss Vinrace is dead,' he said very distinctly.*
>
> *Mrs. Paley merely bent a little towards him and asked, 'Eh?'*
>
> *'Miss Vinrace is dead,' he repeated. It was only by stiffening all the muscles round his mouth that he could prevent himself from bursting into laughter'*

By the mid-sixties, traditional values governing almost every aspect of social conduct are under sustained attack. The holiest cow of all, death, is slaughtered in the 1966 play *Loot*. Its writer, Leicester-born Joe Orton, takes hold of English propriety around death and feeds it to the dogs. At the start of the play the body of Mrs McCleavy lies at rest in a coffin in the family living room. She has been cared for up to her death by a local nurse, Fay, who now has some advice for Mrs McCleavy's bereaved husband:

> Fay: *You've been a widower for three days. Have you considered a second marriage yet?*
> Mr McCleavy: *No.*
> Fay: *Why not?*
> Mr McCleavy: *I've been so busy with the funeral.*

McCleavy is offended by Fay's crass enquiry, but she won't be stayed.

> Fay: *You must marry again after a decent interval of mourning.*
> McCleavy: *What's a decent interval?*

Fay: *A fortnight would be enough to indicate your grief. We must keep abreast of the times*

Meanwhile, Mrs McCleavy's outlaw son Hal is desperate to hide a pile of stolen cash. Deciding to use his mum's coffin, Hal and his lover Dennis lift the box and tip her body directly into a wardrobe, where she ends up stood on her head, minus her dentures. Hal picks these up and clicks them like castanets as he performs impromptu flamenco steps. (Orton's own mother died during the play's run and he unnerved cast members by bringing in her false teeth for use as a prop during rehearsals.)

Even Mrs McCleavy's widowed husband, the one sensitive character in the entire drama, develops a compassion vacuum:

McCleavy: *It's going to take me a long time to believe she's dead. She was such an active sort of person*

McCleavy is rightly appalled when he discovers his son has ejected his wife from her coffin in favour of stolen money. Hal tries to soothe his dad by offering a positive interpretation of events:

You've lost nothing. You began the day with a dead wife. You end it with a dead wife.

Dying for One's Honour

The English excel at risking all for their country, but the idea of putting personal honour before life is more Mediterranean than English, which may explain why Shakespeare uses a Roman, Brutus, to express willingness to die for one's values: '*I love the name of honour more than I fear death.*' But for all his big talk, Brutus can be as hypocritical as the worst politician. Having just helped assassinate Julius Caesar, he declares that by killing Caesar, he and his accomplices have done JC a favour, since they've saved him any future worry about dying! '*...then is death a benefit: so are we Caesar's friends, that have abridged his time of fearing death.*'

Brutus's defence is all the more specious given that Shakespeare's Julius Caesar never feels anxiety about death and has no time for those who allow their lives to be governed by it. His advice is to pay death no heed, as it comes just once, and only when it's good and ready:

> *Cowards die many times before their deaths;*
> *The valiant never taste of death but once.*
> *…. death… Will come when it will come*

In the past, the shame experienced by an unmarried woman at the loss of her virginity, her honour, could be so powerful as to bring her to suicide. Following her rape by the odious Tarquin, Shakespeare's Lucrece can find no way of living with the loss of her virtue, despite her total innocence in the crime. To restore her honour and end her shame, she must kill herself:

> *For in my death I murder shameful scorn:*
> *My shame so dead, mine honour is new born*

Lydia Bennet from Jane Austen's *Pride & Prejudice* has a very different take on honour. She refuses to be ruled by it, and runs off with her lover George Wickham, to live together in sin. As soon as he hears about the scandal, William Collins, a vicar with no spine but two faces, writes gloatingly to Lydia's dad: '*The death of your daughter would have been a blessing in comparison of this.*'

In *Measure for Measure*, the creepy Angelo tells Isabella that he will have her brother executed if she doesn't '*lay down the treasures*' of her body for him. Isabella rejects him, saying it would be better her brother dies once than she dies for ever (i.e. is sent to hell for the sin of fornication). She is certain she has done the right thing, but her brother Claudio doesn't see things exactly the same way. Luckily, as can happen in Shakespeare, someone dresses up as someone else and everything turns out alright.

Death Cafe

On a cold afternoon in December 2016, I chat over Skype to Jon Underwood, a gentle-spoken family man from East London and one of the leading lights of the international Death Cafe movement. Jon is concerned by the way the English still fail to confront death.

> *We've done a lot to banish death in a way, but we compulsively consume a weird kind of death, through news media, films and games. We bring death nearer. The net function of that is to keep death terrifying. It's not like we look away; we almost look too much, rubber-necking around death. As well as making it disappear, we're kind of looking it in the face, but looking in the face in a skewed way.*

Jon points out that there have been numerous experiments that show our attitudes and values can flip when we are subtly reminded that we are going to die one day. The researchers will, for instance, interview people on the street outside either a hairdressers or funeral directors. Those who are interviewed outside the undertakers will, on average express a greater desire for money and luxury goods. Jon sees a simple reason for this:

> *Death denial is the strongest force active in our society. We compulsively consume resources; that greed is strongly related to death denial.*

Not content with eating our way through the planet, we are quite interested in blowing the place up whenever our own deaths creeps into our minds: '*If you ask people about whether it might be a good idea to nuke a fictitious 'rogue' state, they're much more in favour of doing that if they've been prompted with death.*' Worryingly, research shows that if we are unconsciously primed by a passing reference to our own mortality, some of us are up for pressing the button even if that 'rogue' state is no current threat.

125

Jon decided it was time to act. He helped set up the country's first Death Cafe in September 2011.

> *Everyone takes a turn saying what's brought them to Death Cafe, saying whatever's off the top of their head. Sometimes they even surprise themselves with what they say…. then the conversation starts, and it just runs until people have run out of things to say.*

The idea sounds like a non-starter, getting the English to do two things totally opposed to their instincts: embrace cafe society and discuss their own death. But incredibly, Death Cafe is a success: '*We now have 4,000 death cafes in 40 countries.*'

Jon has worked with death (in a hospice), meditated on death (as a practising Buddhist) and talked at length about it (in death cafes). Has all this, I wondered, made him feel easier about reaching his own death day? '*I still fear death. Death is scary. I've got kids; the idea of dying while they're still young, or of their dying, is still quite terrifying.*' But Jon feels that facing facts helps him appreciate his life:

> *We're all going to be parted at some point. For me, remembering that is really useful in terms of avoiding being complacent and trying to appreciate the Now, the present, while it's here. To not let it slip by.*

In November 2017 I receive shocking news: Jon has died suddenly from leukaemia. He was 44. Jon's wife Donna Molloy posted '*I don't think it's an over statement to say he has single handedly started to change cultures around death and end of life awareness, not just in the UK, but across the globe.*' There are now over 5,600 Death cafes in 55 countries.

Working from another direction, artist Damien Hirst has been looking to change modern English attitudes to death. In 1991 he mounted a dead 12-foot tiger shark in a glass tank filled with formaldehyde. He gave this startling piece the clunky title: *The Physical Impossibility of Death in the Mind of Someone Living*. It is hard to imagine oneself dead; the Tibetans say this is because part of us never dies, but art being art, it's hard to say exactly what a dead shark means. It got a bit cruel with Hirst at one point, with trapped flies being electrocuted within his glass-encased piece *A Thousand Years*, but he had a point to make. '*Since I was a child, death is definitely something that I think about every day,*' he told the Daily Telegraph in 2011. '*You try and avoid it, but it's such a big thing that you can't.*' Particularly if you're one of his flies.

Death as a Character

As a blind response to all the havoc and pain that death brings, it's inevitable that we should look for a culprit of sorts. Thus, we have often turned death into a character, a twilight individual with a dreadful day job. In *Paradise Lost*, John Milton has Death as the devil's only son, born of an incestuous relationship between Satan and his daughter Sin. Whoever his parents might be, to many western minds Death is personified by the dreaded Grim Reaper. The Reaper can be traced back to Thanatos, the Greek God of Death, a hooded skeletal phantom, equipped with the twin tools of his trade: the large scythe and a heart of stone.

Just as they near their final moments, some fellow mortals appear to have glimpsed the Reaper. I talked with Jo, a nurse. In 2007 she was working the weekend at a community hospital in the north of the country when a female patient had a heart attack:

We resuscitated her and she was immediately sent over to a cardiac ward for further care. But then she came back to the community hospital and wanted to see me because I was the person who was there when she was having the arrest. She said, 'If that's dying, I'm not scared of it anymore because it felt really nice.' When she came around from the resuscitation, she remembered being on the floor. She said she opened her eyes and had seen me, but behind me there was this man. He was really tall and thin and was dressed completely in black. She said he just looked out of place and she was a bit frightened of him; she asked, 'Who was he then?' I thought, well, there was nobody like that there. The team was just nurses. At one point the emergency ambulance paramedic came, but he wasn't in black. Of course, she had just been defibrillated and it could have been a hallucination. She was desperate to ask me who it was, but I didn't feel it was in her best interest to tell her there was nobody there, so I just said, 'Oh, that was just the Out of Hours Doctor, they share the same building as us.' There was nobody dressed in black and there was nobody who was tall and thin. When I told the other nurses, they were just saying, 'Oh that's the Grim Reaper!', but she didn't say he had a scythe!

Jo's patient wasn't unique. In 1959 Paul Turner wrote a study of a psychic experience shared by several patients in a hospital ward for the terminally ill. They each reported that a lady in grey uniform had been attending them. Six nurses were willing to give signed statements that a patient had 'seen' a woman dressed in grey when there was no one of that description in the room (the nurse uniform at the time was Oxford blue.) Every patient who saw this grim reaper/angel of death died shortly after their experience.

If death really is a person, then why not kill him/her? That would sort the problem out once and for all. The Pardoner in Chaucer's Canterbury Tales tells us about an attempt to do exactly that. The story involves three Belgian lads with a list of bad habits: gambling, drinking, visiting brothels, dancing all night, swearing and (perhaps worst of all) eating cakes. This full-blown party lifestyle made them, says Chaucer, an enemy of Jesus and of God.

One day, they step into a pub just as a customer is being carried out dead; they're told that he's been stabbed through the heart by a serial killer called Death. The landlord tells them he suspects that Death is living in a village a mile down the road, because so many men, women and children have died there recently. The pub locals warn the lads that Death is a very dangerous character to be avoided at all costs. Tempted by the risks, the very drunk Belgian boys decide to go and find this Mr Death and kill him.

En route they come upon an old homeless man who lives a miserable life. He says he'd love to die, but for some reason Death won't oblige. They demand to know Death's whereabouts, and the old man points towards an oak tree, a little up the lane. There's no trace of Death there, but instead they find a huge heap of money – mainly gold coins! They decide to guard the fortune for the rest of the day, then smuggle it home under cover of darkness. The youngest of the three agrees to go into town to get some more booze and a loaf of bread to see them through until nightfall. While he's gone, the two minding the treasure get to thinking how much richer they'd be if they only have to share the cash two ways. Drunk now on greed as well as wine, they agree that when he returns from the shops, they'll ambush their loyal but dim friend and stab him to death.

While he's in town, their not-so loyal nor dim friend starts to imagine what life would be like if all the money were his. He nips into the apothecary and buys some super-strength rat poison, which he mixes in with the wine before heading back to the money tree. As soon as he's back, his two companions set upon and kill him. They toast their success with a full bottle of (poisoned) wine. In no time they too are dead. The only winner, and still undefeated champion of the world, is Mr Death. The Pardoner explains that his tale proves that a life of gambling, sex, drunkenness and cakes will result in terrible retribution. But the real moral of the story seems to be get proper friends.

The poet John Donne had a contempt for death. In his poem *Death, be not Proud*, Donne mocks death for having to keep the company of '*poison, war, and sickness*'. None of us like him, but how does John suggest we beat the Grim Reaper? His answer is not by employing the clumsy Belgian method of trying to murder him, but instead by simply dying ourselves:

> *One short sleep past, we wake eternally,*

> *And death shall be no more; Death, thou shalt die.*

Well I guess we can't die twice, but Donne's idea does sound self-defeating, like kicking over the Monopoly board when we're going bankrupt: we can't lose since the game no longer exists.

Death makes personal appearances in *Midnight Messenger* and *Death and the Lady*. Both poems are around 500 years old; no-one knows the authors. In *Midnight Messenger*, a man who has grown rich via fraud and intimidation is visited one night by Death, who gives him the unwelcome news he has just lived his final day on earth. The rich man tells Death that he's come to the wrong address, because he is as fit as a fiddle. But there's been no mistake: the repugnant millionaire's number is up. The man can't take it in: he has only just bought a massive country estate! Why doesn't Death go to the prison and put a few debtors out of their misery instead? Death is having none of it, and feels no pity for his selfish quarry:

> *Poor parents die, and leave their children small*
> *With nothing to support them here withal*

Mr Rich tries and fails to get Death to take a bribe, and then deteriorates to panic as he reflects on a lifetime spent ripping off the defenceless. Death merely cranks up the pressure by telling his target he has just minutes to live. He offers the rich man some advice:

> *Lift up your heart to God without delay,*
> *Implore his pardon now for what is past.*

Utterly defeated, the Rich Man calls out to his son and daughter, warning them never to base their lives on money. The poem closes with his last words:

> *A painful life I ready am to leave,*
> *Wherefore, in mercy, Lord, my soul receive.*

The poet makes it automatic that we go along with the notion that even the most amoral person can still believe in a god. After all, if Death believes in a supreme being, why shouldn't he? And we? Cleverly, the poet leaves a final twist in the tale for us. With his fate unknown, do we truly want Mr Nasty to end up rotting and roasting in Hell, or are we merciful enough to wish him good luck for the upcoming interview with his maker?

Death and the Lady follows a very similar plot line. This time it is a woman who has come to the top of Death's hit list. Rich and haughty, she insults Death's status and appearance when he appears at her door:

> *Must I, who am a lady, stoop or bow*
> *To such a pale-faced visage? Who art thou?*

Death turns sarcastic in response: '*My name is Death! Have you not heard of me?*'. The rich woman immediately changes her tune, offering Death sacks of gold if only he'd agree to go and cull some random decrepit old folk instead. When this fails, she turns on the charm, pleading with him to let her live to see her daughter married. Death couldn't be less interested. The Lady then decides that a team of doctors will be able to keep her alive, but Death rubbishes this plan. All hope gone, the Lady delivers her dying speech:

> *How shall I stand in the great judgment-day?*
> *…My sins, alas! are many, gross and foul,*
> *Oh, righteous Lord! have mercy on my soul!*

In the final stanza, the poet allows us to visualise our least-favourite celebrity millionaire being dragged into oblivion by a bloke in a hoodie:

> *The grave's the market-place where all men meet,*
> *Both rich and poor, as well as small and great.*
> *If life were merchandise that gold could buy,*
> *The rich would live, the poor alone would die*

Funerals and Etiquette

Wilton Club Reserves 4 – I Tisbury Dynamites

I can't remember if I cried, the day the football died.
Igor Biscan took a moment out of writing his latest theatrical masterpiece
to shed a tear for what was about to occur in the beautiful game.

Jack Marteau, Tisbury Dynamites match report. November 2007

As an indication of the significance funerals held for the stone age inhabitants of England, the earliest human constructions to be found in the country are raised burial mounds, or *barrows*. The simpler of these tombs are mounds of earth heaped over a large flat rock which in turn stands supported on three or four upright stones. The thing is essentially a blanket of soil and turf thrown over a giant stone table. More sophisticated burial mounds have multiple underground chambers. The largest and best preserved of these, West Kennet Long Barrow, in Wiltshire, is among the oldest human constructions in the world. Built around 5,700 years ago, it is 100 metres in length and was the final resting place of around fifty people. The mound is penetrated by a ten-metre long underground stone passageway that serves five subterranean chambers, two opening on either side of the passageway and one located at its far end. Each of these chambers is the size of a small bedroom. Numerous human remains were found when the Long Barrow was excavated in the 1950s.

I first visited Kennet Long Barrow around twenty years ago. I climbed inside and walked from room to room. The experience was both intimate and remote – the builders and occupants had lived and loved just like me, and the entire tomb felt like a hallowed space, but these ancestors' sense of the sacred and my own were thousands of years apart. In their universe, an animal, a river or star would provide care for the departed souls of their dead children. I had no such comfort. Animals are nice but devoid of supernatural talent; although lovely, rivers are 100% water, 0% divine intelligence; stars are globes of compressed hydrogen. Immense but stupid. But in the mire of early grief, the only place I wanted to visit other than the sea was Kennet Long Barrow. It took two hours through winter roads to get there. Stepping into its darkness, I allowed myself to feel the pagan soil and ancient stones hold me with their care for the dead and bereaved. It served as my atheist's temple.

Excavated burial mounds have been found to hold both buried and cremated remains, these two funeral methods being practised up until the arrival of Christianity in England. The intact skeleton of a fairly young man who lived approximately 5,600 years ago was found in a burial chamber in Hazleton North, Gloucestershire. With him were buried a flint and a hammer stone that was used to stroke (or 'knap') the flint into a sharp edge. It's possible those who buried him believed he could use the tool in the next life, or perhaps the man was a commercial flint-knapper and the tools of his trade were put with him to honour his life's work.

The Bronze age, which began some 4,000 years ago, brought a change in funeral customs. Large pottery urns containing cremated remains, sometimes accompanied by smaller food vessels, were interred within burial mounds. For some more important citizens, however, only intact-body burial would do. Among these was a wealthy man known as the Amesbury Archer. His grave, just three miles from Stonehenge, was discovered in 2002 and included 100 objects. Alongside his complete skeleton excavators found three copper knives, five pots, a pair of sandstone wrist-protectors, 16 flint arrowheads and, to the thrill of those working the site, two gold hair tresses, the oldest pieces of goldwork ever found in the UK. The archaeology team worked around the clock to keep their finds safe from graverobbers and complete the dig by the light of car headlights, just hours before work began on the construction of a housing development. Dental analysis showed that the archer had grown up in the Alps and then moved to England, possibly to become involved in the construction of Stonehenge itself.

By around 1,000 BCE cremation took over from burial as the standard funeral method, but burial came back into favour a few hundred years later, sometimes incorporating goods for use in the next world. Some of this equipment was very practical, including sets of tools and even full-sized carts. As a touching sign of devotion, children and young people were sometimes buried under the family home. In Trethellan Farm, Newquay, for instance, a young man was buried beneath the hearth inside one of the houses of a Bronze Age village.

To date very few English Iron Age burial sites have been found, so we remain largely ignorant of funerals practices in the thousand years that precede the Roman invasion. However, an excavated cemetery dating from 400 BCE near Arras, East Yorkshire, included a large grave for a male buried along with two horses, a pair of cart wheels plus, strangely, two pigs' heads: presumably the occupant's favourite take-away. An iron-age warrior found near Mildenhall, Suffolk, was buried with a sword, an axe, a gold neck-ring and two horses. The burial of animals as valuable as horses suggest an active belief among Iron Age people that there is a next world, and that a couple of horses will prove very useful in it.

Cremation burials continued up until the Roman era. Dating from around fifty years prior to the Roman invasion, cremation cemeteries were discovered in the 1920s in Aylesford and Swarling in Kent, and in Welwyn, Hertfordshire. The remains of the dead were housed in decorated pottery urns or, in the case of some more important individuals, within bronze-hooped wooden buckets surrounded by vessels used for drinking or food storage, or even furniture and gaming sets.

The English funeral does not appear to have changed significantly under the Romans, but burial grounds moved from the perimeter of a village to the sides of major roads. Crucially, the Romans brought with them a written language and the tombstone. From this point onward the name of the deceased and a tribute from their bereaved loved ones could live for centuries after their death: a message of devotion and sorrow sent into the future. To date more than 200 Roman tombstones have been found in England. One of the most recent discoveries came in 2015, when a beautifully preserved example was found in Cirencester on the town's Tetbury Road. Carved from Cotswold stone, it carries the inscription, '*To the spirit of the departed Bodica, wife, lived for 27 years.*' A local archaeology team found the skeleton of a young woman beneath the stone. Announcing the find, archaeologist Neil Holbrook commented, '*Perhaps Bodica is a local Gloucestershire girl who's married an incoming Roman or Gaul from France and has adopted this very Roman way of death.*'

Cremation disappeared with the arrival and spread of Christianity. The new religion was clear that come the end of time, or Judgment Day, the bodies of the faithful dead would be raised from the ground and sent, materially complete, to heaven. Cremation would make this an impossibility and was therefore an appalling pagan practice that had to stop. Cremation reappeared with the pagan Anglo-Saxons, often incorporating a simple grave for interment of the ashes. In the epic Anglo-Saxon poem *Beowulf*, the warrior hero is killed while slaying a 50-foot dragon. In line with Beowulf's dying wish, he is burned on a huge funeral pyre. His ashes are then buried in a mound facing the sea, filled with treasure he had taken from the dragon's lair. Real-life royal funerals were no less grand: King Raedwald was buried in a vast 27 metre ship at Sutton Hoo in Suffolk, accompanied by his ornate battle helmet, musical instruments, gold jewellery and fine clothes.

The Vikings eventually turned up to disturb whatever peace was around in Saxon times. With names like Eric Bloodaxe, these people loved violence so much they even believed there was constant fighting in their heaven, Valhalla. Small wonder, as there was limitless alcohol on tap there, and you needed to be killed in battle in order to qualify for entry. The skeleton of a Viking warrior was found at Repton in the East Midlands. He had died from sword wounds, was buried with his weapons, and wore a pendant shaped like Thor's hammer, making him a shoo-in for an eternity of booze and violence in Valhalla.

For anyone planning for death in the Middle Ages, (and why wouldn't they, since there was so much of it about?), a lavish funeral offered a tempting way to sign off. If they had the funds and an ego to match, the sky was no limit. The nobleman John Paton's 1466 funeral cost £230 (equivalent to a whopping £170,000 in 2016). So many candles were burned to light JP's way to heaven that two church windows had to be dismantled to remove all the soot. Although candle bearers would always wear white, black clothing became increasingly common at more expensive funerals from the 13th century. White was preferred for children's funerals, and this custom lasted right into the early 20th century.

The funeral of Queen Mary in 1695 was a huge affair, with a hearse designed by Christopher Wren and music specially composed by Henry Purcell. There was no great outcry that the funeral had cost £50,000 (around £7M in today's money), although a Hertfordshire resident, Abraham de la Pryme, complained that Mary's death had caused the price of black fabric to double overnight.

The class-obsessed English couldn't bring themselves to allow even death to impinge on the distinctions between the great and the not-so-special. Under Tudor law a king was allowed fifteen official mourners at his funeral, an earl could have nine, a knight five, and 'a gentleman' two. The rest of the country could have none. But by the time Queen Mary was having her blinged-up farewell, this system of privilege-even-when-dead was beginning to crumble. Money talked, and death had become a business opportunity: the undertakers entered the fray. Owning a private fleet of hearses and horses, and dozens of drapes, shields and banners, these independent traders were able to put on as lavish a funeral as anyone might wish, at everyday funeral prices. The English traditionalists didn't like it one bit: as one anonymous moaner put it in 1698:

Since the method of these undertakers have got a footing, persons of ordinary rank may, for the value of fifty pounds, make as great a figure as the nobility or gentry did formerly with the expense of more than five hundred pounds.

Thanks to a competitive undertaker and some personal savings, a commoner could now act like a lord, albeit a dead one. But even fifty quid was a lot of money in those days; many couldn't even afford a rock-bottom £2 service. In such cases, the dead were buried at the expense of the local parish. This was the dreaded 'pauper's funeral', infamous because it marked out the dead person as a failure and, worse still, a source of shame for surviving members of the family. Pauper funeral processions would often be heckled or even attacked by members of the public. Surviving relatives were held in equal blame to the deceased, as every family was expected to find the cash to give their relative a decent burial. Such was the level of scorn poured over a pauper funeral that only the most desperate citizen would act as wagon-porter: usually the village drunk. Tragi-comic trips and spillages were almost inevitable.

To help avoid this nightmare scenario, people joined 'friendly societies', or burial clubs as straighter talkers called them. For as little as tuppence a week, club members were guaranteed an elm coffin with 'handsome' handles, some black hat bands and cloaks, and a couple of strong men to help carry them to the church and graveside. Even then, some people didn't have two pennies to their name, and to keep themselves from starvation they were forced to turn themselves into the dreaded workhouse, where they worked for nothing save a greasy dormitory bed and near-poisonous food. And that wasn't the worst of it: when a workhouse resident died their body was likely to be sold, quite legally, to medical schools for trainee doctors to dissect. The thought that they would end up sliced open and carved into pieces was a horror to many poor English citizens of the 18th and 19th century. Ghoulishness and indignity aside, it was still widely believed that a complete body was a prerequisite for entry to heaven come Judgment Day. Once the medical school had finished with you, you'd be in no shape to go anywhere other than hell. Upon entering the dreaded workhouse, you gave up both body and soul.

With the construction of the railways, ordinary people could afford to travel to funerals, and as a result, from the 1840s onwards, the dead could have huge send-offs. The political revolutionary Samuel Holberry, who died in York prison, was given a grand funeral in Sheffield 1842, with tens of thousands of mourners in attendance. In 1844 forty thousand people attended the funeral in Manchester of the chemist John Dalton. The procession was almost a mile long. But biggest by far of these Victorian super-funerals was that of the Duke of Wellington in London. Around half a million people filed past his coffin, and he was then drawn through the streets in a vast 18-ton iron hearse.

Not much could top that, but a far bigger development was in store for the English funeral. In 1879 the country's first crematorium was built in Surrey. Local opposition and some trouble with the law, (people and politicians were scandalised by the very idea of cremation), meant that business was non-existent until 1885, when the actor Jeanette Pickersgill became the first person to be cremated in the country in modern times. With Victorian city cemeteries filled to overcrowding and consequent concerns about the potential for contamination, there was a powerful public hygiene argument for cremation, but it would take another 17 years for it to become truly legal. One hundred years on in an era of restricted carbon emissions, burial now trumps cremation for environmental friendliness.

In another reversal of current English values, sex could never be mentioned in Victorian society, but death was a topic everyone felt free to discuss. The practice of keeping deceased family members at home until the day of the funeral allowed the Victorians to pursue their fascination with mortality. The dead were photographed, painted, recorded in remembrance biographies and had locks of their hair encased in jewellery. Families even posed for photos with their deceased loved-one propped up in the middle of the group, looking pasty but otherwise as lively as anyone else in the portrait. The practice feels somewhere between weird and wrong today.

The reason why so many of us are repulsed by this 19th century act of family devotion may lie in a change in the law during the 1920s that tightened the criteria for post-mortems. As a consequence, many people who died suddenly at home had to be taken to a mortuary by the funeral director for autopsy. Equally, those who died in hospital often had to remain there, in the hospital morgue, until a post-mortem was carried out. In either circumstance, this new law meant that most families no longer had their departed parent, brother, sister or child at home for the days leading up to a funeral. With that person laid out in their coffin in the front room, Victorians grew up familiar with the sight and presence of death. When a neighbour died, they would go next door and pay their respects to the deceased, person to person. In death, someone remained a person to the Victorians; to many English people today, that person becomes immediately invisible, existing as a memory rather than a form. The English have developed a cultural belief that death as well as sickness is the business of the hospital.

There are other factors too of course, for our tendency to call for an ambulance when our 90-year-old granddad is slipping towards death. The verb is the clue. When we slip, we fall. And falling towards death suggests a plunge into the abyss. Perhaps calling the NHS can save us from the horror of mortality. Maybe we should say that at the end of the life we 'slide' towards death, but that won't do either: it sounds too much like an incident at an ice rink. 'Drifting' is no better: that's what happens to a rudderless ship before it is wrecked on some rocks. We need a new more positive lexicon of death, starting with an active verb for our ending. We might say that as we 'move' towards death, granting that the act is not often voluntary. At least we're doing something, even if that something is dying, and we are headed somewhere, even if that somewhere might be nowhere.

Funerals Today

Paul Allcock has been working as funeral director for over thirty years, progressing to his own business in 2000, financed by family members and the proceeds from the sale of his own home. I talked with Paul in June 2018. I was curious about how he got drawn into the work.

I'd seen a programme on TV about an apprentice funeral director when I was off sick from school in my early teens and I thought, 'Oh that's really interesting,' but I never thought any more about it. My father was quite well known locally, he's a former professional footballer with Norwich ...I initially was following in my father's footsteps, I played internationally as a schoolboy, I was on Ipswich's books briefly, but I had an arthritic issue, so essentially, I was out of work. It was probably the only job that was available for my age. I went up for the interview that afternoon. I had long hair, jeans and tee shirt: I was a right scruff and I was given the job!

Working in this role you either fit straight away, or you're gone within a fortnight. You have to be a certain breed. I'm not what I would class a traditionalist funeral director, although we carry out traditional funerals. We have silver vehicles, for example, rather than black. Queen Victoria has a lot to answer for; we mourn death and deal with death by everything being black and dour; you can be respectful and caring without it being a really standard dour occasion. To me it should be uplifting, and very much a celebration of the life of a person, however short that life has been. You're undoubtedly sorry; everybody's going to be distressed, distraught and upset at that time, but you don't need to emphasise that fact. Personally, I feel it's far more healthy to turn that table around, and even in the most difficult situations and scenarios, to just look at it and say, let's celebrate what we had with this person, let's think of all the good times, what it would have been like if we had never had them in our lives at all, how much worse that would have been.

I'm from a Catholic background and I honestly don't feel I could do my job without my faith. There are a lot of funerals we do nowadays that are non-faith based, and they can be very uplifting and have a really good impact on the bereavement process. In my experience of dealing with everybody from all creeds and across the board, the majority now want to have more direct involvement and more of a say in how things should be, and I think that's really healthy. The churches need to be a little bit flexible, otherwise they'll find that an awful lot of people will move away. I think that's been evident over recent years.

Paul regrets that the home of the deceased is no longer the hub for their funeral.

The neighbours used to come out, the funeral would leave from the home because the body had been at home invariably. Funeral directors have been guilty a little bit over the years of taking that away from families, that hands-on privilege that people had years ago.

I asked Paul about new developments in funerals. Things had changed a lot recently, hadn't they?

It's not such a recent thing. I've been experiencing that for many, many years, possibly because we were more open to it than many. Around a year after we started here I had someone who requested they be buried in their own red telephone box. Now that's a challenge that I love to be set. They were saying it in jest initially, ('He'd always said this'), but when we looked into it we were able to achieve it. It meant the use of a JCB and burial on private land rather than a cemetery or church yard. He was buried in a normal coffin, but we buried the phone box, opened the door, took the phone out then lowered the coffin in the normal way, then closed the door on top of it, which the family were over the moon with, because it's what he'd always said. My aim is to always offer and give more than people expect of us.

There's been a lot of good change, different music, natural burials, burial on private land etc. If it's something that people feel comfortable with, at the end of the day that's all that matters: people sending their ashes up in a firework now, for example. The internet has been a huge influence on all of this. If someone could come up with something completely different to anything I've done before, I'd be delighted. I don't think that's very likely though!

The most concerning change for me is what they call the 'direct cremation', which is people being taken directly to the crematorium without any service, straight from the hospital. There seems to be a move to being almost a disposal service. Even government departments seem to be pointing people in that direction if they have financial issues. It just worries me. Obviously, it's the cheapest, but people need to say goodbye.

Three decades of involvement with death have made Paul almost shock-proof.

I can't think of anything that would shock me now, from scenarios leading up to the death, to families fighting at our premises or at the chapel: nothing that we haven't seen or dealt with before!

How, I wondered, does Paul feel about his own mortality?

The one thing I do is I make sure I enjoy myself, because I see far too many people go too young. I believe I'm not afraid of dying, and I'm comfortable with where I'm going afterwards, which makes a huge difference. I think it's my upbringing rather than being work-influenced. I tell everyone to enjoy their life for every minute you've got here, because you never know when it's going to be taken away. You can take me any time now and I'll be quite comfortable!

People say to me, how on earth do you do what you do? To be honest, the dead are no problem at all to us, it's always those who are left that cause us any issues. It's a wonderful job. No two days are the same, no two funerals are the same. No two relationships within the families you deal with are the same. It's hard work: you have to be available or have someone available constantly. You might have been up two or three times through the night, but you still have to be up at nine for the first funeral that's going out at ten, and not look too tired or miserable or knackered. The friends you make and the gratitude you receive are so rewarding, they're beyond comprehension. And that means everything to me.

Reincarnation

Top 5 Horrific Horror Movie Taglines. Cherry Falls (2000)

Tagline: 'Get Laid… Or Die!'
HAHAHA really? I think I'll take the former. Yes, that's my final answer

Jack Marteau, Student Direct Magazine 2009

In 1785, the first English translation was published of the Hindu religious text, the *Bhagavad Gita*. It included the following:

> *As a man casts off worn-out garments and puts on new ones, so the embodied soul casts off the worn-out body and enters other new ones.*

With this one line, the idea of reincarnation or rebirth finds a way back into the English imagination, perhaps for the first time since the Druids. There had been some conversations about a mysterious couple of lines in the Bible that seemed to point to reincarnation: '*Do not marvel that I said to you, "You must be born again"*.' and, '*if you care to accept it, he* [John the Baptist] *himself is Elijah, who was to come.*' But aside from these puzzling quotes, there are no hints at reincarnation in any Christian scriptures.

Artists and scholars were among the first to take account of Hindu and Buddhist teachings on rebirth. William Blake, writing to a friend in September 1800 said,

> *I am more famed in Heaven for my works than I could well conceive. In my brain are studies & chambers filled with books & pictures of old, which I wrote & painted in ages of Eternity before my mortal life; & those works are the delight & Study of Archangels.*

It's the sort of statement that gets you noticed. Although not strictly talking about reincarnation, Blake is asserting that someone may exist long before they are born. As much as Blake revered the Bible (he thought it the true and perfect word of God), he used his imagination to travel beyond its limits. As we will find, to Blake imagination is a long way from make-believe.

Although it gained little support among the wider English population, reincarnation attracted the fascination of several artists. The London-born painter and poet Dante Gabriel Rossetti wrote an unfinished short story about an artist who paints the portrait of a woman he loves. The painter learns there exists an uncannily similar portrait painted four centuries earlier by an Italian artist. He travels to Florence to find it and discovers that the face it depicts is truly that of the woman he loves, and moreover a self-portrait beside it shows its 15th century creator to be identical in appearance to the author of the story. He realises in that moment that both he and his lover/model are the Italian couple reincarnated.

In 1850, still entranced by the plot of his story, Rossetti met and fell in love with Elizabeth Siddal. He went on to write the poem *Sudden Light*, which opens as follows:

> *I have been here before,*
> *But when or how I cannot tell:*
> *I know the grass beyond the door,*
> *The sweet keen smell,*
> *The sighing sound, the lights around the shore.*
>
> *You have been mine before, —*
> *How long ago I may not know*

At the close of the 19th Century a new religion, Theosophy, surfaced in England. Blending mystical East and Middle-Eastern teachings, Theosophy preached the reality of reincarnation and drew followers from among the adventurous and curious. Never likely to achieve mass appeal, Theosophy took an embarrassing fall when its leader 'Madame' Helena Blavatsky was caught faking a communication with some long-dead gurus.

Reincarnation has been accepted by some followers of Wicca, a modern take on witchcraft created in Hampshire in 1949. Some Wiccans believe in reincarnation, involving a series of returns to Earth until the soul has learned all they can, after which they progress to a place called 'Summerland', which sounds like a leisure park off the A349.

In many ways reincarnation is a tougher idea than heaven and hell, which at least provide a decisive result. Reincarnation, with its back-to-square-one-and-baby-food recycle is a tough ask. How many times do we have to come back? Once was bad enough. Will I have to spend chunks of my next turn with more people I don't much like? And go to work again for several more decades? And have to be as neurotic next time round?

There have been many reports of very young children advising their parents they have lived a previous life. At times these infant testimonies include names and places that can be verified. The world's number one reincarnation researcher, Professor Iain Stevenson devoted his working life to investigating these cases. The English writer Ian Wilson took a cool look at Stevenson's published evidence and pointed out that eight of Stevenson's more dramatic cases from Sri Lanka and India involved children from humble or relatively poor families claiming to be a reincarnation of a member of a wealthy family. '*This trend is so marked across so many of Stevenson's cases that it surely indicates only one thing: a motive*'. There is, however, another interesting pattern to Stevenson's data that appears unconnected to money: a half of all the cases reported to him from India involved a violent death. This is almost ten times the national average. Taken in this context, reincarnation represents natural justice: those whose lives are cut short deserve another go.

In reading through many of the stories from around the world, another big theme emerges. The person reporting reincarnation is usually a child, generally aged between two and four years old. At this stage, the sense of having lived before, (or of even living another life currently), is at its strongest. The journalist Tom Shroder accompanied Stevenson, then an old

146

man, on trips around India, Lebanon and the USA, interviewing children who believed they had another life. Shroder noted that, '*When the subjects are young children, they say, 'I have a wife', or 'I am a doctor'... They are the previous personality, and they resist the imposition of a new identity*'.

Anita Moorjani is an English-school-educated resident of Singapore. In February 2006 she almost died from lymphoma. As she lay in a coma in her hospital bed, Anita had a convincing sense, like the children Shroder interviewed, that she had other lives running concurrent with her conscious life. In one of these, her elder brother Anoop is/was actually younger than her:

> *I became conscious of what seemed to be simultaneous lives playing out. I seemed to have a younger brother in one incarnation, and I was protective of him. But I knew that this sibling's essence was the same as Anoop's, only in that existence he was younger instead of older than I was.*

For Anita, reincarnation was not rebirth as such, but more a case of multiple, simultaneous births. Her explanation is that '*time just is*' and it is we that are moving through it, rather than it rolling past us. Anita goes on: '*This means that not only do all points of time exist simultaneously, but also that in the other realm, we can go faster, slower, or even backward and sideways.*' Oh dear, sideways through time in the other realm: the closer we look at reincarnation, the more slippery it becomes.

The most celebrated English story of rebirth is the account of Jenny Cockell, a mother of two from Northamptonshire. As a young child growing up in the 1950s Jenny had a pair of invisible friends. Not so strange, except these were both adult males and not particularly interested in Jenny. They just sort of hung around. Jenny had other strange experiences too. From a very early age she could, in her own words, '*remember past lives, gain glimpses of the future and experience the feelings of others through means such as telepathy.*'

147

The most pressing of Jenny's 'memories' was of being a mother in the 1920s and 30s. *'I don't remember a point where the memories started,'* said Jenny. *'I presume they were with me from birth. I always knew that my name was Mary and that I lived in Ireland.... The memories were just like any memories of the past'.*

Jenny believed Mary had been a mother to eight children. Besides memories of particular events, (the children trapping a hare, cooking a family meal, standing on a jetty with a shawl around her shoulders), Jenny's overriding recollection and concern was that she had died young, leaving her children vulnerable: *'I was a mother who had left children behind'.*

As a child Jenny would sketch buildings from her 'memories' as Mary: the family's cottage and a distinctive-looking chapel. She would draw maps of Mary's village, incorporating a train station, chapel, shops and Mary's home. In looking at a map of Ireland in her school atlas, Jenny found herself drawn repeatedly to a place called Malahide, a town north of Dublin.

In her mid-twenties, still anxious at the fate of her 'remembered' children, Jenny decided to take things further. She ordered a map of north-east Ireland from a local bookshop and in comparing her childhood sketch of her home area with a map of the village of Malahide, she found, *'all the roads were right, including the one leading to Dublin, which I had marked, 'To the City'.'* In 1989 Jenny got to travel to Malahide and walk its streets, to its chapel and jetty. The place was familiar (*'I didn't need a map, I knew my way around'*), but Jenny could not find Mary's cottage. She asked around, but no-one could recall any house occupied by a Mary with eight children. Jenny returned home, confused.

Soon after the trip, a letter arrived from Ireland, from an older resident of Malahide who suggested the woman whose story she was looking to trace may well have been Mary Sutton. Mary had died following the birth of Betty, her 8th baby, in 1932. The children were split up after Mary's death. They were put into care separately, except for Sonny, who was left to keep house for his alcoholic father. The family home was later abandoned and collapsed into a ruin. Jenny got hold of Sonny's number and phoned him out of the blue, narrating to him some of her memories of Sutton family life. The call rocked Sonny:

> *I turned around to my wife and she said, 'What's wrong with you? You look like a ghost?' I said, 'I think I've been talking to a ghost?'.... the things that she told me, nobody else could know. Not even my brothers know. It kind of frightened me.*

After further detective work, Jenny was able to contact Mary's four other surviving children: Phyllis, Christy, Frank and Betty. Betty had always believed she was an only child. The five were reunited for the first time in 61 years in 1993. Jenny was there. Did they believe that the young English woman really was their re-incarnated mother? Phyllis saw things this way: *'Jenny's dreams are mummy's thoughts.'* Christy went a bit further about her mother's fate: *'Jenny was the lucky one; she put her soul into Jenny.'* And Sonny, the eldest, was convinced that Jenny was the reincarnation of his mother, who had died when he was thirteen: *'She is back again. I believe that my mother hasn't 'passed over' as we say. The wounds of not knowing where my brothers and sisters were, those wounds Jenny has healed now.'* In summing up her own part in the Sutton family reunion, Jenny said, *'That part of me that was Mary needed to see the children happy.'*

As if that weren't enough, Jenny has memories of other past lives, but as these extend back before Mary Sutton's birth, they can never be validated by anyone still living. She has some recollection, for instance, of being Anna, an illiterate French girl who in 1716 was sold into the service of a rich family in Boulogne: *'I recalled being taken by my father on a cart ride into the city; he was quiet and looked very sombre...I was taken to a small bare room high up in the attics; the walls were of slightly yellowing plaster and the only furniture was a wooden bed. My grief and fear were overwhelming.'*

It can be argued that Anna sounds like a character from a TV costume drama and the Sutton family story may be no more than a case of happy coincidence: it's likely that almost every village in early 20ᵗʰ century Ireland would have a resident by the name of Mary with several children. Jenny resists the thought that her memories of other lives are merely romantic fantasies. '*None of my past-life memories have put me in a prominent position, or even in particularly dramatic times. I missed the French revolution by a few years and was a very young child during the Second World War. I never knew anyone famous.*' It may be of significance that Jenny and the Sutton siblings remained in contact after all the TV and press attention had died away.

In total, Jenny reckons she has had ten lives. But can Jenny recall anything that happened after any one of her deaths? Yes, she can:

> *I found myself floating inside something like a soap bubble; above, below and all around me were other bubbles that I knew to be people...The sensation was of being almost like a single cell within a whole constellation of cells...Every bubble glowed brightly with an energy that I took to be the basic life energy that is ourselves...Enveloping everything was a feeling of calm, a unique calm in which nothing seemed to matter or hurt or worry.*

On occasions, the past has broken into her present. In 1981 she and her husband Steve visited a blue john mine in Yorkshire. Miners were working from ropes and ladders in the main cavern, chipping at the rock-face. Back above ground, Jenny mentioned their activity to Steve. He told her there had been absolutely no-one other than themselves in the cavern. On checking she found he was right: mining had stopped there some years past.

And Jenny's glimpses of the future? She has 'seen' that next up she's going to be Nadia, a Nepalese lass born around 2040. She has also had the presentiment that in 2190 she will return as an American woman called Janice Thorp, and in 2285 she is/was/will be a Californian, Sheryl

Vaughan. Will humanity have managed to survive to the 23rd century? Yes again, but something substantial must have occured between now and then, as there will be a '*Much smaller world population*,' but there will be '*very little violence, if any*.' I'm happy to go along with just about all of this, but humans giving up violence? That's a hard one to swallow.

A past-lives movement has gained popularity in recent years, drawing the interest of some psychotherapists. The thinking here is that one of our previous lives included a traumatic event that still screws us up today. Seems like a long shot, but many of us appreciate an explanation why we're such nervous wrecks. Anyway, the treatment for previous life trauma involves hypnosis, with subjects being put into a trance then invited by the hypnotist to go back to a time before they were born. Rather than saying nothing, or telling the hypnotist to stop wasting their time, subjects often begin to recall a life that was complete news to them. They may change sex, finding themselves a milk-maid from 300 years back, instead of a present-day plasterer. They can give a detailed description of their 18th Century surroundings and a convincing account of the past life they are revisiting, as if they have genuinely travelled back in time.

I had a go myself. I was hypnotised, but instead of going back to a previous life as instructed, I decided to head off in to space. I ended up hovering above some distant planet with a landscape comprising wave-like rocks. Below me were grazing a pair of alien cattle that resembled giant maggots. Glancing up, they were genuinely angry with me for disturbing their day. I decided to retreat to earth. This session was thirty years back and remains a vivid memory, but I'm now pretty sure that I invented the whole scenario while under the spell of hypnosis. I've come to realise that the wave-like rocks had been lifted by my unconscious mind from a photo I'd once seen of Wave Rock, a geological formation in Western Australia. I'm not sure about the origin of the alien maggots: probably an old episode of Dr Who. The experience taught me that when the human brain is put in a trance and invited to explore an area outside the limits of its daily existence, it can

151

quickly cobble together an impressively detailed, wholly false, three-dimensional world.

In the small world of English research into reincarnation, one name stands out above all others: Joe Keeton. Joe was born in Derbyshire in 1920 and spent much of his adult life developing his skills and experience as a hypnotherapist. These included the doubtful art of past-life regression. Regardless of whether we choose to believe our next-door neighbour was a 16th century highwayman, Joe's commitment to the investigation of past-life regression cannot be doubted. He would often work unpaid all weekend, acting as lead hypnotherapist for a group that included interested fellow travellers and people needing help with a variety of health problems. The stories he and they uncovered have been explained by psychologists as examples of *cryptamnesia*, the brain's ability to stitch together images and old tales to form a coherent false memory, as per my adventure with the space maggots.

Keeton did encounter this problem among some of his hypnotised subjects, but said, '*It is usually not difficult to recognize an example of cryptamnesia.*' He did this by asking questions that required specific factual knowledge. He gave the following example: a young woman claimed to be the Empress Josephine who was sailing to France to meet her husband Napoleon. Joe Keeton asked her whether her ship was made of overlapping or butted-together timber. She said it was neither; it was built of metal. Joe Keeton knew that the first metal-hulled ship was built thirty years after Josephine and Napoleon had died. The Josephine story sank like a stone.

Keeton used this same technique, (asking his subject seemingly innocuous questions, the answers to which he already knew), when working with Ann Dowling, who had come for help with recurrent nightmares. Under hypnosis, Ann '*regressed* to Sarah Williams, a scouse girl living on the streets of Everton in the early 1800s. Keeping his intentions hidden, Joe asked Ann/Sarah to go back to 12th July 1835. On reaching that date, she said she was staying off the streets because of '*Them Irish. They're mad, fighting all over the place.'* When it was put to Sarah that the situation couldn't be so dangerous, she replied, '*It is. They've 'ad to fetch the soldiers out.'* In fact, there had been a serious riot in Liverpool that day, and the military had been called in to restore order. When asked to go to January 1839, Ann/Sarah reported an awful storm, '*blowin' roofs off and howlin'* There had been a devastating hurricane across Liverpool on 6th January 1839. Invited to travel to 1848, Ann/Sarah reported that the wife of the wife of the Mayor of the city had given birth to a '*babby*' and, scandalously, Queen Victoria's husband Albert was the father ('*Everybody knows it. He's been carryin' on wi'' Mayor's wife*'). She added that Albert gave her a cradle. Investigation by Joe Keeton revealed that the Mayoress of Liverpool had indeed had a baby in October 1848 and had been presented with a miniature silver cradle to mark the happy event. No-one appears to have ever suggested in print that the child was the product of an affair with the Prince. Ann's story is intriguing, but the trail goes cold as no record could be found of a woman called Sarah Williams living homeless in Everton in the first half of the 19th century.

The next case does offer such evidence. Pat Roberts, another of Joe's volunteers/patients, came from Liverpool but had limited knowledge of local history. When in a trance, she claimed to be Frances Mary Rodriguez and gave her address as 10 Bankfield Street in Bootle. She said her dad was a cobbler called Joe. A search of *Gore's Liverpool Directories* of 1888 and 1889 revealed a cobbler named Joe Rodriguez listed at no 10 Bankfield Street, Bootle. Pat/Frances claimed to have been married in '*the little relief church.*' Although no record seemed to exist of this church, subsequent research found that a St Mary's church had been built in Bootle in 1827 as a '*relief church*' to manage the spiritual needs of a growing population, and that this church was destroyed in WW2. It was never rebuilt and had been forgotten by just about everyone except Pat/Frances. '*Frances*' said that she had been married to an accountant called Frederick Jones. A search of the parish register of the destroyed St Mary's revealed that the churchyard had contained a grave bearing the inscription '*Frances Jones, died 17th of*

September 1913,' with the added ironic tribute, *'Gone but not Forgotten.'* The chances of someone with a limited interest in local history knowing the name, occupation and exact address of a 19th century tradesman seemed remote to Joe Keeton. He began to form a theory to explain what might be happening.

Our bodies, says Keeton, are sculpted by our genes. It has been my great fortune to inherit my father's big Belgian nose, my mother's drainpipe ankles and my grandad's baldness. So, if DNA carries the physical history of our ancestors, couldn't it, he wondered, carry some of their personalities and memories too? Red hair can skip several generations, and then suddenly appear in a child of two dark-haired parents. Keeton felt that in the same way, a recording of the thoughts and memories of a distant ancestor might be passed down through the generations until they are reactivated in the brain of you, me or whoever. It's a neat theory, but in many of Joe's cases there appeared to be no possibility that the person being remembered was a blood-ancestor of the individual under hypnosis. Time for more cases.

Cliff Pattinson, another of Joe Keeton's cases, *'regressed* to a boy called Jim Jackson. The son of a blacksmith on a Yorkshire estate in Ainderby Steeple in North Yorkshire, Jim was afflicted with what he called *'the palsy'* (loss of muscle control) which kept him from attending school. When he was well enough, he helped in the squire's stables.

Cliff/Jim mentioned the preacher at the local chapel was called Mr Hirst. This checked out. The librarian in Huddersfield, Judy Sissons, found an old book in Leeds Reference Library called *On Sea and Shore*. Published in the late 19th century, it is an autobiography of an old sailor, Thomas Hedger, who spent the first 13 years of his life in Ainderby Steeple, a few years before Jim's time. I doubt it was a best-seller. Judy Sissons takes up the story:

> *Armed with obscure information from this dusty old book, at the next regression group Joe Keeton first put Cliff through his own*

life to any time he was reading On Sea and Shore. There was no trace of Cliff ever having heard of [the book].

During Cliff's regression to Jim, I questioned him using the names of people taken from the book, all of whom Jim should have known about.... Someone asked if he knew Rachel, giving him no information other than the name. Yes, he did know 'Spike Rachel', as he called her, and he didn't much like her, despite the fact that she made sweets and did 'a bit of baking'. She also made baskets. The book tells us that Rachel was known as 'Spice Rachel'. She was the wife of the basket-maker and supplied the village children with toffee.

Cliff/Jim was asked if he recognised the names George Calvert or Neddy Henderson. These were young men who regularly won local running races. Cliff/Jim said he knew one of these men and added that he was a good runner. Despite this impressive showing, Judy was unable to find any record of a Jim Jackson in local census forms.

Another of Joe's cases relates to a woman whose life is a matter of public record. Under hypnosis, Liz Howard, a biologist, became a Tudor woman called Elizabeth Fytton. a handmaiden to Anne Boleyn, one of Henry VIII's unluckier wives. Thinking her story to be exactly that, Keeton cross-examined Liz under hypnosis, asking her the meaning of one hundred highly unusual words and phrases taken from a dictionary of slang expressions of the Tudor period, such as *'gander-mooner.'* Liz/Elizabeth got all one hundred correct. A gander-mooner, by the way, is a man who is unfaithful to his wife during the month that follows childbirth.

Liz/Elizabeth was able to describe in detail her family home, Gawsworth Hall in Cheshire, despite Liz never having visited the place. Keeton contacted the then owners of Gawsworth Hall, Tim and Elizabeth Richards, who were able to confirm Liz's descriptions of the house from their records. E(Liz)abeth also correctly named various members of the Fytton family and gave details of several events which the Richards were again able to verify.

Looking back, Liz recalled, *'I refused to believe a word of my hypnotic ramblings,'* but she was forced to accept they were valid when *'painstaking research would only prove my unconscious mind right... How such a wealth of information could have been absorbed and stored while the conscious mind remained completely ignorant of the fact will always be a mystery.'* Liz could not bring herself to believe in reincarnation, but she'd *'reluctantly'* concluded that she may have somehow inherited the memory of a woman who had been dead for four hundred years.

As we have seen, Joe Keeton was swayed by the idea of inherited memory. Like Liz Howard, however, he was, very cautious about rebirth: *'I am not about to commit myself to the theory of reincarnation,'* he said.

Spiritualism

Top 5 Movies that Star Bald Guys: Con Air (1997)

For some reason a lot of bad guys are bald, possibly because they are so evil that all their hair runs away in fear. I used to have a shaved head, during which time I stole a sachet of tomato ketchup and some Softmints. Coincidence?

Jack Marteau Student Direct Magazine 2009

In February 2010 I went to a Spiritualist church with my wife Debbie. I had no desire to go, but as we were still floundering in the depths of grief, I came along; it was the least I could do. We parked a couple of streets away. Before getting out the car, concerned that she might be prey to some phoney manipulation, I asked Debbie what she hoped to get out of the evening. *'I want to know if we got there in time, and if Jack heard what we said.'* Inside, the church was laid out like a conventional Anglican church. The congregation was largely female and getting on in years. One of the faithful was playing Victorian hymns on an electronic keyboard, and prayer books were set evenly across vacant pews. So far, so regular.

Departure from convention came with the introduction of a medium, a volunteer who had driven across two counties in bad winter weather to attend, apparently at her own expense. She got straight down to it. Who, she asked, had come tonight in the hope of contacting a departed loved one? A good crop of hands went up, and for the next hour and a half the medium attempted to transmit messages from the other side to the bereft of middle England. It was tiring enough to just sit and watch as she closed her eyes tight and concentrated with what appeared to be all her might. I need to brave and add here that at the age of forty I suddenly found I had an ability to see human 'auras'. This was a bit inconvenient for a sceptic, although my rational side was able to write off this new talent as my visual cortex going on the blink. These 'auras' are a glowing mobile pearl-white fringe surrounding a person's outline, about three inches wide and ragged-edged. They are semi-transparent, allowing me to see the walls, scenery or sky behind, while laying a narrow pale filter over each of these. For every waking hour of most days I cannot see any 'aura,' but at times they appear vividly. The only pattern I've noticed is that they almost always appear when people are talking honestly about an emotionally significant event.

Anyway, as I was sat through the Spiritualist church service, wondering when we could all go home, the distinctive flame-like borders of an aura formed around the head and body of the hard-pressed medium. I watched curiously and was amazed to notice that immediately before the medium scored a bullseye, the aura became so bright and obvious that I almost wondered how others failed to notice it. Conversely, just before the medium drew a blank over some dead chap called Stan or Sam, or mentioned the name of a dog nobody had ever heard of, her aura dimmed and shrank to the point of disappearance.

The medium was trying to offer comfort to a family who had lost a child when her aura began to grow and glow brightly. Very abruptly, the soft soap ran out: '*There was shouting; doors were slammed.*' The family all nodded in sorry unison; she'd somehow picked up that their loved one had died after a horrible row.

The medium looked mentally and emotionally exhausted as she neared the end of her stint. She asked if anyone had lost a loved one in the night. Debbie and I both put a hand up and she turned her full attention on us. Her eyes were very wide. '*There were three of you got there. Or four.*' She was unsure. Three of us had in fact gone to Jack's bedside, but a fourth, Debbie's sister Denny, arrived the next day. '*You got there in time and he heard every word you said.*' This was almost a word-for-word answer to Debbie's questions; for an instant I had the paranoid thought our car had been bugged. This level of performance is, however, hard to sustain: '*and there's something about Tottenham football club...*'. Had I been taking account of the medium's 'aura' at this point, I'm confident I'd have noticed it fade to zero. No, we told her, Jack was Liverpool full stop.

Seances and Mediums

The first record of a seance comes from the Bible's *Book of Samuel*. King Saul consults a medium, with a view to contacting the long-dead Samuel. The medium manages to locate the expired prophet, who is not happy to be disturbed. Eventually he calms down and gives Saul helpful advice on problems he'd been having with the Philistines. But elsewhere in the Bible, any communication with, '*the spirits of the dead* is strictly forbidden, and by consequence seances were outlawed in England. As we've seen, John Dee and several other Tudor chancers gave it a go, but involvement in seances remained illegal until the 19th century.

Many have claimed to have received internal telepathic messages from the spirit world, but three sisters, Kate, Margaretta and Leah Fox, were the first to make sonic contact with the dead. In 1848 their New York state home began to echo with loud knocking sounds with no apparent earthly cause. When the 'energy' behind these sounds was invited to give three knocks to confirm that she or he was a discarnate spirit, three solid thumps would follow. A sequence of public demonstrations of the sisters' powers were held across America, and a craze of mediumship and seances was born. Among the attendees at one of these events was a Yorkshireman, David Richmond. Upon returning home in 1853, Richmond gave the people of Keighley, crammed into the town's Working Men's Hall, a performance of mediumship, the receipt and transmission of messages from the dead. He divided the audience into small groups sat around tables, and then invited them to call upon the spirits. The resulting rocking and tipping of tables under the downturned palms of the startled townsfolk created wonder, joy and fear...spiritualism had arrived.

Among those who came through this newly established conduit was a deceased radical preacher called John Mason. Having not had enough of telling fellow citizens how to behave while he was alive, Mason dictated a lengthy sermon from beyond the grave. While a religious professional like Mason might have been expected to turn up, few would have predicted the appearance of the great Robert Burns, who took the opportunity to dictate a poem about his life as a dead person. It was a long way short of Robbie's finest work, allowing sceptics a field day. Sceptics were in fact about to have a century of field days, as bogus mediums battled to separate naive Victorians from their cash. Red Indian spirit guides, ectoplasm, voices out of thin air, ghost limbs, random bumps, small explosions and many other sensations and marvels were conjured up to blow the individual minds and empty the collective wallets of the unwitting.

Back in the USA, forty years on from the extraordinary events in the Fox family home, middle sister Maggie confessed to the *New York World* newspaper that none of the Fox women owned a single supernatural power. All they ever possessed was a set of uncommonly noisy toe joints, which they'd cracked in response to the stock, '*Is there anybody out there?*' question. The whole thing had been a hoax. News that the entire spiritualist movement was built on a lie did not, however, trigger its collapse. True believers – some of whom had turned to spiritualism for relief from the agonies of grief – chose to keep the faith.

These were times alive with a sense of the dead, and people tried every wild idea to break through to the other side. William Britten, a German who moved to England in the 1870s found himself among a group of people experimenting with: '*pungent essences, or narcotics; the action of clamorous noise or soothing music; the process of looking into glittering stones and crystals; excessive and violent action, especially in a circular direction; and lastly, through the exhalations proceeding from the warm blood of animated beings.*' They'd even brought a levitating Shaman over to London from Siberia. He banged his ceremonial drum and chanted with enthusiasm, but failed to leave the ground. His host explained that this was because the bloke needed to be on home soil.

The most famous medium of the age, Daniel Dunglas Home, was also reputed to levitate. He boasted other powers too, including the ability to make instruments play themselves. Today's illusionists would have little difficulty replicating many of Home's tricks (the self-playing musical instruments, for instance, were positioned under a table, right next to his feet). The level of gullibility of intelligent investigators duped by the 'magical' powers of the mediums was so immense that even now, 130 years on, we can feel embarrassed for them. Home was smart enough never to get caught out, but others weren't so clever. Florence Cook, for instance, would somehow make a white spirit materialise in darkened seance rooms while she was sat securely behind a curtain, immersed in trance. During one of Florence's performances in 1880, the psychic investigator George Sitwell rugby tackled a pale phantom as it ghosted past his seat. When the lights came on, (for some reason these conjured-up spirits refused to appear in anything other than near-pitch darkness), it was clear as day that he had hold of Florence herself, dressed only in pale but durable Marks & Spencer underwear.

In the belief that there might still be something in spiritualism, and that other mysteries such as telepathy deserved to be investigated, a group of scientists formed the Society for Psychical Research in London in January 1882. While, as we shall see, there were far more promising areas to investigate, the SPR, led by its first president Henry Sidgwick, wasted years of energy and thousands of boat miles putting professional mediums to the test across England, mainland Europe and Asia. Among these was an Italian woman, Eusapia Palladino. As proof of her preternatural powers, unattended tables were tapped, untouched musical instruments played, and isolated furniture rearranged itself in the course of a standard Eusapia seance. At the SPR's suggestion, she came to England to give a demonstration of her unearthly talents in Cambridge in 1895. It was a personal disaster for Eusapia, who was found to have freed up one of her hands in the dark to make things move and – hardly worthy of Jonathan Creek this – kicked stuff around.

The SPR had a reasonable track record in detecting frauds, to the point where almost every spiritualist quit the Society, complaining it was run by sceptics. It was, however, caught out itself on occasion. The American professional medium Leonora Piper claimed to receive messages from the dead, which she passed on with her own voice or via automatic writing. Her contacts with spirits were established by a number of afterlife *'controls.'* These dead middle-men included Julius Caesar and a French doctor called Phinuit. It's often fishy when either Caesar or Cleopatra turn up, and when famous but dead Sir Walter Scott put in an appearance at one of Piper's seances, most of the open-minded observers packed their bags and went home. More dubious still, French Dr Phinuit didn't appear to remember much medicine or, for that matter, French. Similarly, Piper produced no evidence that Julius Caesar could speak a word of Latin.

Piper was investigated by the SPR, and predictably most of the Society were satisfied she was a fake, but two of its members, Richard Hodgson and Oliver Lodge, felt certain Piper was the real deal. It's hard to know how this apparently smart pair (Hodgson was a Doctor of Law and Lodge an inventor) could have fallen for such tosh. Robert T Carroll of skepdic.com has a simple theory: *'they believed that since they were brilliant men, they couldn't be tricked.'* The illusionist Harry Houdini was equally clear why so many eminent people were taken in by fake mediums: *'Scientists, philosophers, and psychologists live in circles where honesty is taken for granted...They fail to realize that they're working hand in glove with members of one of the most unclean professions in the world.'*

Hodgson, Lodge and many others were tricked because they needed to be tricked: they were desperate for the existence of an afterlife. Hodge became so fixated on Leonora Piper that some friends believed he had lost hold of reality. Lodge, pulverised by grief following the death in a WWI battle of his son Raymond, turned to mediums for comfort, principally Gladys Leonard from Lytham in Lancashire. Gladys claimed to be in communication with the departed spirit of Raymond, and Lodge was willing to clutch at this hope that his son lived on in a happier other world. The bereft scientist was not alone in this regard: the number of spiritualist churches in England doubled between 1914 and 1920 as people tried desperately to contact the 750,000 husbands and sons who had died in the First World War. Spiritualism would never be as popular again; it has declined gradually over these past one hundred years, but it is far from dead. In fact, it is in resurgence.

I met with Phyllis Rumney a medium, and President of Christchurch Spiritualist Church, Dorset. She is in her seventies, has two grown-up daughters, and lives with her husband in a bright, well-kept home. I asked Phyllis what led her to become a medium:

First of all, losing my mother when I was nine; my father had already walked out on the family when I was three and a half. I never knew my grandparents. Mum died working to keep us. After she had passed, I always knew that I would find my mum; I believed a mother would not leave her young child willingly. I was kicked out of home when I was fifteen into service, because I was being brought up by a brother. I went into nursing. There was an oral exam I was having to sit, and I thought, 'Oh god, I can't stand this!' I got really uptight and nervous over these things. And as I was studying, sat up in bed, I looked up, and there was my mum's face…. this was ten years after she had died. I saw my mum. The feeling I had was 'You've found me; you hadn't left me.' This gave me peace in my heart, and all I said was, 'I knew I'd find you mum'. I passed the exam the next day, and I really felt that she was with me at that time. All through my life I've always known that I've had someone with me.

As an example, I was on an orthopaedic ward one night, and I was the only qualified nurse on duty. I was unable to leave the ward as there'd been six operations that day and I only had auxiliaries [unqualified nursing

163

assistants] *with me. We had some of the patients on intravenous drips. I was sitting in the dayroom with my feet up on a stool during my break. I'd said to the auxiliaries, 'Come and get me if I'm needed.' And the stool was pulled out from underneath my feet, and I automatically said, 'Stop playing silly fools!' and I got up and I went to the bed where I was needed. If I hadn't gone at the time, I wouldn't like to imagine the consequences. And this happened time and time again. So, these are my experiences of the Spirit, people working with me or my sub-conscious. I could go up to someone's bed and tell them where they had the pain. I could sense their pain. I would hold my stomach where their pain was. Or they would have toothache and I would know.*

And then I had another real trauma in my life, and I was left with two girls to bring up on my own; and I started to know if something was going to go wrong when they were going anywhere.

Talking it over with my friend, we thought it was about time we went to a Spiritualist church, just to see what it's all about. My goodness, I was scared stiff when I walked into the church...I saw this little old lady sitting at the front, and I thought, 'Oh my, that's Mrs Bygraves!'...I went up to her and I said, 'You're Mrs Bygraves, aren't you?' and she said, 'Who are you?!' in a very angry way...then she said, 'My goodness', and she told me of a guide that was standing with me. That made me feel quite cold, because I knew nothing about guides or helpers.

Another time I went, there was a medium there and she said to me, 'It's about time you sat in circle and realised what you are seeing, what you're feeling, what you're sensing.'....A circle is a group of people who come together for meditation, who want to progress more with the spirit world....For five years I sat in a circle and said, 'I don't get anything. I don't get anything. I don't get anything.' But of course, for five years I had been doing meditation and I was absorbing the energy. And for the first time I said, 'I've got someone who wants to speak.' And my mentor said, 'Tell them 'stand back' and they can speak later.' She wanted to make sure that I was in charge. And even today, if I go on the platform, I don't have anybody speak until I get on that platform. Because I'm in charge of my life, and if I'm going to do a service, I'll let the spirit come through then. I'll give myself to them, and my voice may change.

I can do platform work and when I come home I have to tell them to be quiet, because they're still with me. It's not you that's being used: it's their energy you're using.....so you're not tired. You can come off a platform and you're alive with it.

We are all the same when we go over. We're not going to change and become Miss Goody-Goody when we're on the other side. If you were a 'baddie', let's put it that way, always robbing and thumping, that energy is still going to go up there...your soul is still the person you were down here. It sometimes takes years of I could say remorse, or growing up, for you to learn and change.

If you have love in your heart, you're not going to be infected by bad spirits...Love is the most important thing in life.

I've been doing this now for 30-odd years. I've given people a message, and they say, 'Tell him to go away, he gave me enough hell on Earth. I don't want to speak to him now!' I can understand that, even though they might be coming through to ask for forgiveness. They wouldn't come through if they had no reason. I mean, I've had my dad through. I could have throttled him, but he has the energy, so there must be a reason why he wanted to come through and speak to me. And out of sheer respect – he's my dad – you give him the time.

I asked Phyllis if she considered this life as completely real.

Life is an illusion. All of life is an illusion. You have to think of it as an illusion. You have to think there's just <u>Now</u>. What has happened has gone, passed. There is only now. So, everything else has got to be an illusion, because there is only this second. Everything is an illusion; there's no 'time' *in the spirit world. But the past includes the future. Life is inclusive of the past and the future.*

Phyllis is a strong believer in reincarnation and, like some modern physicists, in the existence of multiple universes:

I met this girl called Maria at antenatal clinic. We became great friends. Molly, her elder daughter, was always this very strange girl...she turned around when she was five and said, 'I didn't ask to be born this time.' So when you ask me about reincarnation, that's very vivid, from a young child.... When Molly was in a coma, before she died, I could feel her going around, in a circle. She'd left her body. She'd said, 'I was born on a Sunday, so I'll die on a Sunday,' and she did. [The dying] leave their bodies, so they know who's there; they're looking down. Molly was looking down on us. She was, to me, like losing a daughter.

I asked Phyllis if she believes everything has a spirit or a soul:

Yes, even a piece of lettuce, a lettuce leaf. Everything's alive. It's all got that energy, it's all part of that universal energy. People say, 'I'm vegetarian,' and I think, 'What are you eating that lettuce for?' It's exactly the same [as meat]....If you're vegetarian, that's up to you. It's each person to their own point of view. I don't mind!

Coincidences are never coincidences. They're meant to happen: everything's connected. To me, we are the spark of the spirit... We are in everything. The universal. It's God if you want to call it 'God,' or whatever.

My meeting with Phyllis left me not knowing what to believe. Here was a sane and, in many ways very conventional woman telling me that she speaks with the dead. I decided to do some reading around what makes a medium. I found there's a significant link between traumatic events in childhood and 'seeing' and/or 'hearing' the dead. The UK's most famous medium Gordon Smith was subjected to violence and sexual abuse in his childhood. During these terrible events, Gordon would leave his body and enter another realm:

166

'*I started seeing dead people. I'd tell my mum and she'd get angry. I saw Ummy, my grandmother's partner, as clear as day. He'd died the week before and I hadn't known about it.*' Phyllis's father had left her when she was three and a half, and when her mother died Phyllis was still only nine.

It's likely that the dreadful things that happened to both Phyllis and Gordon made them hyper-vigilant, ever primed for some new danger. Their minds would have needed to operate in a far more extended way than those of most other nine-year-olds. Tuned in to everyone around them, they would have the ability to see and read the smallest change in another person's appearance and behaviour: a slight crease at the corner of the eye, the merest shift in the pitch of someone's voice, a micro-second's hesitation in a response to an everyday question. The endangered child's ability to notice signs that almost all of us miss, and then interpret the driving force behind these signs (lust, pain, excitement, fear) is tantamount to mind-reading. A young traumatised person can, it seems, develop an extraordinary ability to register the concealed emotions, thoughts and intentions of others. Furthermore, this reading might happen at a completely unconscious level. We could call this unwitting cold reading. Such a mechanism goes some way to explaining mediumship: the psychic individual is unconsciously picking up tiny cues from the sitter. We may, however, have to look elsewhere to explain how Gordon Smith could '*see*' his grandmother's dead partner when he had no knowledge that person had died, or how Phyllis knew when her patients were in crisis.

Throughout all our childhoods our brains carry out a substantial piece of internal reconstruction. Encased in the skull, the brain cannot increase in size, and yet we need it to retain enough capacity to take in new information and learn new skills. The brain's solution to this problem is to cut away parts of itself that are surplus to requirement, thereby freeing up space for more efficient networks of communication. Small groups of brain tissue that form little-used connections are removed, allowing other busier networks to grow and strengthen: a tangle of meandering B-roads swept aside to accommodate widened neural highways. This process, known as synaptic pruning, is completed in adolescence, by which time the total number of connections between our brain cells has been halved.

Given that the brains of some deeply vulnerable children need to develop in highly unusual ways to see them safely through to adulthood, it seems possible that these (path)ways are spared the onslaught of synaptic pruning, allowing unusual abilities to persist.

In a large survey of more than 3,000 American adults, almost half (42%) reported having had some sort of psychic experience. These 1,270 volunteers often reported a range of uncanny experiences. These included: a sense they were standing next to themselves and watching themselves as though they were a separate person; an impression that objects, other people and the world around them were not real; the sensation that their body didn't belong to them; or the feeling that, because they act so differently on separate occasions, they might be two different people. At the far end of these kind of experiences lies what used to be called Multiple Personality Disorder, but these twelve hundred or so psychic experience volunteers were within the recognised healthy range of psychological functioning (i.e. not so unusual that a psychiatrist might be interested in them). Surprisingly, other studies have found that mediums are, on average, in better mental health and socially more capable than the rest of us.

Jack's death and my brush with mediumship set me to thinking about the working of my own brain, particularly in the early years of my childhood. The world to me then was a vivid place, vibrating with intrinsic life. I could feel no separation between me and it. I was in the world and the world was in me. Everything was almost too bright and alive – it overwhelmed me. The sky, trees, buildings, the ground under my feet were all suffused with life and appeared to move around each other like the components of a giant living kaleidoscope. To push this effect to the limit, I would grab hold of our garden washing line post and run as fast as I could in tight circles around it. When giddiness took over, I would fall onto my back and watch the

168

clouds spin above while the planet pitched and heaved beneath me. I was falling through space, thrilled.

I had little sense of time back then. Occasionally past, present and future would fold into one, which seemed absolutely natural to me. At such moments I immediately knew who was going to speak next, and exactly what they were going to say. Often, I was two or three lines of dialogue in front of the real world. I'd never heard the term déjà vu. All I knew was that I really disliked these events. Dread would come over me and I would feel a constriction across my chest as soon as it started. I 'knew' Theresa will say, *'There's a new girl started at school'* and Elizabeth will reply *'I know – her name's Angela and she's got a sister and two brothers.'* And sure enough, they'd recite these lines, word perfect. While this was going on further lines were coming into my mind, and these again would be spoken two or three seconds later by whoever was in the room. Eventually the present would detach itself from the future and I'd receive no more dialogue, my bones would thaw, and the world would resettle to normality. One bad variant had the déjà vu laying out for me about three or four turns of a conversation between others in the room, but with the additional presentiment that after a while I would be bound to say something specific but nonsensical, such as *'I like the one with elephants and stars.'* To thwart this predestination, I'd promise myself that no matter what was about to happen, I will never utter these words. Shouldn't be difficult, as my sister and I had been talking about a thing completely unrelated, such as the repair of the local swimming pool. But suddenly the subject shifts to some pictures of fabrics in a magazine one of my sisters is reading. I'd not seen it before. She holds up a page and asks me which print I like best. I fight to keep my teeth clenched shut, but my mouth moves outside my control and I hear myself speak the words, *'I like the one with elephant and stars.'* With that the wave breaks, and I can breathe freely once more. *'Yes, it's my favourite too,'* says one of my sisters.

One dream, the same dream, kept troubling me in my very early years. It would come back every few weeks, clamping my spine. It would start with me entering a long, narrow high-ceilinged room, at the far end of which are two glass boxes, one much larger than the other. I am drawn, against my will, towards these boxes, aware that they hold a horrible secret. On reaching them I look down to see they contain human skeletons, one adult, the other a child. The dream would always end at this point. The thing plagued me for two years or more.

One day, I guess I was six years old, we were out as a family visiting some museum or national trust place (my mum loved these outings, the rest of us didn't), and we turned from a corridor into a long, narrow high-ceilinged room. It was *the* room. Sure enough, at the end were two glass cases, side by side. I stayed close to my mum as we walked up to the glass coffins and gazed at the skeletons for a while. My mum read from a plaque on the wall that they were thought to be a mother and baby, and that it was believed that they both died during the child's birth. '*Have we ever been here before?!*' I asked my mother, in a bewildered panic. Deep down, I knew we hadn't. '*No*', she said, '*we haven't.*' There was no-one else in my life who would ever take me to historic sites, so I could see no way I had been in that building before that day.

I was left certain that I had dreamt about that room months, years even, before I physically saw it. Perhaps I had seen the room on telly when very young, and replayed its shocking image in my sleep? I really don't believe so, because the room from floor to ceiling was so complete in my dream. I have concluded, however absurd, that my unconscious brain had drawn material from my future life to help me process a big problem; the dream was plainly about the horror of death. From the day I walked into that room, I never had the nightmare again, and I have had no fear of my death since that visit. To borrow Russell Brand's joke, I'm more afraid of life.

My sense that there was another reality capable of breaking into this one in defiance of the laws of time, stayed with me until I was around nine or ten years old. At this point the déjà vu that would take over my mind without warning, and the prospect that I might dream again about the future, melted away for good. My universe resolved itself into a solid, material reality. Synaptic pruning had shut off my looking-glass world for good. I wasn't sorry. I didn't need or want it.

Sickness, War and other Disasters

Top 5 Crap Remakes. The Lake House (2006)

Here's one for you Bullock: Keanu is dead, you saw him die. His death led you to quit your job as a doctor...Oh, your letters travelled through time and now he's alive? So who died? No one? Get back to work then.

Jack Marteau Student Direct Magazine 2008

Prior to the development of modern medicines, death was a constant companion to all. If a rogue bacterium didn't get them, there was a good chance a foreign war would see off many young males. And it wasn't necessary to catch a disease or fight in battle to meet a premature end: the murder rate in medieval England was ten times that of today, and death through famine or fire could never be ruled out.

Sickness

The earliest report we have of a plague in England comes from the grumpy historian Gildas, writing around 540 AD. It had occurred around a hundred years before, and according to Gildas, his ancestors had no-one to blame but themselves: '*A pestilential disease mortally affected the foolish people, which, without the sword, cut off so large a number of persons, that the living were not able to bury them.*' Proof the plague had been visited on these '*foolish people*' by God was to be found in their shameful behaviour; the population had developed a respect for '*wickedness rather than goodness, the love of darkness instead of the sun, the admission of Satan as an angel of light.*' Trusting Gildas' version of events, Bede decided that the people at the time had been suffering from '*spiritual death*'.

A plague of sorts returned in 664. Describing it as a '*sudden pestilence*', Bede said that it spread throughout Britain and Ireland and '*ravaged the country far and near and destroyed a great multitude of men*'. Sighere, the

172

king of Essex, was so alarmed by the epidemic that he and his subjects gave up Christianity as a bad job and took to worshipping the old Saxon gods.

For the many diseases that failed to respond to folk remedies, the Supernatural remained the last potential cure. Of necessity, belief in miraculous healing was common in medieval England. At the spot where King Oswald of Northumbria was killed in battle in 642, people would gather up the soil and mix it with water to make a medicine that was good for humans and animals alike. It cured a horse of epilepsy and a local innkeeper's daughter of palsy. Demand for the magic dust was so great that a six-foot hole developed on the site.

In 1347 a new and terrible disease arrived in Sicily and began to spread death and destruction across the Mediterranean. The Black Death, or bubonic plague, was a bacterial infection believed to have been carried by black rats and spread via their fleas to humans. In the months that followed, word spread of the severity of the problem devastating Southern Europe and of its advance towards the English Channel. In July 1348, Archbishop Zouche of York writes that a '*mortal pestilence and infection of the atmosphere is hanging over various parts of the world, and especially England*' As we would expect, he is certain that the plague is '*caused by the sins of men who, made callous by prosperity, neglect to remember the benefits of the Supreme Giver.*' Zouche's remedy is an increase in daily prayers. But hope and prayer are to prove no defence, as within days a ship will dock in Weymouth bearing the sickness that will turn to ruin an entire nation.

Many communities put themselves in quarantine to keep the plague at bay. A few succeeded; most did not. Geoffrey the Baker was living in Oxfordshire at the time. He wrote of what he knew of the plague:

> It came to England and first began in the towns and ports joining on the seacoasts, in Dorsetshire, where, as in other counties, it made the country quite void of inhabitants so that there were almost none

left alive. From there it passed into Devonshire and Somersetshire, even unto Bristol, and raged in such sort that the Gloucestershire men would not suffer the Bristol men to have access to them by any means. But at length it came to Gloucester, yea even to Oxford and to London, and finally it spread over all England and so wasted the people that scarce the tenth person of any sort was left alive.

Henry Knighton, who lived through the plague, recalled that in Bristol, *'the grass grew several inches high in the High St and in Broad St...virtually the whole town was annihilated.'* Knighton, recorded the horrific impact of *'the sorrow-bearing pestilence,'* on, his home city, Leicester: *'almost the whole strength of the town died as if struck with sudden death, for there were few who kept their beds beyond three or two days or even half a day.'* Knighton, who knew his history, compared the Black Death to the great plague of 664. Sheep were struck down too. 5,000 died on just one farm. Surviving farm animals were left to wander and fend for themselves. Land was left to waste; harvests went un-gathered. Dazed by the size of the calamity, Knighton recalls *'no one knew what to do.'*

Overcrowding and dreadful sanitation made cities particularly vulnerable. As established graveyards in London ran out of space, new cemeteries were opened, but within weeks these too were filled. Alongside one of these burial grounds (which carried the grim name No Man's Land), a huge 13.5-acre cemetery was created, Spittle Croft. No one knows exactly how many people were buried there, but the king's own records put the number at a staggering 50,000.

Ralph Higden was living in Chester at the time of the plague. Looking back, he wrote that, *'scarcely a tenth of mankind was left alive'*. A chronicle at St Mary's Abbey, York stated that, *'there were hardly enough living to care for the sick and bury the dead*

For any healthy person, death might be just hours away. Many turned to 'shriving', formally confessing their sins in the hope they'd be spared the horrors of hell. Some engaged in self-flagellation, trusting God would regard them as purified and therefore undeserving of death. Knowing the disease to be highly contagious (a simple sneeze could transmit it), the townspeople of Winchester demanded a new cemetery be created on church land far out of town, and when a monk called Ralph de Saunton refused this, they set upon and almost killed him.

In dread of the disease, a number of clergymen abandoned their flock and fled to open country. The Bishop of Salisbury wrote in April 1350 that that some priests, '*have most shamefully absented themselves for their churches,*' leaving them to '*birds and beasts.*' These defections had, he said, brought '*danger to many souls.*', with no priests on hand to deliver *extreme unction* to save the dying from damnation.

Meanwhile, a war was going on, and the people of Portsmouth wrote to the king saying they were '*very much depressed…both by the pestilence and by the burning and destruction of the place by our enemies*' and could not therefore pay him any tax. The king accepted the situation. He had little choice: the entire country was in chaos. Much of the 14th century was a catastrophe for England. A run of three bad summers from 1315 to 1317 ruined the harvests and caused a deadly famine. Twenty years later England got involved in an exhausting war with France that would last for almost a century. After doing almost immeasurable damage in 1348-9, the plague returned in 1361, 1369 and again 1378. Although it didn't kill nearly as many people as the terrible first epidemic, (it couldn't), these later outbreaks took the lives of many children and young people, weakening the country for a further generation. Many felt the end of the world had come.

The medieval poem 'A Death' sums up a fatalistic attitude, with the paltry consolation that when the plague has taken you off, you will be past caring.

> *When my eyes mist up*
> *And there's hissing in my ears,*
> *And my nose grows cold*

And my tongue folds
And my cheeks sag
And my lips turn black
And my mouth grimaces
And my spittle flows
And my hair falls out
And my heart is panicked
And my hand shakes
And my feet stiffen,
All too late, all too late
When death is at the gate

So I shall move
From my bed to the floor
From the floor to a shroud
From my shroud to a funeral bier
And from bier to the grave;
Then my house lies on my nose
And I couldn't give a fig for all of this world

All together now!

In 1665 the bubonic plague returned to England with lethal ferocity. Writing on 31st August of that year, Samuel Pepys tracked the spread of the disease through London:

> *Every day sadder and sadder news of its increase. In the City died this week 7,496 and of them 6,102 of the plague. But it is feared that the true number of the dead, this week is near 10,000.*

There were reports of dying people digging their own graves, since anyone else capable of wielding a shovel had either fled or expired. Richer Londoners, including the king, judiciary and parliament, took off for the country. The poor remained, alongside those who chose not to abandon their businesses. Among them was Daniel Defoe's uncle Henry Foe who had a saddler's shop to safeguard. Henry survived, and told his story to his fascinated nephew, who went on to write an account of it, imaging himself as Henry, living through the entire outbreak. As the plague approached, Henry told his elder brother that since God decides who lives or dies, he intended to stay at his shop and trust the divine ruler will protect him from the plague. Henry's brother, a conspicuously religious person, couldn't help but laugh at Henry's naïve plan. He'd just returned from Asia, where he'd seen the plague first hand; those who kept well away survived, while those who hung around generally died. The Almighty didn't appear to get involved. His advice for his kid brother was blunt: '*Save yourself*'. But Foe, like Pepys, stayed on through the mayhem and horror.

In the early days of the plague the churches of London were crammed with people praying for God's mercy. Fortune tellers, astrologers and magicians set up make-shift businesses and did brisk trade predicting the survival of any desperate punter who would cross their palms with silver. Delirious with fear, some Londoners began to see demons and angels in the sky, and when Foe tells a crowd of people gazing up at a supposed angel that, frankly, he can see nothing, he is met with a torrent of scorn and abuse and has to quit the scene for his own safety.

People had every reason to go half-crazy. Foe remembers that:

> *The shrieks of women and children at the windows and doors of their houses, where their dearest relations were perhaps dying, or just dead, were so frequent to be heard as we passed the streets, that it was enough to pierce the stoutest heart in the world to hear them.*

Yet as the disease progressed, '*men's hearts were hardened, and death was so always before their eyes, that they did not so much concern themselves for the loss of their friends.*' By October 1665 Pepys has become so accustomed to the sight of dead bodies that '*I am come almost to think nothing of it.*' Defoe felt that people had become indifferent to the death of others, even their friends, because they fully expected it would be their turn next. When the plague reached its height relatively few people risked going to church, for fear of becoming infected there. Drinkers were less cautious, and the beer house carried on business even as the 'dead-carts' trundled their grizzly cargo past the pub's open doors.

In September 1665 Pepys passed by a farm *'where about twenty-one people have died of the plague.'* An armed guard had been placed around the farm, to prevent the few workers still alive from getting out and contaminating others. He was shocked at *'the plague making us cruel, as dogs, one to another.'* City homes where someone had come down with the plague were similarly 'shut up'. A padlock was put on the door and a 24-hour guard was placed outside. After 28 days the house was unlocked, and anyone within that had survived was free to come out. If a nurse who had been attending a plague patient wished to leave the sick house during these 28 days of quarantine, she had to go straight home where she in turn would be locked up for 28 days. Some people kicked against this imprisonment, escaping via upstairs windows and back doors, or even bashing out their own front door and attacking the guard outside. Many more were too weak to even think of escape, and instead died in their captivity.

Defying a ban, Foe sneaked a look at a huge plague pit in Aldgate, East London. He estimated it was 40 feet in length, 15 feet wide and 20 feet deep. In just 14 days it was full. Foe reported that some people at death's door would simply stagger to the nearest plague pit and thrown themselves in.

The swollen buboes or glands that gave the plague its name were so painful that people would roar with the agony, or as Foe witnessed, shoot themselves or leap to their deaths rather than endure their final hours. Surviving in dread among all this mayhem, Foe *'wished often'* that he had taken his brother's advice and left London while he still had the chance (the roads through towns and villages outside of London were now blocked by constables and wardens). In an effort to portray in our imagination the full horror of the great plague of 1665, Daniel reports Foe as saying,

> *it is impossible to say anything that is able to give a true idea of it to those who did not see it, other than this, that it was indeed very, very, very dreadful, and such as no tongue can express.*

He claims that several people expired through pure fear, literally frightened to death. Things in London couldn't get any worse. Except they could. The following year most of the city burned to the ground. Again, Pepys was around to witness disaster: '*it made me weep to see it. The churches, houses, and all on fire, and flaming at once; and a horrid noise the flames made.*'

From here, the only way was up. And it's largely true: by good fortune the plague of 1665, which had killed one sixth of London in less than 18 months, was the last instance of mega-death in England. That's not to say that we all lived happily ever: death still picked us off with impressive frequency, via outbreaks of infections such as smallpox, cholera and, most recently, the 1918 Spanish flu pandemic that claimed around 150,000 English lives. '*The funeral corteges followed each other through the town,*' recalled an eyewitness from Leicester in 1973, 55 years on the from the catastrophe. '*Often there was more than one coffin in a hearse.*' Although they needed no assistance, humankind has been an active contributor to the dirty work of viruses and bacteria, via its own lethal epidemic: war.

War, what is it good for!

Throughout my childhood there was unlimited talk about The War. Almost every adult recollection seemed to reference it ('*That was just before The War broke out*'; '*Of course, The War was on then*'; '*He'd just come back from The War and..*'). Life was a drama in three acts: before, during and 'just after' The War. Every Sunday there was some dreary and violent film on the telly about *The War.* During the week ITV ran *All Our*

Yesterdays, a documentary series about *The War* that ran even longer than the thing itself.

My dad had enlisted at nineteen years old. He was put in the tank regiment and shipped across the channel to fight the German army. He told us nothing of what had happened over there when we were kids, and almost nothing when we were adults. He did describe once how he had looked on, powerless, as one of his mates, Ginger, was cut in two trying to exit his toppling tank. He also described having to blow up a house filled with a squad of German soldiers, young Europeans, just like himself. Piet's brother, my Uncle Louis, had enlisted too, but never got sent over to fight. He was shaken by the change in Piet and his comrades when they returned to England. '*They were never the same,*' he said.

When Winston Churchill died, they broadcast his funeral live on the telly and almost everyone watched. It went on all day. I was six years old and resentful that kids tv had been hijacked by such a boring show, I complained at the big fuss over some stupid old man. My dad, who was always slow to anger and never violent, lost it completely and went for me. I ran but he caught me on the stairs and gave me a proper hiding. I couldn't know what Churchill represented to Piet – his friends blown to pieces, everything risked, principles lost and so much sacrificed for a future generation. A generation that, as it turned out, could only sneer. The Beatles movie *Hard Day's Night* had just come out. My parents didn't go and see it, but us kids did:

> Man in Bowler Hat: *Don't take that tone with me, young man. I fought the war for your sort.*
> Ringo: *I bet you're sorry you won.*

As well as disappointment at how the next generation had turned out (the 'pill' and a low appetite for key values of the past such as unquestioning service to the nation), the wartime generation felt the loss of something else: the thrill of war. The genuine sense that life might finish at any moment combined with the knowledge that they were positioned, in the prime of their lives, at the very centre of history, generated an electric excitement in my parents and their friends, the afterglow of which shone from their eyes whenever the subject turned — as it frequently did — to *The* (capital t), *War* (capital w). The comedian and war veteran Spike Milligan captured this lost excitement in a TV sketch. An elderly couple, safe but deeply bored in their 1980s English home, dance for joy on hearing on the radio that after 40 years of peace, World War II is to restart, due to popular demand.

Assuming any war can ever be worse than another, civil war stands out as uniquely horrific. Brother kills brother, son kills father, father kills son. With Henry VII's decisive victory in 1485, England's longest civil war, the War of the Roses ended. It's likely that accounts of the war still ran through conversations during Shakespeare's time, a little over 100 years on. He put these words into Henry's mouth:

> *England hath long been mad and scarred herself.*
> *The brother blindly shed the brother's blood.*
> *The father rashly slaughtered his own son.*
> *The son, compelled, been butcher to the sire*

Stupidly, just fifty years on the country would throw itself into another bloody civil conflict. For England and so many other nations, war seems unavoidable; there's a terrible force of logic that acts like an undertow, dragging all down into calamitous violence: if you don't kill, you'll be killed.

Shakespeare sets out this dilemma in *Richard II*. The Bishop of Carlisle, who doesn't let the odd Commandment stand in the way of organised slaughter, tries to convince the King to go into battle against Henry Bolingbroke. He warns Richard that if he shies away from the fight, his enemies will only become stronger, and kill him. So, according to the less-than-spiritual Bishop, seeing as he's as good as dead already, Richard might as well fight: '*Fear, and be slain. No worse can come to fight.*' This all makes pretty good sense so far, but the Bishop goes further, telling the nervy King that if worst should come to worst, and he is killed in the battle, his death will obliterate death: '*fight and die is death destroying death*'.

It's hard to see how death can destroy death, particularly for poor Richard, who's the one who has to do the dying. But strangely reassured, Richard says he's up for the fight. He soon changes his mind though and makes a run for the Welsh hills. Ultimately it does him no good as his enemies capture him there and kill him, just as the good Bishop had predicted.

So in a few lines of drama, Shakespeare sums up the riddle that neither war nor peace can solve: do nothing and you may get killed; do something and you may get killed.

But if you do stand and fight, at least people can say you were brave; and if you don't stand and fight, you run the risk of looking a pussy, like Richard. These twin imperatives, to show courage and to resist cowardice, combine to drive the spiritual characteristic that the English recognise most readily and value so highly: fighting spirit. Who else to turn to here but Winston Churchill?

Like the Bishop of Carlisle, Churchill wasn't too squeamish about making war. Particularly against Johnny Foreigner. He took his inspiration from a legendary English warrior, King Arthur:

> *let us then declare that king Arthur and his noble knights,*
> *guarding the Sacred Flame of Christianity and the theme of world*
> *order, sustained by valour, physical strength, and good horses and*
> *armour, slaughtered innumerable hosts of foul barbarians and set*
> *decent folk an example for all time*

There are many who argue that Arthur never really existed, or – worse still – that he did, and he was from France. But that wouldn't have troubled Churchill in the slightest. His ultimate hero was French: Joan of Arc.

> *Joan was a being so uplifted from the ordinary run of mankind*
> *that she finds no equal in a thousand years.*

The quality Churchill so admired in Joan was her willingness to risk everything for the defence of her country. Writing about the English response to a potential French invasion in 1690, Churchill refers to the '*spirit of the nation*,' which showed itself when, '*The whole country took up what arms they could find.*' In dark times, far from being wrong to kill others, it was morally right. If angels saw a defenceless woman being attacked in the street, would they fold their wings? At the darkest of times, 1940, Churchill took a rare trip to church to read out a passage he'd chosen from the Bible. It began, '*Arm yourselves and be ye men of valour.*'

But what of the absolute Christian commandment, Thou Shall Not Kill? Well, despite his stirring acclaim of the '*sacred flame of Christianity*', Winston was not much of a believer. In a letter home from Sudan written in 1898, Churchill states his faith on the eve of a battle, '*I can assure you I do not flinch—though I do not accept the Christian or any other form of religious belief.*' His friend Charles Wilson summarised: '*King and country, in that order, that's about the only religion Winston has.*' But Churchill did hold belief in a protective supernatural force. He had good reason: he'd nearly drowned, survived a plane crash, been shot at, blown up, and even run over, but still lived to the age of 91. '*Over me beat invisible wings*,' was how he explained his freakish run of good luck.

At the simplest level, Winston loved a good scrap. Writing to his friend Violet Asquith from the trenches in 1916, Churchill says, '*I love this war. I know it's smashing and shattering the lives of thousands every moment - & yet - I can't help it - I enjoy every second of it.*'

A warrior to the end, Churchill chose, *The Battle Hymn of the Republic* and *Fight the Good Fight* as hymns for his own funeral. The old man would have been chuffed to learn that he is today worshipped alongside his hero Joan of Arc as a saint by the followers of the Cao Dai religion in Vietnam.

In its purest sense the fighting spirit is the act of self-sacrifice, among the greatest example of which is the charge of the Light Brigade. On October

25th 1854, six hundred soldiers, armed only with swords, charged across an open plain in Crimea in a suicidal attempt to capture a rank of Russian cannon. Their chance of success was zero. William Russell, a London journalist, was there that day:

> *with a halo of flashing steel above their heads, and with a cheer which was many a noble fellow's death cry, they flew into the smoke of the batteries; but ere they were lost from view, the plain was strewed with their bodies.*

Although it was and still is rightly regarded as the Everest of courage, back in the UK there was a national outcry, as the charge had been ordered in error. Tennyson, was moved to write his most famous poem:

> *Boldly they rode and well,*
> *Into the jaws of Death,*
> *Into the mouth of hell*
> *Rode the six hundred.*

Such is the prominence and power of the fighting spirit within English culture, even pacifists can catch it. Wilfred Owen was born in Oswestry, Shropshire. His one ambition was to become a great poet. Achieving this would cost him his life.

Wilfred is 21 years old and living in the south of France on the day the First World War breaks out. A Christian and a pacifist, he sums up his turn-the-other cheek values in a letter to his mother: '*Be bullied, be outraged, be killed, but do not kill.*' He hates war, but he hates injustice and cowardice just as deeply. What to do? On his return to England in 1915, Wilfred settles the dilemma by signing up and undergoing military training. He then finds himself dropped mid-winter into the grotesque hell of the trenches. To communicate this world gone to horror he writes poetry that is so unflinching and accurate that it is as obscene as war itself. In six nightmarish lines, Wilfred takes us with him, to help collect the body of one of his comrades, just killed by mustard gas:

If in some smothering dreams, you too could pace
Behind the wagon that we flung him in,
And watch the white eyes writhing in his face,
His hanging face, like a devil's sick of sin;
If you could hear, at every jolt, the blood
Come gargling from the froth-corrupted lungs

The point is no longer to live a virtuous life and avoid hell; the point now is to avoid a ridiculously early death and live any sort of life at all. By 1917 Wilfred's nerves are shredded. The last mental straw comes when he is trapped for three days beside the blown-up remains of a friend as shells explode incessantly around him. Owen is declared unfit to fight and shipped to a hospital in Edinburgh. He is safe at last, but in September 1918, dismissing the pleas of friends and family, Wilfred resolves to return to the battlefield. His friend and fellow patient Siegfried Sassoon begs Owen not to go, even threatening to stab him in the leg to stop him. Owen knows that going back will be the death of him; the war has stripped him of all illusions. He tells his brother, '*I know I shall be killed. But it's the only place I can make my protest from.*'

On 1st October 1918 Wilfred captured a German machine gun post almost single-handedly, killing several soldiers and taking many others prisoner. As a result, he is awarded a Military Cross. In describing the action, Wilfred writes to his mother that he had '*fought like an angel*'. It is a strange phrase, articulating the near-spiritual relationship the English can have with war. One month later, and just seven days before the end of the war, Wilfred is killed. His mother will receive the news on Armistice Day.

Not every pacifist could be persuaded of the necessity to fight. Thousands refused to serve in the British forces during the two world wars. Although many went to prison during WWI, very few were killed for their principles. This was not always the case. On 8 August 1643, a crowd of women wearing hats decorated with white ribbon, marched on the House of

Commons, calling for an end to the civil war. Thomas Knyvett, an MP, was there: '*On Tuesday morning a large group of women came and demanded peace. The next day they came again in a far greater number...they became unruly and many women were killed by the trained guard.*' I don't know how trained the guard were, but the worst way of convincing any protester that your way is correct would be to kill them.

Enthusiasm for the civil war was rarely high: in general, it is easier to convince someone to fight a foreign enemy, as this involves protecting the homeland and all that they hold dear within its shores. Asking someone to go to war against their own countrymen is trickier. One way round this problem is to convince them that the opposition are working for Satan. This kind of thinking embedded itself within both armies fighting the English Civil War. Lucy Hutchinson was working as a nurse for the parliamentary army, attending to Roundhead soldiers injured in battle:

> *In the encounter only five of our men were hurt...we dressed all their wounds with such success that they were all cured...Seeing three of the prisoners badly bleeding, I dressed their wounds also...Captain Palmer came in and told me not to help the enemies of God. I replied, I had a duty to treat them as men, not as enemies.*

Go Lucy!

According to one eyewitness account of the Battle of Edgehill in 1642, there was a genuine appetite for the civil war among the foot-soldiers that fought that day on the Royalist side:

> *Arms were the great deficiency, and the men stood up in the same garments in which they left their native fields; and with scythes, pitchforks, and even sickles in their hands, they cheerfully took the field, and literally like reapers descended to the harvest of death.*

There are several ways in which someone can descend into a harvest of death, but cheerfully would be among the rarest. This eyewitness seems to have been at a different battle to Edmund Verney. A Royalist officer at Edgehill, Verney who wrote to his son: '*Our men are very raw, our victuals scarce and provisions for horses worse. I daresay there was never so raw, so unskilful and so unwilling an army brought to fight.*' In case you were wondering, it ended a draw.

Unlike an overseas conflict, in the civil war loved ones were close enough to visit their soldier husband or son. In January 1644, Mary Springate heard that her husband, William, was seriously ill with '*camp fever*' [probably typhoid] in Sussex. Although heavily pregnant, Mary made a dangerous journey from London to Arundel, through ice and winter floods. '*It was about twelve at night when we arrived...Seeing me...he sprang up as if he would come out of his bed, saying, 'Let me embrace you before I die. I am going to my God.'...He died two days later.*' Mary gave birth a few days after, but to double her terrible sorrow, the baby was born dead.

The English could not find a way to collectively mourn the dead from the Civil War. It would take the mass slaughter of the First World War to produce a day, time and national method of commemoration. The two minutes' silence began on 11th November 1919, marking the burial in Westminster Abbey of the body of the Unknown Warrior, a soldier exhumed from a battlefield grave in Flanders.

Once the thing is done and won, fiction is free to make war appear glorious. *The Dam Busters* and *633 Squadron*, made a decade or so after WW2, are examples of the trigger-happy genre. Both show RAF planes dropping high explosives, but the suffering of those below the bombs are ignored or portrayed as the just deserts of a cartoonish gang of Nazi baddies. Films made during WW2 were generally far more realistic and mature. *In Which We Serve*, made in 1942, has at its centre the sinking of a British warship, HMS Torrin. It goes down in the Mediterranean, along with most of its crew. Back in London, others are killed in the Blitz. The primary message of the film could not have been clearer: war is death and suffering. The secondary message is equally plain: keep calm and carry on. Amidst all the sorrow and mayhem, no one in the film dissolves into panic, grief or psychological freefall. Personal loss is borne with quiet acceptance. The future of the nation demands that all should be prepared to make noble sacrifices and set each other examples of patriotic emotional restraint.

But films promoting too much self-sacrifice would make anyone seeking escapism at the cinema want to scream; light was needed to hold dark at bay. Charlie Chaplain provided this in one of his finest moments, playing the fascist buffoon Adenoid Hynkel in *The Great Dictator*. In a scene that is a masterpiece of physical comedy and satire, Hynkel toys endlessly with a giant inflatable globe, like a child playing with a balloon.

A different message winds its way through the *Life and Death of Colonel Blimp*, a weird epic that begins and finishes in London during WW2, but flashes backwards to the Boer War, WWI and the stretches of peacetime in between. There's some propaganda in there (Blimp's wife refers to the Germans as '*butchers*'), but for much of the film the non-Nazi Germans are friendly and polite. More surprising still for a film released in 1943, the movie is built around a deep friendship between an English and a German soldier (Clive Candy and Theo Kretschmar-Schuldorff). The two get on so well they almost seem to be on the same side. As the film reaches WW2, Clive, (by now a grumpy old colonel), is booked to give a talk on the BBC about the retreat from Dunkirk, but as a result of political pressure his broadcast is pulled.

A wartime film that has a very likeable German as one of its central characters and a sub-plot involving political censorship of the BBC was never going to be a hit with the politicians. Churchill is said to have hated it, but *Blimp* did make it to the cinema. In a sense the real subject of the film is not war, but the process of ageing and dying. Towards the end of the film, Clive stands by the bombed-out shell of his marital home. He gazes at a pool of rainwater that has filled the exposed foundations, and his eye fixes on a dry, dead leaf floating on its surface. At that moment Clive realises that in the late autumn of his life, he must, like every other old soldier, simply fade away.

Exactly where Clive Candy fades away to, along with all the others who were to die in WW2, became the subject of Powell and Pressburger's 1946 *A Matter of Life and Death*. The film begins with Peter Carter bailing out of his burning RAF fighter plane without a parachute. By rights he should die, but he comes to on an English beach, washed ashore thanks to some heavenly cock-up. Deep in the cosmos, in the giant city of the Afterlife, steps are being taken to correct this mistake. A messenger calling himself Conductor 71 is sent down from Afterlife to tell Peter his number's up and he must accompany him to the next world. But Peter has just met and fallen in love with an American radio operator called June; he has no intention of going anywhere. A heavenly court is set up to decide Peter Carter's case: should he be allowed to stay on earth, or must he take his place in the next world? The consistent jokey take on death (bungling immigration control at heaven's gate, angels with detachable wings, cheery newly killed soldiers) and the absence of any recognisable godhead must have offended a proportion of the many bereaved cinema-goers, but the film is crammed with charm, and the idea of an atheist heaven is a creative masterstroke.

By 1969 heaven of any sort is out of fashion and is replaced by the tomb-black humour of *Oh! What a Lovely War*. Religion is the comfort of fools, and the prospect of an afterlife is worse than the carnage of the trenches. Soldiers sing a mindless music-hall song, *The Bells of Hell Go Ting-a-ling-a-ling*, after dropping numerous dead comrades into a mass grave. Jack Smith, the only surviving son of the Smith family, is shot at two minutes to eleven on Armistice Day, 1918. '*You're the last one*' says a mysterious officer, who goes on to tell Jack to follow a blood-red tape, which leads right past four old generals signing the peace treaty, (none of whom can see him), and out into a poppy field where his family are picnicking in the summer sun. Again, they can't see Jack, although his mum does sense something strange. Smith then encounters his fellow soldiers, lying on the grass. They don't speak. He lays down beside them, and they each morph into an individual white cross. As the camera pulls back, hundreds and then thousands of crosses fill the screen, as small and insignificant as pixels. A similar image was developed in 2014 to create an art installation at the Tower of London. 888,246 ceramic poppies, one for each British Empire soldier killed in WWI, were set around the Tower, to form a blood-sea of sorrow.

By the time he came to write *Gulliver's Travels*, Irishman Jonathan Swift had lived through English military campaigns against Spain, France, Native Americans, Scotland, Ulster, the Cornish, the Dutch, the Swedes, Turks, Bavarians and Hungarians. Swift wasn't buying the kill or be killed imperative for wars, and to be fair it's hard to see how Cornwall could have represented a deadly threat to the whole of England. In Swift's book, war is an avoidable catastrophe caused by pig-headed political leaders. When Gulliver stumbles upon a conflict in Lilliput, he learns that it all sprang from a command by the Emperor that the nation should only open boiled eggs at their narrower tip, instead of at the customary wider end. The ensuing row escalates into a full-blown war in which eleven thousand people are killed, '*rather than submit to break their eggs at the smaller end.*'

Swift was right to be sceptical about the necessity for every war: the historian Stuart Laycock has calculated that of the 194 countries that make up our world, Britain has invaded 178 of them, including the ever-dangerous Iceland and the super-power that is Narau (eight square miles, total population 9,500, but why take chances?) No, there seems to be a national appetite for a fight that can take the English half way round the planet in search of the next bit of organised violence.

If further words were needed to underline the horror of war, Corporal Joe Hayles recalled his experience of the Battle of the Somme:

There was a terrible smell. It was so awful it nearly poisoned you. A smell of rotten flesh. The old German front line was covered with bodies – they were seven and eight deep and they had all gone black. These people had been lying since the First of July. Wicked it was! Bodies all over the place. I'll never forget it. I was only eighteen, but I thought, 'There's something wrong here!'

From the safe side of the English Channel, foreign wars can be clean and odour free causes for celebration and even glee. In June 1665, 700 naval officers and crew were killed in a sea battle with the Dutch. Making no mention of the death toll, Samuel Pepys is thrilled by the victory, which he shares the next morning with the family of William Penn, who had commanded the English fleet: *'with my heart full of joy…to my Lady Penn's, where they are all joyed and not a little puffed up at the good success of their father'*. Pepys may have felt differently had he been manning one of the cannon-blasted ships; it's easy to celebrate when you're not the one doing the fighting.

Victorian Horror

Top 5 Horrific Horror Movie Taglines: Alien vs. Predator (2004)
Tagline: 'Whoever wins, we lose'

This movie is such shite that it would be better described in full as
'Whoever wins, we lose 90 minutes of our lives,' 'Whoever wins, we lose
the will to live' *or* 'Whoever wins, we're glad we downloaded the film
from BitTorrent and didn't pay to see it.'

Jack Marteau, Student Direct Magazine 2009

Among the superstitious practices that were common at the start of the 19th
century, covering the home's mirror (there was usually only one) is the most
intriguing. No-one can say with confidence how it began. One common
theory is that it prevented the dearly departed from catching sight of their
own reflection and becoming trapped in the house, a ghost unable to cross
over to the next world. A competing explanation is that the use of a mirror
by the bereaved was an act of vanity, disrespectful to the deceased. Others
believed that whoever looks in the mirror next would be the next to die,
reason enough to keep the thing covered indefinitely.

While unskilled workers and the sick lived in terrible deprivation
throughout much of the Victorian era, industrialisation and the spread of
Empire swelled the ranks of the middle classes, providing them enough spare
money to turn grief into commodity, with its own consumer must-haves and
dress-codes. Older superstitious practices such as covering the mirror and
drawing the curtains became part of full-blown ritual: clocks were stopped
(either to signify that time had ended, prohibit the intrusion of hourly
chimes, or simply record the moment of death), the piano was locked so no
music could be played, and family members, servants and even carriages were
draped in coal-black crepe. The purchase of sombre fabric, full mourning
wear, jet jewellery and elaborate headstones was wholly consistent with
funereal fashion, but it also represented activity to stave off anxiety about

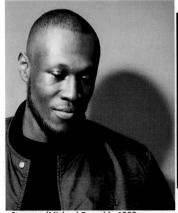

Philosopher Margaret Cavendish (1623-1673), who suggested atoms might be *knowing bodies*

Stormzy, (Michael Owuo) b. 1993, composer of *Blinded by Your Grace*

Prometheus Bound, by William Blake

Portrait of Virginia Woolf by Roger Fry, 1917

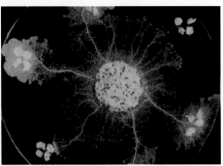

Slime Mold (Physarum Polycephalum), a single-cell creature with an ability to solve problems

Jack at 3 years old

Jack in Sicily, aged 21

My sister Elizabeth, c. 1983

From left to right: Me, Jack, Debbie and Rosie, September 12th 2009

Jack with fellow language students in Sicily, Autumn 2009

Innermost chamber inside West Kennet Burial Long Barrow, Wiltshire

Front entrance, West Kennet Long Barrow

The Book of the Dead (2019) by Brixham-based artist Ian Watson

death. As the research psychologist Sheldon Solomon has found, we spend and consume more when we are reminded of our mortality. Faced with death, the Victorians chose to go shopping.

But for the luckless, the reign of Victoria was a time of unmatched prospect and prosperity. The writer Charles Kingsley, drunk on the success of the times, gushed, '*England is...inventing, producing, exporting, importing, till it seems as if the whole human race, and every land from the equator to the pole must henceforth bear the indelible impress and sign-manual of English science.*' As the Cambridge historian Hilary Carey has pointed out, the Christian churches fostered the sentiment that in building its empire, Britain was serving God's plan to salvage souls across the globe. Doing well and doing good, the future was iridescent.

The only blot on the horizon was the horizon itself: the visible limit of our existence. Even for the wealthy in mid-Victorian England, life expectancy was 45 years. You could live to a ripe old age, but all the evidence around suggested you wouldn't. And the evidence was both rife and persuasive: hospitals were such disease colonies that the sick often preferred to take their chances at home, where they would pine away, sometimes assailed by the most alarming symptoms.

English science had conquered nature, England may have conquered much of the world, but the English were doomed to lose their last and most important battle. Moreover, in pursuing two of its great obsessions, scientific advancement and the construction of Empire, the English had brought into doubt mortality's one certain consolation, that there is Christian god who will make everything alright when death comes to call. The relatively new science of geology established that the world was very likely to be many millions of years old, thoroughly refuting the six-thousand-year age tag suggested by the Old Testament; and rather than representing a hotchpotch of crude pagan beliefs, scholars discovered that Indian religions incorporated scientifically valid insights (the non-absoluteness of time, the vast energy within the atomic world) developed

193

long before the earliest days of Christianity. What's worse, some of these ideas, particularly the existence of a timeless, bodiless soul, had travelled in the opposite direction, informing the work of Socrates and Plato, which in turn had influenced Christianity. The irony for the modern Victorians was the tighter their collective grip grew on the physical world, the looser their hold became on the certainty of a Christian god whose divine laws are expressed in one irrefutable book.

Faced with a crisis of faith, the Victorians resorted to a strategy favoured by many of us today: they became more adamant and emphatic. If smallpox had taken their child away, it was for the purpose of setting them down among the angels of heaven. The child's grave would therefore be attended by a brace of seven-foot high stone angels. Similarly, if a devoted wife and mother died during childbirth, then she had been called from her earthly family to join the divine family above. She should therefore be laid to rest in a symbolic new home, a shining marble mausoleum. By such grand gestures the Victorians declared their belief in the life everlasting. But as teams of jet-black horses crested with black feathers drew glass hearses containing ornate coffins, statement began to look very much like overstatement, and in proclaiming a faith founded on humility, the Victorians seemed to have neglected that vital spiritual ingredient. They had protested too much. Christianity had solved the problem of death for the English, but the age of science had left the faithful seemingly more spooked than ever by their mortality. Rather than shrinking into denial to save themselves from horror, many Victorians employed their customary purposefulness to look death straight in his dark eye.

In *Jude the Obscure* written by Thomas Hardy in 1895, the elder of Jude's sons, Jude junior, has been talking to his step-mother Sue about the family's dire straits: virtually homeless with three children to feed. Things seem more hopeless still when Sue tells him she has another baby on the way. The boy takes himself off to bed, muttering to himself, '*If we children was gone there'd be no trouble at all!*' Sue overhears him and tells him not to think

194

that way, but she cannot guess the direction his thoughts will take him. The following morning, Jude and Sue enter their children's bedroom and their world implodes in horror:

> *At the back of the door were fixed two hooks for hanging garments, and from these the forms of the two youngest children were suspended, by a piece of box-cord round each of their necks, while from a nail a few yards off the body of little Jude was hanging in a similar manner. An overturned chair was near the elder boy....a piece of paper was found upon the floor, on which was written, in the boy's hand, with the bit of lead pencil that he carried: 'Done because we are too menny.'*

Although we know the story to be a complete fiction, Sue's despair is still too horrible for us to imagine. Even by Hardy's advanced standards of misery, the tale of Jude's three children is unbearably tragic. The childish misspelling of the word 'many' cements the scene's dreadful realism.

There's a fair slice of suffering in Charles Dickens' *Bleak House*, where Esther gives what care she can to Jenny's dead baby.

> *Presently I took the light burden from her lap, did what I could to make the baby's rest the prettier and gentler, laid it on a shelf, and covered it with my own handkerchief. We tried to comfort the mother, and we whispered to her what Our Saviour said of children. She answered nothing, but sat weeping—weeping very much.*

Unlike Hardy, Dickens finds at least one prospect of consolation in the death of a child. The schoolmaster in the *Old Curiosity Shop* says, '*An infant, a prattling child, dying in its cradle, will live again in the better thoughts of those who loved it, and will play its part, through them, in the redeeming actions of the world.*'

This small cause for optimism leaves Dickens free to kill off not only Jenny's baby, but young Paul Domby in *Domby and Sons*, and Little Nell in the

Old Curiosity Shop. Readers were confused and angry, furious even, that Dickens should decide to kill sweet Little Nell just as she had defeated all her troubles and was set to live happily ever after. Dickens' plot becomes easier to understand in the knowledge that he'd based Nell on his sister-in-law, Mary, whom Dickens idolised and who died suddenly aged just 17. Nell's death is pure Dickens. She lies on her deathbed, comforted by her grandfather. At the moment of her death, Nell *'turned to the old man with a lovely smile upon her face – such, they said, as they had never seen, and never could forget – and clung with both her arms about his neck'.* Nell's grandfather spends the remainder of his days at her graveside, eventually dying there from a broken heart. Oscar Wilde commented, *'one must have a heart of stone to read the death of Little Nell without laughing.'* Wilde was in truth a big Dickens fan, but he could never resist an opportunity for a one-liner.

Of all deaths, the death of a child, an innocent, seems to be the most senseless. The idea there is a kindly creator up there doesn't hold up at all well when a child dies. This contradiction (there is a very good god, but very bad things happen) has bothered English Christians for as long as they have been able to write about it. Julian of Norwich, an 14th century holy woman, saw everything, including dreadful stuff, as God's work and therefore beyond wrong:

> *For a man beholdeth some deeds well done and some deeds evil, but our Lord beholdeth them not so: for as all that hath being in nature is of Godly making, so is all that is done, in property of God's doing.*

Fairly easy to say but very hard to believe if, for instance, your child has been murdered. How can there be any meaning to life when children are killed by cancers or psychopaths, fires or floods? William Blake called such questions Contrarieties. He believed that the terrible and the wonderful eventually come together and are settled: *'There is a place where*

Contrarieties are equally true. This place is called Beulah, it is a pleasant lovely shadow where no dispute can come.' We just need to find Beulah.

Shakespeare's Hamlet has an answer that doesn't require any hidden world: no event is wonderful or terrible, not even child birth or child death. They are only wonderful or terrible as a consequence of us believing them to be so: *'there is nothing either good or bad, but thinking makes it so'*. This makes some sense: if Roman reports are correct, two thousand years ago people were making human sacrifices on English soil, an action we view as beyond repugnant, but the Druids might have regarded as acceptable. To Egyptian monarchs, incest was not criminal, but divinely ordained. Numerous tribes of homo sapiens have practised cannibalism, presumably with little or no sense of wrong-doing. It seems one would have to be at a higher level, raised above the visual threshold of one's own time, to see the absolute rightness or wrongness of any action. One would have to be a kind of god. Perhaps we create gods for want of a preternatural periscope, to see above and beyond our current moral horizons.

The Orphan

Prior to the establishment of Barnados homes in the 19th century, orphans were generally the responsibility of the church. As if they hadn't suffered enough, many orphans received no charity at all: exploitation, malnutrition and deaths were commonplace. Known as 'parish children,' orphans who did receive help often found themselves blamed, distrusted or resented. This callousness originated from a medieval superstition that some children have the power to cause the death of their parents, an idea played out in the 1976 horror movie *The Omen*. More simply, orphans were resented because life was hard enough; an extra mouth to feed and body to clothe pushed the entire family closer to ruin.

Perhaps England's most famous orphan, Oliver Twist, is in Dickens' words, *'a parish child—the orphan of a workhouse.... despised by all, and pitied by none.'* Middle class orphans were less cursed, frequently becoming the wards of some relative or other, but often resented all the same. In Jane Austen's Emma, orphaned Jane Fairfax is brought up by her Gran. The Fairfaxes were once reasonably happy, but after a double tragedy of parental death, all that remained of the family was '*the melancholy remembrance of him dying in action abroad—of his widow sinking under consumption and grief soon afterwards—and this girl.*' 'Girl' as in 'dog.'

Charlotte Bronte's Jane Eyre is another of fiction's great orphans. Jane is sent to live with her Aunt, Mrs Reed, who is horrible; so are her horrible kids, especially her horrible son John, who assaults Jane and then claims Jane had attacked him. Miss Abbot, Mrs Reed's maid, grabs and confronts Jane

> '*What shocking conduct, Miss Eyre, to strike a young gentleman, your benefactress's son! Your young master.*'
> '*Master! How is he my master? Am I a servant?*'
> '*No; you are less than a servant, for you do nothing for your keep.*'

It's a simple value system. Orphans occupy the bottom of the pile, deserving no pity. This left them without a right to feel grief. Guilt should be their prevailing emotion.

The Death Penalty

Top 5 Political Movies. JFK (1991)

I was hoping for a murder mystery but it turns out they already got the guy

Jack Marteau, Student Direct Magazine, 2009

The early 18th century marked the high-tide of the death penalty in England: you could be hanged for any one of 220 different offences, including *'being in the company of gypsies for one month.'* Today, we'd have to call that harsh. At its absurd peak, the law permitted a sentence of hanging for damaging a bridge, impersonating a Chelsea Pensioner or *'being out at night with a blackened face.'* Many of these fabulously unjust punishments were ended by the 1800s, but until deep into the 20th century there was little appetite for the complete abolition of the death penalty.

In the poem *The Plain-Dealing Man*, published over 400 years ago, the anonymous author reflects a contemporary lack of public sympathy for petty criminals sentenced to hang:

> *O fie upon cheaters and thieves,*
> *That liveth by fraud and deceit;*
> *The gallows do for such blades groan,*
> *And the hangmen do for their clothes wait.*

Fifty or so years later, Samuel Pepys shows a similar approval for capital punishment when he writes in his diary that he had been, *'reading of the trials of the late men that were hanged for the King's death and found good satisfaction in reading thereof.'* In January 1664 Pepys even attends the public execution of a Colonel Turner, who had been found guilty of stealing £5,000. Pepys knew and disliked Turner, summing him up as *'a mad, swearing, confident fellow...a known rogue,'* adding that everyone on hearing of the guilty verdict was *'desirous of his being hanged.'* For all the serves-him-right pub talk, when the big day arrives Pepys doesn't sound so fixed on his opinion:

> *I got for a shilling to stand upon the wheel of a cart, in great pain, above an hour before the execution was done; he* [Turner] *delaying the time by long discourses and prayers one after another, in hopes of a reprieve; but none came, and at last was flung off the ladder in his cloak. A comely-looked man he was, and kept his countenance to the end: I was sorry to see him.*

Witnessing a London execution first-hand may have given Pepys mixed feelings about capital punishment, but if the historian Harold Wheeler is correct, few Londoners shared these finer feelings. '*The condemned met their end in the atmosphere of a rowdy Bank Holiday,*' he wrote. The procession of carts transporting the condemned to the gallows at Tyburn was, Wheeler noted, all part of the savage theatre:

> *As the carts slowly trundled along Holborn and Oxford Street the crowd cheered or jeered or abused their inmates according as they were popular or not. No noble or tender emotion ever swayed that mob; it applauded or execrated, but never pitied.*

But when confronted by the barbarity of a child hanging, surely a crowd had to be moved to pity and even anger? In 1829 a broadside pamphlet was published describing '*The Dreadful Life and Confession of a Boy Aged Twelve Years, Who was Condemn'd to Die at last Old Bailey Sessions.*' The son of petty East London crooks, the unnamed lad began thieving at an early age, eventually joining a criminal gang that sent him down the chimney of a jewellers. The burglary was foiled, the boy was arrested, tried at the Old Bailey and hanged for his crime. The broadside included a poem that expressed the shock and sorrow caused by the death sentence:

> *when he was sentenced at the Bar,*
> *The Court was drowned in tears,*
> *To see a child so soon cut off*

All in his infant years.

The tragedy to both writer and readers of the pamphlet did not, however, appear to be that the nation had executed a child. No, this was depicted as an awful but necessary response to the boy's descent into crime. The tragedy was the lad's dissolute life, which necessitated his death. In 1815, the death penalty was available to children as young as seven; in the eyes of the hangman and the law, if you were bad enough, you were old enough.

Charles Dickens was one of England's most famous critics of the death penalty. In A Tale of Two Cities, he attacks capital punishment for its injustice, brutality and most tellingly of all, because the ultimate deterrent was ultimately no deterrent at all:

> *the forger was put to Death; the utterer of a bad note was put to Death; the unlawful opener of a letter was put to Death; the purloiner of forty shillings and sixpence was put to Death; the holder of a horse...who made off with it, was put to Death; the coiner of a bad shilling was put to Death...Not that it did the least good in the way of prevention—it might almost have been worth remarking that the fact was exactly the reverse.*

Taking time out from writing novels about people with names like Ronnie Muggeltwat, Dickens put his personal reputation on the line to fight the death penalty. In January 1840 he took up the cause of Eliza Burgess, a servant girl accused of killing her new-born child. Facing a hostile jury at the baby's inquest, Dickens argued persuasively on Eliza's behalf, and then paid a top barrister, Richard Doane, to represent her at the subsequent murder trial. The jury found Eliza guilty of concealing her child's death, but not guilty of murder. She was spared the gallows.

If Dickens was the death penalty's best-known opponent, Violet Van Der Elst was its most flamboyant. Born into poverty in Feltham Middlesex in 1884, Violet made a fortune in cosmetics and went on to spend most of it campaigning against capital punishment. On the morning of an execution she would turn up at the prison in a chauffeur-driven Rolls-Royce to protest in person, paying for a light aircraft to fly overhead, trailing a banner demanding an end to hanging.

Violet's first demonstration took place in 1935 outside Pentonville prison on the day of the execution of a Charles March. She paid 60 men to march around the prison walls wearing slogans on sandwich-boards while a full brass band, also hired by Violet, played hymns. Seen by many as an irritating lunatic, (as a woman questioning male authority, she had to be mad), Violet was frequently arrested but refused to be silenced. Eventually all the money ran out, and fearless Violet ended life as she had begun it: penniless. Happily, she lived long enough to see capital punishment ended in 1964.

Public reaction to three particular executions led politicians to abolish the death penalty: those of Derek Bentley, James Hanratty and Ruth Ellis.

On 2ⁿᵈ November 1952, 19-year-old Derek Bentley and 16-year-old Christopher Craig attempted to break into a confectionary warehouse in Croydon, Surrey. Bentley came armed with a knife and a knuckle duster; Craig was carrying a gun. Suspicious neighbours rang 999 and the pair were confronted on the warehouse roof by two police officers. DC Fairfax got hold of Bentley, and Craig pulled out his gun and fired, wounding Fairfax in the shoulder. At some point Bentley is alleged to have called out, '*Let him have it, Chris.*'

Police reinforcements arrived minutes later, the first of whom, PC Sidney Miles was shot by Craig as he stepped through the door to the roof. Miles died instantly. When he ran out of ammunition, Craig attempted escape by jumping from the 30-foot-high roof. The fall broke his back. Bentley was detained at the scene.

Christopher Craig and Derek Bentley were held jointly responsible for the murder under the legal principle of common purpose, which holds that if two (or more) people commit a crime and it is established that they both (or all) intended or could have reasonably foreseen the outcome, they may be regarded as equally responsible. They were both found guilty of the murder of PC Miles, but as he was legally a minor Chris avoided the death penalty. Derek, however, was sentenced by Judge Lord Goddard, to be hanged. Because he hadn't fired a single shot, the jury recommended clemency for Bentley, but Goddard would not support their appeal. Two hundred MPs signed a petition calling for his reprieve, but the Home Secretary David Maxwell Fyfe refused, saying, '*There is no possibility of an innocent man being hanged in this country.*' Many disagreed, including Derek's former school teacher Hugh Maw, who said, '*If there was a fight he was a coward, which always brings me to the crucial words at his trial: 'Let him have it, Chris.' This was typical - Give in and not kill him.*' A crowd of 5,000 people gathered outside Wandsworth prison on the eve of the execution. Chanting, '*Murder!*' they tore down and burned the death notice pinned to the gates. Forty-five years after the events on that warehouse roof, Derek Bentley's case was reviewed at the Court of Appeal, and in July 1998 his conviction was declared unsafe.

In 1953 Ruth Ellis was 28 years old and managing a London nightclub. It was there she met 25-year-old David Blakely. The two moved in together and shared a tempestuous relationship involving alcohol, obsession, mistrust and violence. On one occasion Blakeley punched Ruth so hard in the stomach, it caused her to miscarry. By Easter 1955 their relationship had collapsed: Ruth was cheating with a former bomber pilot called Desmond Cussens, and she suspected David of the same with a nanny they'd hired to care for Ruth's son and daughter. David moved out and refused to see Ruth. On the 10th of April 1955, Ruth Ellis persuaded Cussens to drive her to the Magdala public house in Hampstead where David and a male friend were drinking. Ruth waited by the pub door and when David emerged at 9.30 p.m., she called out to him. He ignored her, so she fired at him with a .38 calibre Smith & Wesson revolver. David tried to run away, but her second shot brought him down. Ruth stood over her wounded lover and shot the remaining four bullets into him.

When asked by prosecuting counsel Christmas Humphreys, '*Mrs. Ellis, when you fired that revolver at close range into the body of David Blakely what did you intend to do?*' she answered plainly, '*It was obvious that when I shot him, I intended to kill him.*' Ruth being of sound mind, this response left Mr. Justice Havers with no option other than to sentence her to death. Ruth thanked him, gave a smile to her supporters in the gallery and walked calmly from the dock. But for one tearful episode in the 'Condemned Suite' of Holloway prison, Ruth faced her fate without apparent distress. She refused to appeal her sentence or beg for clemency. Following his final visit with Ruth, her brother Granville Neilson, told reporters, '*she seemed absolutely calm and unafraid of what was going to happen to her.*'

With less than 24 hours before she was due to hang, Ruth was visited by her lawyer Leon Simmons. Another solicitor, Victor Mishcon was there, and he recalled Ruth's exact words:

'*I am now completely composed. I know that I am going to die, and I'm ready to do so. You won't hear anything from me that says I didn't kill David. I did kill him. And whatever the circumstances you as a lawyer will appreciate that it's a life for a life. Isn't that just?*'

On Wednesday, the 13th of July 1955 Ruth Ellis became the last woman to be executed in Britain. To answer Ruth's question, according to the law of 1955, her death sentence was wholly 'just'. She had planned the David Blakely's murder, she did not intend for him to survive her attack, and she had not acted in self-defence. But the state execution of a mother of two for the killing of a violent man made many feel the law was at fault: Ruth Ellis represented no threat to the public at large. To many, Ruth's hanging amounted to automated state vengeance, and public appetite for the death penalty diminished as a result.

Towards the end of the 1950s Valerie Storie and Michael Gregsten, colleagues at the Road Research Laboratory in Slough, were having an affair. Michael was married but Valerie, nine years his junior, was single. On Tuesday the 22nd of August 1961 they had gone out for a drive in Gregsten's Morris Minor and were parked in a lane near Windsor when a man tapped on the driver-side window. Michael wound it down and the stranger, the lower half of his face covered with a handkerchief, produced a gun. He forced the couple to drive to the ominously named Deadman's Hill, where he took their valuables. He tied them up, shot Michael dead, raped Valerie and then shot her three times. One of the bullets severed her spine. Valerie survived, but was crippled for life. Some days later the murder weapon was found wrapped in a handkerchief and lodged behind the back seat of a number 36A bus parked in Peckham bus station.

Investigation led to James Hanratty, a 25-year-old small-time criminal, with no history of violence. Although Valerie had picked him out in an identity parade, the assailant's use of a mask put Hanratty's involvement in some doubt. James maintained he had been in Liverpool on the night of the shooting, but later changed his account to locate himself in Rhyl. This shift fatally undermined his defence, and on the 17th February 1962, at the close of what had been the longest murder case in English history, James Hanratty was found guilty and sentenced to death. James protested his innocence throughout but was hanged at Bedford prison on 4th April 1962.

There was real controversy following his execution. The evidence had been far from conclusive and alongside Hanratty's mother and brother Michael, prominent journalists and the Beatles' John Lennon campaigned for his name to be cleared.

Four decades on, with the emergence of DNA profiling, the opportunity to prove James Hanratty's innocence had come. At the request of his family James Hanratty's body was exhumed in 2001 and his DNA compared with samples of semen taken from Valerie Storie's underwear and mucus from the handkerchief that had been wrapped around the murder weapon. To the shock of many, they provided an exact match. This was a potently ironic result, as it had been the Hanratty case, above any other, that had convinced parliament to end the death penalty.

The majority of the public remained firmly in support of corporal punishment for many years after its abolition. For this reason, successive governments resisted every call for a referendum on the matter. It wasn't until 2006 that support for restoration of the death penalty in Great Britain fell below 50%.

Suicide

We humans are more likely to kill ourselves than any other person: globally 870,000 of us took our own lives in 2014, compared with a total of 812,000 victims of homicide and war. In the United Kingdom the ratio is far starker: we are ten times more likely to die by our own hand than by another's: around 6,000 UK residents take their own lives each year; there are 600 victims of homicide per annum.

Taking one's own life is almost a human right now, but throughout recorded English history it has been both a criminal and spiritual offence. Even today, we speak of someone *committing* suicide, as someone commits a robbery. Self robbery. Those of us who remain after suicide may certainly feel robbed.

To the medieval mind, suicide was just about the worst thing you could do. Why this should have been equal to, (let alone worse than), the taking of another's life seems very strange to modern thinking, but to earlier minds suicide guaranteed a place in hell. Any property the unhappy soul left behind was usually confiscated by the king, and a church burial was generally forbidden. If a place in the churchyard were provided, it would be on its god-forsaken northern side. According to historian Alexander Murray, there was a medieval belief God would punish an entire community where a member had taken their own life. A bad harvest, for example, was blamed on a suicide among a town's population, or on undue gentleness by the townspeople in dealing with the offender's corpse. For centuries the English belief that suicide was a danger to the whole community generated anger and resentment towards those who took their own lives. Until relatively modern times, suicide was regarded as the work of the devil. When, for instance, in 18th Century London resident Emanuel Swedenborg considered taking his own life, he was certain that his suicidal thoughts had been put into his head by demons as he slept. He failed to see any relationship between his self-destructive urges and any emotional pain he experienced in his waking hours.

The event that pushed the public towards a more enlightened opinion of suicide came in 1770, when 17-year-old Thomas Chatterton from Bristol died having taken poison. Thomas was a gifted poet, and his death was regarded as a romantic tragedy rather than a criminal act, with Chatterton the innocent victim of an uncaring materialist world. Chatterton was buried in a mass grave at Shoe Lane Workhouse Cemetery in London. Several 19th century artists were inspired by his brief life and work, including Keats, who wrote a sonnet to his memory, reassuring Thomas than rather being sent to Hell, he had earned a place, '*among the stars of highest Heaven*'. Ironically, after inspiring a revolution in the national attitude to suicide, it now appears that Chatterton's death was accidental, the young poet having dosed himself with arsenic in an effort to treat a sexually transmitted infection.

Elizabeth, My Sister

Elizabeth was the sister closest to me in age. My elder by almost three years, she had a rich laugh, but was gentle and nervous, like a bird. Until I was about eight years old, Elizabeth and I shared a bedroom. I didn't think it was so odd at the time, but before turning in each night she would have to count and re-count almost every article in the bedroom – toys, bedding, books, items of clothing. But to recall it to this day, I must have thought it a bit strange. She was a thoughtful girl, with a tendency to frown, as if preoccupied by some invisible puzzle. She had one or two friends, quiet ones. Elizabeth was sometimes so quiet, it was as if she had made herself magically disappear. As it happened, she was working on precisely this trick; when Theresa (second born, and Elizabeth's immediately elder sister) came back from her first term at University, she cried out in shock at how thin Elizabeth had become. At five feet five, she weighed under six stone. She looked like a stick drawing. I don't know how I hadn't noticed. She'd been standard sized in September, and with the loss of a little weight every day since, each morning's silhouette looked much like the previous day's, blinding me to the reality that over three months Elizabeth had been starving herself towards death. Anorexia Nervosa the doctors called it. A police-state feeding regime pushed Elizabeth's weight back up. She was better. '*Part of me still wants to be thin*,' she told me later. That shocked me, but since just a year earlier every part of her had wanted to be thin, it probably shouldn't have.

Somehow, three years on, Elizabeth managed to pass three A Levels and left home that Autumn to study at Oxford Poly. I don't know the detail – who truly wants to know detail of suffering endured by someone they love? – but things began to go wrong for Elizabeth, so wrong that before the Christmas break she had a major psychological breakdown. Dad drove down to Oxford to bring her home, but as we'd only weeks earlier moved to small village a hundred miles from where she'd grown up in London, home really wasn't home to Elizabeth. Her distress increased, she wailed, rattled off incomprehensible asides, picked at her face, and gave up sleeping for frenzied pacing and chain smoking. Mum and Dad were out of their depth. Jacqueline, my eldest sister, had married and emigrated to Australia the previous summer and Theresa was still away at University. That just left me, then fifteen, and eleven-year-old Clare, confused and anguished. A doctor came out, and Elizabeth was taken to hospital in Leicester, where she remained, filled with tranquillisers, until Christmas. Slowly the pieces of her fractured self began to re-settle into the familiar gentle personality of my absent, lovely sister. There was cautious optimism. Elizabeth got a volunteer job helping out at a learning disability school. When that went OK she moved in with friends in London and got a desk job at the Department of Social Security. Perhaps she might even go back to college to complete her studies. But what looked like rehabilitation was more a high-wire act: the further she dared to tread, the narrower and shakier became the rope under her feet. Eventually she lost her balance and fell, crash-landing as an in-patient on another psychiatric unit. One doctor told her she had manic-depression, another said she had schizophrenia, and another said she had schizoaffective disorder. Diagnoses notwithstanding, she had to take a range of noxious medications from the 1970s pharmacopeia of hell…Largactyl, Melleril, Haloperidol.

When Elizabeth went down, she ground to a psychic halt, barely able to speak or eat. When she went up, she shot out of earth's orbit (she was once arrested for dancing in the middle of the street). Both the low and high roads led to the portals of psychiatry and the evaporation of all she had struggled to build – employment, peace of mind, a future. Trapped within one of these black mental implosions, Elizabeth turned to me and said, '*I'm basically a bad person.*' She was basically a very good person. I recognised the primary guilt of a Catholic; a soul, like mine, complicit in the Original Sin.

Sick of the crushing effects of more than a decade of psychiatric drugs, and too honest to simply flush them down the toilet, Elizabeth persuaded her psychiatrist to stop prescribing them to her. He agreed, for the present. Before long, Elizabeth found her mind begin to take its first slow turn inward and downward. Years before, naïve to what this signified, she would not have panicked at what most of us would take to be a 'bad day', but now she knew too much. She realised she was headed towards one dreaded destination, and nothing on this earth could stop the slide; its motion would increase as she caught the rim of the vortex of madness, drawing her down in an accelerating spiral into mental twilight. In just days insanity would again swallow her whole. She had had enough. Theresa met with her in town, tried to lift her spirits but couldn't know as Elizabeth knew that any effort was futile. As Theresa saw her onto a Piccadilly Line train back to the parental home, Elizabeth said flatly and out of the blue, '*You'll not see me alive again.*' '*Don't be ridiculous,*' Theresa responded, in the desperate hope that Elizabeth was playing with melodrama.

The next day, Elizabeth was missing. After a few days things looked serious. '*Aren't you worried?*' Debbie asked me, '*No, she'll turn up,*' I answered, unaware of what Elizabeth had said to Theresa at Kings Cross station. At the weekend we visited friends in the East End. They had no phone. Suddenly Deb's brother Kev was at the door – he'd ridden up from Croydon. He took off his helmet and told me Elizabeth was dead. Her body had been found at the foot of Beachy Head cliff. Kev's words struck me in the solar plexus, but my mind would only take a portion of the blow. I was abstracted. *'I'd better go to my mum and dad's,'* was all I could find to say. Realising I was in no state to drive, Charlie took me there. We stopped for petrol on the way. Charlie went off to pay. Some medical students in fancy dress were collecting money for a local hospital. I stayed in my seat, cocooned in shock, gazing at nothing through the passenger window. Suddenly a clown's face appeared just inches from my own. He leered at me and shook a bucket of coins. I felt I was in a Fellini film.

My tears came when I got to my parents' house. I was mainly crying for myself. I had to be almost happy for Elizabeth: she had got what she wanted, an end to her every living pain. But for that ending she had to pay the ultimate price: she had to embrace the end. No more flashes of joy, not one more moment of love, no further sunshine, not a note of music. Nothing, forever.

I looked around for someone to blame. I didn't have to look far. Just a few months earlier Elizabeth had asked me if she and her boyfriend could move in with Debbie, me and our baby daughter Rosie. I had a spare room, but I couldn't face the chaos of insomnia, mess and random behaviours. I said no. I said no, and Elizabeth had gone on to take her own life. What if I had said yes? Could I have saved her? These two questions churned through my mind for months on end. After a year, unanswered, they exhausted themselves.

I draw some consolation from the thought that Elizabeth has to suffer no more. I admire her bravery, sacrificing her life to defeat her troubled mind. But as much as suicide demands courage, it can never be heroic. It throws too many others – parents, siblings, children, lovers – into torment. Often, it's a tragic error; a gentle soul taking their own life for a fallacy, the mistaken

211

belief that the world would be a better place without them. The truth is that while the planet may get by very nicely with two or three fewer brutal dictators or violent bullies, it gains nothing from the disappearance of any troubled but gentle individual. Shock waves radiate in every direction from the awful event, expanding to affect anyone who has truly known that person. Tracking the disturbance to its source, the violence of impact increases with each concentric ring. Those closest to the epicentre can be all but destroyed by the catastrophe. Indeed, they may be so distraught they kill themselves. Alexandra Pitman, a researcher working at the University of London, has found that people bereaved by the suicide of a friend or family member are 65% more likely to go on to take their own lives. Suicide can be contagious. Stressing the need to reach out to someone bereaved through suicide, Dr Pitman concludes, *'Saying something is often better than saying nothing.'*

For a while I had a job in a hospital, working with and trying to safeguard people who were suicidal. For the most part it was possible to stop someone in time, but I failed once, and a woman died in front of my helpless eyes. This was just two years after Elizabeth had taken her own life. It's easy to blame oneself in the event of suicide; it's very hard not to.

When a new patient arrived on the hospital ward, staff would ask them to complete a questionnaire, to help assess his or her risk of suicide. The form included the straight question: *'Have you ever thought of taking your own life? If, yes, what prevented you from doing so?'* A very glum youngish man filled in the form and handed it to me. Yes, he had thought of ending it all, but he had decided against it because, in his words, *'the next world will probably be as bad as this one.'* I was so taken aback by the utter hopelessness of his answer that I almost laughed; I'd never come across this idea, but had I read *Hamlet* I would have known Shakespeare already had it covered. In his famous *'To be or not to be?'* soliloquy, Hamlet dithers about whether to take revenge on his uncle Claudius for murdering his dad. Hamlet talks himself out of risking his life in an attack; he reasons that what follows death might be significantly worse than all the hard knocks we face in this world: *'the dread of something after death... makes us rather bear those ills we have than fly to others that we know not of'*. Even if dying is, as many of us believe, just like falling asleep, Hamlet still sees a problem: what kinds of nightmare might we have? (*'For in that sleep of death what dreams may come?'*)

John Milton saw suicide as an urge and act as old as humanity. In *Paradise Lost*, Eve suggests a suicide pact to Adam, to escape the punishment of a furious god for eating from the tree of life. Adam can't see the idea working, and talks her out of it:

> *Death So snatcht will not exempt us from the pain*
> *We are by doom to pay*

Their decision to live on means the human species survives but will forever be tempted to end it all in the flawed new world created by Adam and Eve's fruit-centred misdemeanour.

A character in Virginia Woolf's novel *Mrs Dalloway*, a First World War veteran called Septimus, takes his own life. Instead of feeling sorrow for the man, Clarissa Dalloway admires his courage:

> *Death was defiance. Death was an attempt to communicate ...There was an embrace in death...She felt somehow very like him – the young man who had killed himself. She felt glad that he had done it; thrown it away.*

Like her character Clarissa Dalloway, Virginia Woolf was drawn to the idea of throwing it all away. In *Street Haunting*, Virginia returned to the subject of suicide, describing a walk she takes through central London. Stopping to gaze at the Thames from its north bank, she recalls seeing a less troubled person, a man, stood at the same spot studying the same stretch of river six months earlier. Virginia doesn't say what happened to him, but it seems he jumped: '*His is the happiness of death; ours the insecurity of life. He has no future; the future is even now invading our peace.*'

For Virginia, the future is the enemy: what is to come will hurt you. Like my own lovely sister Elizabeth, Virginia Woolf was battered by bouts of mental anguish, and like Elizabeth, Virginia took her own life in Sussex; thoughts of horror and blackness closed in for one episode more than either of them could bear.

In 1964, teenage songwriter Twinkle had a hit with *Terry*, a morbid song about the apparent suicide of a biker following a row with his girlfriend:

> *He rode into the night*
> *Accelerated his motorbike*
> *I cried to him in fright*
> *'Don't do it, don't do it, don't do it!'*
> *…. One day he'll know how hard I prayed for him to live*
> *Please wait at the gate of heaven for me, Terry*

Politicians queued up to denounce Terry as '*sick*' and a '*death record*'; it was banned by BBC radio, and even the knowingly hip TV music show *Ready, Steady, Go* wouldn't play the song, its presenter Keith Fordyce informing viewers: '*You have not heard that record on this programme, and you won't be hearing it, either!*' For all its taste for rebellion, the Sixties had no appetite to confront suicide. The silence was broken by a 1972 ITV play, *Whose Life is it Anyway?* The power of the story and the brilliance of Brian Clark's writing saw the play turned into a major Hollywood film. The hero, Ken Harrison, is smart, funny and paralysed from the neck down. He is only kept alive by medical science, and he reaches a point where he wants to refuse all help and be left to die: '*For me life is over. I want it recognised because I can't do the things that I want to do.*' For Ken, a life without pleasure is no life at all: '*Of course I want to live but as far as I am concerned, I'm dead already.*' Ken and his doctor Michael Emerson do battle over Ken's demands to be left in peace. The argument is finally settled in court, with

Ken winning the right to discharge himself from hospital and die. As one reviewer put it, '*Whose Life is It Anyway? may be the only film in which a person's right to self-destruction is regarded as a happy ending.*'

From what I've seen in my private and working life, I have come to feel that some people find the decision to take their own lives the easiest as well as the hardest choice to make. Assailed from all corners by hostility or unachievable expectation, they can't find the fire to tell others to fuck off and leave them in peace. Instead, they elect to fuck themselves off. They find their only way out.

I have no evidence to support this impression, and I would add that hostility and unfeasible expectation may well come from within, in the guise of extreme self-dislike or self-criticism. Plus, sometimes it pays not to get too psychological: as a solid rule, the further someone lives from the Equator, the higher the chance they'll take our own life. England is only 38 degrees of latitude away from the North Pole.

Assisted Dying

Assisted dying involves a terminally ill person engaging the help of another person to hasten their death. As it requires the active involvement of a third party, assisted dying is significantly different from suicide per se, and remains illegal in the UK. A clear majority of the public (one survey put it at 82%) support legalisation of assisted dying for terminally ill, mentally competent adults.

Diane Pretty from Luton was one of the first persons to test the law on assisted dying. Terminally ill from Motor Neurone Disease, 42-year-old Diane wanted to choose the time and way of her death. Paralysis meant she would need the help of her husband Brian to die. In August 2001 she wrote to the government, requesting that Brian be immune from prosecution should he help her to die. This plea was denied, so Diane pursued her case through the English legal system, asserting that legislation discriminated against her and other persons with a disability: she was allowed by law to end her own life, she wanted to exercise this right, but the State denied her this as she would require the help of another person, her husband Brian.

After the English Courts and the House of Lords rejected Diane's argument, she turned to the European Court of Human Rights, claiming that the right to life included a right to choose whether to carry on living. The judges in Strasbourg ruled that Diane's right to respect for private life included a right to choose how to end her life. They decided, however, that the ban on assisted dying in the UK could be justified as a protection for vulnerable people. This logic is shaky, as it carries an assumption that it would be too hard for the UK system to distinguish between vulnerable and non-vulnerable citizens, judgements that the NHS, education and social services make every day.

In 1995 Debbie Purdy, a journalist from Bradford, was diagnosed with Multiple Sclerosis (MS). She was 32 at the time. As the MS progressed, Debbie felt that increasing pain and immobility would eventually make her life intolerable. She was also aware that if she chose to end her life, her condition meant she'd require the help of her husband, Omar Puente. Knowing that this decision would leave Omar facing a lengthy prison sentence, Debbie went to court to argue that it was contrary to her human rights to not know if her husband would be liable to prosecution if he were to accompany her to Switzerland to die. In 2009, Debbie won her case in the House of Lords. The judges ruled the law was unclear on when a person would be prosecuted for encouraging or assisting suicide. They ordered the Director of Public Prosecutions (DPP) to produce guidance on how to decide whether a case should result in prosecution. While full of helpful common sense, this guidance gave no guarantee that Omar Puente or any other citizen of England or Wales would be immune from prosecution if they were to help their desperate and determined loved one to either plan or carry out suicide. No doubt worried by the poor protection the guidance offered Omar, Debbie decided against taking her own life, although she did refuse food in her final days. She died in Bradford's Marie Curie Hospice on 23rd December 2014. Debbie never managed to change the law on assisted suicide, but her and Diane Pretty's struggles have moved the country closer to the point where new legislation will be passed.

The most recent attempt to change the law was rejected by the Court of Appeal in June 2018. Noel Conway, a retired lecturer suffering with motor neurone disease had attempted to overturn a High Court decision that he cannot be lawfully helped to die. Noel, who strikingly described himself as *'entombed'* by the paralysing effect of his condition, reflected that the Appeal Court's decision had left with the *'barbaric'* option to either *'effectively suffocate'* by disconnecting his ventilator, or have his family risk prosecution by escorting him to Switzerland. He vowed to, *'keep fighting for myself and all terminally ill people who want the right to die peacefully, with dignity and on our own terms.'* A subsequent appeal to the Supreme Court was also rejected, a ruling that Noel criticised as, *'downright cruel'*

Visions of Another World

Worst 5 Vegetables: Lettuce

These are just leaves. They look and taste like leaves. They are definitely leaves.

Jack Marteau Blog, April 2009

On the morning of 7th November 2010, a Sunday, Deb and I didn't feel like getting up. We were sat up in bed when the sun came streaming through the window, lighting up the room. Deb became very excited at its appearance: *'Can you see that?!'* she asked, *'The sun's bright red!'* It wasn't. *'Can't you see it?! It's bright red with concentric rings around it.'* She was astounded; she'd never seen the sun look anything like that. It wasn't dawn — the sun had been up for two or three hours, but perhaps it was an effect of dazzling, the sunlight exciting veins around her retina, or maybe haemoglobin in her eyelids had acted as a crimson filter. Debbie wasn't having any of these theories. Three or four weekends later, the same thing happened. The sun, standard white/yellow as usual to me, again turned red to Deb's eyes, surrounded as before by a succession of scarlet rings. Once again, Deb was really surprised I couldn't see this effect, which lasted for some minutes. She has not had a similar experience since; it happened just twice, when Deb was at the first, deepest year of her grief. She later summarised it as, *'The most out-there thing that's happened to me in my 51 years.'* Watching her at the time, it seemed to me she might have been seeing things as they truly are, rather than as they appear to our limited everyday perception. In the inverted physics of grief, the lower you go, the further you might see.

Although someway short of the Middle East or India, England has had a fair sprinkling of mystics, seers and visionaries across the span of written history. The first report we have of a supernatural experience comes from a man who lived in the Midlands in the first few years of the 8th century. We

218

don't know his name, but this is what he said to the monk Bede in describing a vision he had that began promisingly with a couple of likeable angels:

> 'there came into this room two fair youths, and sat down by me, the one at my head, and the other at my feet. One of them drew forth a book most beautiful, but very small, and gave it me to read; looking into it, I there found all the good actions I had ever done in my life written down, and they were very few and inconsiderable.'

If we begin to wonder about the dimensions of Book Two, we soon have our answer. An 'army of evil spirits of hideous countenance' turn up carrying a book that is 'of a monstrous size, and of almost insupportable weight.' The boss of the demons orders the monk to read the whole thing, which he duly does. 'Having read it, I found therein most plainly written in hideous characters, all the crimes I ever committed, not only in word and deed, but even in the least thought.'

The man's goose looks to be thoroughly cooked. He takes up the story again as Mr Nasty turns to the two nice lads with the microscopic good book, and asks them,

> 'Why sit ye here, since ye know of a surety that this man is ours?' They answered, 'Ye speak truly; take him and lead him away to fill up the measure of your damnation.' This said, they forthwith vanished, and two wicked spirits arose, having in their hands ploughshares [the cutting blade of a plough], and one of them struck me on the head, and the other on the foot. And these ploughshares are now with great torment creeping into the inward parts of my body, and as soon as they meet I shall die, and the devils being ready to snatch me away, I shall be dragged into the dungeons of hell.

That's bad! Did his luck improve at all? Not really. Bede tells us that he died 'soon after'. Oh dear. The story will leave a few of us hoping that those hideous demons don't come around our place with a giant book and some agricultural equipment. And if they do, we would hope for angels with more bottle than those two pushovers.

The next account is marginally more hopeful, but still holds its share of horror. In 1206 an Essex peasant named Thurkill has a strange dream in which he is visited by a saint, St Julian, who takes him on a journey to another world. Thurkill has fiddled his tax return, and he is shown how things will end up if he doesn't mend his ways. There's a cold, salty lake, a horrid bridge bristling with thorns and wooden stakes, and of course, some diabolical fire. He sees heaven too, which is filled with saints including St James, St Peter and St Paul. The Archangel Michael is there, and the devil puts in an appearance, riding on the back of an upper-class Englishman.

Thurkhill watches as St Paul and a devil stand either side of a set of scales to weigh the souls of new arrivals. Good souls tip the scales in the direction of Paul, sinners drop down on the side of the devil, who then grabs hold of them. St Peter cheats by throwing a holy water sprinkler into one of the pans, causing a heavy weight on the opposing side to catapult out, and land on the devil's foot. Hooray! Scales have been a significant piece of after-world equipment since the days of ancient Egypt when Thoth in his ibis-headed form weighed a dead person's heart against a feather. If the heart is weighed down by guilt from things done wrong in life, its owner cannot enter the otherworld. Instead, the heart is eaten by Ammit, a demon that is part crocodile, part lion and part hippo, a very poor result for any dead person. If, however, they pass the scales test, she or he is accompanied by Horus to the house of Osiris, for an eternal life of bread and beer. It's unclear what would be offered to a gluten-intolerant non-drinker.

According to Thurkill's vivid dream, souls are punished in a theatre. They are sat in uncomfortable seats and then are obliged to come up on stage to re-enact their sins, following which they are tortured by demons, to the delight of an all-demon audience. Among the tortured are a proud man, a crooked priest, a murdering soldier, a corrupt lawyer, and a mixed group of adulterers, thieves, heretics and general trouble-makers. Theatres feature in

220

several English visionary reports from across the centuries, including, as we will see, near death experiences.

Thurkill says that when he got back to earth he kept this story to himself, but in a further dream he was told (thankfully for us) that he must make others know about it, so they might benefit from his experience. On waking, he recounted everything that he had seen to the local priest who duly recorded his story.

Although it's likely Thurkill existed, it's equally probable that much of his tale has been changed by others over time. He comes, for instance, across his father in the afterworld. The old boy is in a bad way, which he attributes to a sinful life. He instructs Thurkill junior that as soon as he gets back to earth he must pay to have masses sung to end his father's torment. This bit may well have been added by the priest who transcribed Thurkill's story. Being illiterate, Thurkhill would have been unable to spot the commercial break.

In contrast to Thurkill's dream, some medieval visions were demon-free and 100% spiritually positive. The Virgin Mary appeared in a vision to Richeldis de Faverches, a serious-minded Saxon woman, in 1061 in Walsingham, Norfolk. On Mary's instruction, Richeldis built a shrine on the spot. It would become one of the busiest pilgrimage destinations in the country. Simon Stock, an Englishman who lived in the 13th century, is also said to have been visited by the Virgin Mary, who encouraged his decision to live as a monk.

Julian of Norwich

The delightful *Revelations of Divine Love* is probably the first book written in the English language by a woman. Its author, Julian of Norwich, took her name from the church where she lived for most of her life. Julian's book centres on a sequence of Christian visions that, in her words, '*were shewed to a simple creature unlettered, the year of our Lord 1373, the Thirteenth day of May*. Julian was 30 at the time and seriously ill. In the course of this sickness she had a total of fifteen visions, featuring telepathic conversations between herself and a man she took to be Jesus (*'I conceived truly and mightily that it was Himself.'*) The Virgin Mary also appeared to her, as did several dead prophets and seers, including the English saint, John of Beverley. She subsequently recovered her health and lived into old age.

The Jesus who Julian encounters in her visions is a gentle mystic. He reassures her with the words:

> *All shall be well, and all shall be well, and all manner of thing shall be well.*

The pedant in me wishes he had put an 's' at the end of 'thing', but in every other respect this is one of most comforting quotes in the English spiritual canon.

Julian comes to regard Jesus as all we need:

> *He is to us everything that is good and comfortable for us: He is our clothing that for love wrappeth us, claspeth us, and all encloseth us for tender love.*

That's all very nice, but what about all the suffering in the world; after all Julian lived in the most death-filled century of the lot, the 1300s? Julian has an answer to this: it's all part of some hidden natural plan: '*I saw truly that nothing is done by hap nor by adventure.*'

Julian reckons we can't see this world of Jesus and the Grand Design on account of the way we are made. She says we are '*sense-souls*'. I take this to mean we are built to experience everything through our five senses; anything outside of these will be a closed book to us. We don't realise we are supernatural ourselves: '*our passing life that we have here in our sense-soul knoweth not what our Self is.*'

Things get easier to follow when Julian describes her god as '*the endlessness*'. I know what she means; I had a neighbour like that.

Julian did not think she'd been given these visions as a reward for being more spiritually advanced or special than the rest of us: she describes herself '*a simple creature*', adding, '*I am right nought*'. But it turns out that as well as being nothing, '*right nought*' might be a right lot: following her otherworldly experiences, Julian tells us, '*after this I saw God in a Point...I saw that He is in all things*.' Her idea that the most significant or powerful thing can be found in the smallest possible space – a point – comes several hundred years before science calculated that the entire Universe probably sprang from an enormous source of energy held within a microscopic area, the singularity – a Point in other words. Julian would have had no problem with Big Bang theory.

Bur perhaps Julian's most cosmic moment comes when, in her vision, Jesus helps her see how much matter there is in the Universe:

> *He showed me a little thing, the quantity of an hazel-nut, in the palm of my hand; and it was as round as a ball. I looked thereupon with eye of my understanding, and thought: What may this be? And it was answered generally thus: 'It is all that is made'.*

It's unlikely that any scientist in the medieval world would have agreed that all the stars, planets and comets in the Universe might condense to a lump no bigger than a hazel-nut, but as we will see, Julian may have been very close to the truth.

Maybe Shakespeare had read Julian's book, because he has Hamlet say something that would have had Jules nodding in agreement or emailing her copyright lawyer: '*I could be bounded in a nutshell and count myself a king of infinite space*'.

For spiritual reasons, Julian chose to live as a hermit, locked in a single room for much of her life. It's therefore incorrect to think of her having mates as such, but by chance she did spend some time in the company of one of the middle ages' most extraordinary women: look out, here she comes…...

Margery Kempe

In 1373, the very year Julian of Norwich had her fifteen visions, one of England's greatest and wildest mystics was born. Part visionary, part celebrity, proto-feminist, businesswoman, wife, mother of fourteen and would-be saint, Margery Kempe dictated her event-packed autobiography towards the end of her life. At the book's opening, newly married Margery is twenty years old, living in Norfolk and expecting her first child. It's a difficult pregnancy, and Margery is very ill after the birth, going, as she puts it '*out of her mind* (Margery always talks about herself in the third person. As we shall discover, this is not her most irritating habit). For the next eight months Margery is tormented by visions of demons: '*in this time she saw, as she thought, devils opening their mouths all alight with burning flames of fire, as if they would have swallowed her in.*' We may choose to see this as a post-natal psychosis, but to Margery the experience is a supernatural instruction to mend her ways: up to this point she has been extremely vain and an arch-materialist:

> She was enormously envious of her neighbours if they were dressed as well as she was…. she always craved more and more.

The big change came as she lay in bed one night and heard what she took to be heavenly music, a '*melody so sweet that it surpassed all the melody that might be heard in this world, without any comparison.*' Soon after the music stopped, Jesus Christ and his mother Mary appeared to Margery, urging her to live a more religious life. From here on she would direct herself to more spiritual matters. Out went the fancy clothes, in came hours of prayer and meditation. At the same time, Margery developed the unusual habit of extended loud weeping and dramatic wailing:

Her weeping was so plentiful and so continuous that many people wondered that she might start and then stop when she pleased, and therefore many men said she was a false hypocrite.

In truth, Margery couldn't stop; when she tried to hold it back, the sobbing just got worse: *'The more she laboured to keep it in or suppress it, so much the more would she cry, and the louder.'* Anything would set Margery off: regrets over her past selfish ways; the suffering of others; and the biggest cause of all, thoughts of the crucifixion of Jesus. Along with these hours of weeping and wailing, Margery felt compelled to tell neighbours/friends/anybody that they needed to change their ways. People began to avoid her like another outbreak of the plague.

This reformed Margery resolved to lead a celibate life:

And after this time she never had any desire to have sexual intercourse with her husband...[it] was so abominable to her that she would rather, she thought, have eaten and drunk the ooze and muck in the gutter.

That was that then. Inspired by her personal revolution, Margery puts her celibacy plan to her husband, John. While not opposed to it in principle, he suggests they wait for two or three years, and then come back to the subject. Unhappy with John's lack of enthusiasm, Margery begins to refuse all sexual activity. One hot mid-summer evening Margery and John are travelling back to Kings Lynn from York. She has a bottle of beer in her hand and John, for some reason, has a cake tucked inside his shirt. In a higher-stakes game of Snog, Marry, Avoid, John turns to Margery and asks her to suppose that someone turns up with a sword and says that unless Margery agrees to make love to her husband, he will cut off John's head; what would she do? Margery thinks for a moment and then says, *'Truly, I would rather see you being killed.* This isn't the answer Mr Kempe has hoped for; he walks off muttering *'You are no good, wife.'*

Margery turned to Christ to solve this conjugal problem. She received the following answer to her prayers: '*On Fridays you must go without both food and drink, and your wish will be granted before Whit Sunday, for I will suddenly strike your husband dead!*' It seems Christ had lost his touch, because John Kempe lived for a further thirty years. But mindful that there was a heavenly contract out on him, JK agreed to the celibacy deal.

Jesus doesn't appear in person to Margery as such, but he instead talks quite frequently to her '*in her mind*', covering a range of subjects, including the fate of others. Utilising this information, Margery claimed to be very accurate in predicting the recovery of people who seem to be at death's door, and in anticipating when apparently fit people are about to die a sudden death. Jesus, again speaking inside Margery's mind, revealed to her the after-life destination of many of her neighbours. It upset her to be told that anyone was to be sent to hell, but Jesus explained, '*Daughter, you must hear of the damned as well as of the saved.*' Margery recalls visiting '*a very respectable lady*' to tell her,

> Madam, our Lord Jesus Christ bade me tell you that [your] husband is currently in purgatory and he won't be coming out for a long time.

The widow turns furious with Margery, refusing to believe her departed husband would be found in any sub-celestial setting.

In speaking to Margery, Jesus almost always takes the role of kindly parent, but on occasions he appears to want to move their relationship on to a different level. At one point he tells her,

> '*I must be intimate with you and lie in your bed with you. Daughter, you greatly desire to see me, and you may boldly, when you are in bed, take me to you as your wedded husband.*'

That's a bit weird. But Margery remains pretty solid that all her messages come from God, although she wonders at times if the devil might be speaking to her, posing as either Jesus, Mary or one of the good angels. To

226

sort out this confusion Margery visits our good friend Julian of Norwich. You'll recall that despite her name, Julian is a woman too, but a far more introspective and calmer person than Margery. Having spent much of her life in religious contemplation and having had visions of her own, Julian is well placed to give Margery an expert opinion. They spend several days together, during which Julian advises her to obey whatever message she receives from God, provided it, '*were not against the worship of God and the profit of her fellow Christians.*' Margery finds this very helpful.

In one of his messages, Jesus commands Margery to go on pilgrimages to Santiago, Rome and Jerusalem. Margery wonders where she will find the money to fund these trips. Jesus answers that he will send her enough generous friends as she travels across England, reassuring her, '*daughter, I shall lead you there and bring you back again in safety, and no Englishman shall die in the ship you are in*'. He adds that he wants her to become a vegetarian and only dress in white. This last direction will come to cause problems.

And so, in her mid-30s, Margery sets off with a group of English pilgrims for Jerusalem. The plan is to travel overland to Venice, where they will board a ship for the Holy Land. The spiritual purpose of a pilgrimage in no way lessens Margery's habit of extended loud weeping. Her incessant high-volume wailing causes her compatriots a discomfort that no right-headed English citizen can endure: sustained social embarrassment. By the time they reach the Alps, her fellow pilgrims fix on a desperate remedy: they chop up her gown so that it looks like a crazy mini-dress, stick a canvas apron on top, and tell everyone she's a lunatic.

When even this tactic fails to ameliorate Margery's wailing, they abandon her by the side of the road. According to Margery, they take most of her money too. It's very dangerous to be a woman alone on a pilgrimage in the 1400s: muggers, rapists and murderers prowl the route to pick off vulnerable prey. Rather than giving up though, Margery busies herself, cadging a sequence of lifts. As a result, she reaches Venice before her duplicitous fellow Brits, and takes great satisfaction watching their collective jaws drop as they eventually arrive, only to see Guess-Who waiting for them at the docks. On her return from Jerusalem, and on subsequent adventures to Rome, Santiago and Poland, Margery is again abandoned by other sets of fellow travellers who can't abide her constant sobbing and wailing.

It's men that give Margery the most trouble. At one point she is arrested by the Mayor of Leicester, who tells her, '*you are a false strumpet...I shall have you in prison.*' This is no idle threat; Margery is in danger of being executed for heresy. The Mayor goes on, '*I want to know why you go about in white clothes, for I believe you have come here to lure away our wives from us.*' Her response is straightforward, '*Sir, you shall not know from my mouth why I go about in white clothes; you are not worthy to know it.*' If she'd had one, her lawyer would have despaired at this point. Eventually Margery is taken before the Archbishop of York on a charge of preaching, an illegal activity for a woman. There's every chance she'll be burnt at the stake. After roundly criticising Margery for all her loud weeping, the Bishop goes in for the kill: '*I hear it said that you are a very wicked woman.*' Margery won't be bullied: '*Sir, I also hear it said that you are a wicked man.*' She adds that he might consider fixing his ways if he has any ambition of heaven. The Bishop all but blows a fuse, and can find no more to say than, '*Why you!...*'

God knows how, but she gets out of that one. She also manages to walk free from imprisonment by the Duke of Bedford, then the most powerful man in the country. Even everyday citizens can be a jeopardy to Margery: when she boards a ship at the start of her pilgrimage to Santiago in Spain, the superstitious crew are so concerned she might be possessed by demons that, '*if they had any storm, they would throw her into the sea.*' Luckily, it's a smooth crossing.

It is 23rd January 1421, and Margery is in church in Kings Lynn when a terrible fire takes hold in the town centre. The sky is filled with flame, smoke and sparks. The Guildhall burns to destruction, and it looks like the whole town will follow. Margery gets praying and before long heavy snow starts to fall. The town is saved! Margery is the hero of the hour.

She could be a highly irritating, but as much as some wished her ill, Margery never (outside an isolated spat with her daughter-in-law) seemed to hold any ill intention towards them. She had the courage to never back down, even when threatened with execution, and was often called to the deathbeds of neighbours, to help smooth their pathway into the next life: '*Though they loved not her weeping nor her crying in* [their] *life-time, they desired that she should when they were dying, and so she did.*'

Unlike some of today's mystics, Margery never believed she had communicated with the recent dead – all her supernatural contacts were with the Biblical inhabitants of heaven and hell: demons, angels, God, Jesus Christ, the Virgin Mary and Mary Magdalene. Margery's visions and the voices in her head belonged to her era, the early 1400s. There were no aliens or extraplanetary spirits. Whatever she saw or heard, it was real enough to Margery for her to risk her life proclaiming and defending. If Margery's courageous and whacky life can teach us anything about the supernatural, it is perhaps that if by any chance there is anything 'out there', we may only experience it through the filters of our own minds, beliefs and times.

As she surely would have demanded, we will leave the last word to Margery. She claimed Jesus had said to her, '*Daughter, I shall make the whole world wonder at you*', and six hundred years on he looks to have kept his word.

In 1794 Richard Brothers, a retired Royal Naval officer, published *The Revealed Knowledge of the Prophecies and Times*, a record of psychic communications between God and Lieutenant Brothers. Among several divine messages, the Almighty assured Brothers that unless England stopped fighting Napoleon, London would be destroyed by an earthquake on June 4th, 1795. England didn't, and London wasn't. Most likely at the suggestion of others, Richard checked himself into a private asylum, from where he wrote further pamphlets containing additional wild prophesies. Many of his readers kept faith with him, but when Richard predicted that come November 19, 1795 he would be revealed as Prince of the Hebrews and Ruler of the World, and that day came and went without Richard inheriting any part of the planet, these embarrassed supporters melted away. With a new century about to dawn, many still held to the millenarian belief that a new spiritual age was imminent, and they soon found another and better herald of its arrival: Joanna Southcott.

Joanna was born in East Devon in 1750. She was eighteen and working as a servant girl when she had her first otherworldly experience, a visit from a being she named *The Spirit of Truth*. When she reached the age of 42, God appeared in person to Joanna, to warn her of, '*what was coming upon the whole earth.*' In this year she began writing down prophesies dictated to her by the Spirit of Truth. The most important of these predictions were sealed in a box (*The Great Box*) and left in the custody of one of her friends. '*I have fresh things revealed to me every day,*' she wrote, '*I feel as though I was surrounded by angels feeling a heavenly joy which I cannot describe. It has taken from me all natural appetite, yet I feel no want of food.*'

So strong was her conviction she was being guided by inhabitants of heaven that Joanna spent her life savings publishing pamphlets detailing many of their divine revelations. The pamphlets sold like hot cakes, and Joanna became a national celebrity, with thousands of pre-Twitter followers. In 1796 she predicted that the perfectly healthy Bishop of Exeter, wouldn't live to enjoy Christmas. He died on December 12th1796. That same year she correctly predicted Lord Malmesbury's peace mission to France would end in failure. Joanna also forecast that the thrown-together French revolutionary army would conquer Italy. She was right about that too. Joanna had, however, a few failures, and this caused her to wonder if she were truly in contact with the Big Man and his team. But by this point so many people were making good money off her back that it was impossible for Joanna to quit and go home to the West Country.

In 1813 Joanna announced that though she was still a virgin and 63 years old, she was carrying a child that would become the new Messiah. Several doctors examined her and confirmed that Joanna was indeed pregnant. The baby was due in July 1814 but come November it had still not arrived. Joanna experienced a crisis of faith, wondering if she had been completely deluded. Her health collapsed, and she died soon after, on 16th December 1814. On her deathbed Joanna made a will in which she declared she had come to believe the Devil had deceived her. The will directed that all gifts intended for the coming Messiah (including a luxurious £200 crib) should be returned to their donors.

It's unclear where Joanna's great box is now: it might be in the British Museum, although they seem to have mislaid it; the Panacea Society, a modern-day group of Southcott followers based in Bedford, reckon they have it, and as evidence there's a photo of a sealed-up old box on their website. According to Joanna's instructions, it may only be opened in the presence of 24 bishops of the Church of England. Seeing that precisely zero bishops want to get involved, and the whereabouts of the box remains at question, the mystery is set to run for a further 200 years.

Emanuel Swedenborg

To encounter our greatest visionary, we travel back to the mid-1700s and an unusual church in Fetter Lane, off London's Fleet Street. The Church of Moravia at this time emphasised the spiritual importance of marital sex, to the point where they considered orgasm a mystical experience connecting humans to Christ. They went further, worshipping male and female genitalia on the slightly thin grounds that Jesus would have had a penis, and he must have entered this world through a vagina. Married couples were not regarded as lawfully wedded by the church, '*unless they performed the conjugal duties in the presence of the Elders'* (or the Dirty Old Men as we might know them today). The Moravians became fixated on the story of Christ's execution, and in particular the piercing of his side by a soldier's spear. This wound they somehow equated with a vagina. With a commendable enthusiasm for First Aid, they chanted prayers about sucking it clean or kissing it better. According to one source, this healthy religious interest in genitalia culminated in, *'sexual perversions such as orgies of group sex'.* People had to make their own entertainment back then. Around this time, the Fetter Lane congregation included an occasional visitor to England, a Swedish man who was to have a significant impact on the way the English came to view death.

Emanuel Swedenborg was born in Stockholm in 1688. One of the great scientists of his day, Swedenborg designed prototypes for aircraft and submarines. He also made a strikingly accurate prediction of the structure of the atom and deduced the existence of oxygen some fifty years before its discovery. By the age of fifty-five Emanuel could consider himself a conspicuous success: he had secured international renown and held a handsomely paid post, employed by the king of Sweden. It was at this point Swedenborg began to act strangely, this odd behaviour included rolling around in the street. The Monrovia Church records mention one of these episodes: *'The Swedishman...that was lately besides himself is now better again.'*

As Swedenborg recovered in his London lodgings, a daytime vision of a man appeared in his room. This visitor introduced himself as God and bestowed on Swedenborg a free pass to roam the next world. Swedenborg took up the offer, and for the next 25 years spent a chunk of his spare time mooching around the afterlife, chatting with angels and steering clear of demons. He mapped out the hereafter in a sequence of books that divided opinion across Europe and America, with readers regarding Swedenborg variously as a modern-day prophet, a fraud or a lunatic.

So what did Swedenborg see when exploring the next life? The set-up was, to his eyes, fairly straightforward: when we die, we go to a sort of holding camp called the *Spirit World*. We are dead, and we are now spirits, but we look exactly as we did on one of our better days on planet Earth. We even sport the same clothes we preferred to wear down here. We can remain in the spirit world, Swedenborg learns, for a fair while, but the absolute maximum stay is 30 years. It's OK there, but Swedenborg complained it had more than its fair share of evil spirits from the Christian church who were obsessed, as he put it, by '*how to become the greatest and to possess all things*'. Swedenborg took this as a strong signal that Judgment Day was nearby, but of course we're still waiting on that.

When we have to move on from the spirit world, it's the usual story: we go either upstairs or down. Should we strike lucky, we discover that there are three levels to Swedenborg's heaven. They are arranged like a set of rings surrounding a spiritual bulls-eye. The outer circle is the third heaven. It's not too bad. Nice and bright. The middle ring is very bright and shiny, a genuine step-up from heaven 3.0. The inner ring is super-brilliant, easily the best paradise out there. It embraces the core, which is a constant wonderful light. For those of us who get sent in the other direction, there are, according to Swedenborg, three hells. One is shit, the second is shittier, and the third is unbelievably shit.

Where we end up is down to us. Those of us who are perfect '*in love, wisdom, and intelligence*' get a place in heaven number one. The next best group go to the middle section, and the likeable but less impressive of us are headed for the outer zone. Readers at this point should feel free to imagine how close they'll find themselves to the heavenly light bulb. I'm picturing myself at the rear of tourist-class heaven, vulnerable to a sudden fall out the back door....Swedenborg's advice to me and other spiritually compromised folk is that we should mend some of our ways ASAP, because (contrary to what we've always been told) we can, and will, take stuff with us: our bad habits. And these are far harder to drop in the next life:

a man takes with him his favourite inclinations and opinions, and
it is very difficult to be divested of them. We ought therefore to lay
them aside here.

We don't have to turn ourselves into saints in order to get to heaven, says Swedenborg, but simply act with honesty and show some kindness to others. While touring through heaven, Swedenborg bumped into two people he had known in this material world. They told him life up there was great, miles better than the best day they'd ever experienced on earth. So good, in fact, they didn't have the words to describe the zenith of joy they felt.

In addition to these recent arrivals in heaven, Swedenborg claimed to have encountered spirits who had died two thousand years earlier. Old testament prophets, including Abraham, Jacob and Moses were up there and happy to chat. They hadn't aged a bit.

Swedenborg notes that as soon as they land in their patch of heaven, people are free to associate with like-minded spirits, forming groups and societies. Rather than sitting on a cloud with a harp, everyone *'pursues a life similar to that which he had led in the body'*. There are houses, gardens, parks and public squares, all of which are loads better than our earthly versions:

> *I have seen palaces in heaven that were so splendid as to be beyond description. Their upper stories shone as though they were made of pure gold, and their lower ones as though they were made of precious gems.*

Travel from one corner of the next world to the other is instant, but you can drag your heels if you wish:

> *when any one goes from one place to another, whether it be in his own city, or in courts or in gardens, or to others out of his own society, he arrives more quickly when he eagerly desires it, and less quickly when he does not.*

There's some church-going to be done in heaven, (see the heel-dragging point above) but all sermons are platinum standard, so this is not much of a chore. Confining himself to the upper levels of the after-world, Swedenborg found that the angels made pretty good company, although they couldn't answer all his questions: *'angels have no notion or idea of time and space; and this so completely that they do not even know at all what time and space are.'*

If you fancy moving up to a higher heaven, no-one will try and stop you, but the result is always the same: *'One ascending from a lower heaven is seized with a distress even to anguish, and is unable to see those who are there, still less to talk with them'.* Similarly, if you are in the nice end of heaven and you fancy slumming it by drifting out to one of the outer rings, you soon realise your mistake: *'one descending from a higher heaven is deprived of his wisdom, stammers in his speech, and is in despair.'* The most common attempts to gate-crash any heaven come, of course, from the occupants of hell. These never meet with success:

> *as soon as those who are in the love of self and of the world draw near the first threshold of that heaven, they begin to be distressed and so tortured inwardly as to feel hell rather than heaven to be in them; and in consequence they cast themselves down headlong therefrom, and do not rest until they come into the hells among their like.*

The angels don't mind giving the hapless demons a helping shove; Swedenborg said that he himself had seen, *'hundreds of thousands of evil spirits dispersed by angels and cast down into hell'.* That's not the end of their hopes though; some demons are better behaved than others, and after a while these spirits are raised up to the outer suburbs of paradise, where they can start life afresh, in a lovely new home just inside the celestial M25.

Swedenborg gives us a vivid description of gaping portals to hell, but he shows no desire to drop in for a nose around. We can almost see him swerve and double his step as he nears these mouths to the underworld: '*Through these caverns nauseous and fetid stenches exhale, which good spirits flee from because they abominate them, but evil spirits seek for them because they delight in them.*' Like attracts like, and this world's baddies feel quite at home in the underworld. Denizens of hell look fine to one another, but to the goodie two-shoes of heaven, they appear repulsive:

> *In general their faces are hideous, and void of life like those of corpses; the faces of some are black, others fiery like torches, others disfigured with pimples, warts, and ulcers; some seem to have no face, but in its stead something hairy or bony; and with some only the teeth are seen; their bodies also are monstrous; and their speech is like the speech of anger or of hatred or of revenge*

But God is not up for punishing poor devils, because She/He's not like that. No, it's the bad spirits that make their own hell, tormenting and bullying one another. Swedenborg assures us that there are some bad sorts down there, but no super villain, no Devil, Satan, or Nasty Nick, or whatever we might call him.

With his Scandinavian eye for good order, Swedenborg notices that there are many types of government in heaven, although the place pretty well runs itself. Governing hell, on the other hand, turns out to be a nightmare, with spite and double-dealing featuring heavily.

Swedenborg claimed that he'd been lucky enough to be present at a review of the life of a new arrival into the Spirit World holding camp. Rather than a checklist of their good and bad deeds being itemised by a superior being, (a scenario set out in the Bible's book of Revelations), Swedenborg saw the arrival's whole life played out as a kind of 3-D video, featuring characters who had been involved in important events in the newly dead person's time on earth.

> *all their deeds were disclosed and reviewed from their memory in order, from their earliest to their latest years.... Others who had*

236

enticed maidens to shame or had violated chastity were called to a like judgment; and the details of their crimes were drawn forth from their memory and reviewed. The very faces of the maidens and women were also exhibited as if present, with the places, words and intentions, and this as suddenly as when a scene is presented to the sight, the exhibitions continuing sometimes for hours.

Swedenborg's account of the holographic Life Review, his mention of dead friends who tell him the afterlife is super-brilliant, and his report that time and space don't exist for residents of the next world are all echoed in modern accounts of Near Death Experiences, which we come to later.

As modern people we are satisfied that our thoughts are our own. They stay encased within our skulls; no one can tell exactly what we're thinking. Swedenborg's wanderings in the next life convinced him otherwise. Thought transfer was the method for all communication, every private thought or secret intention becoming immediately apparent to all. This prompted Swedenborg to give us a warning: '*There are some who do not believe that thoughts and affections really extend* [beyond] *themselves....such are greatly mistaken.*'

Swedenborg's angels come from all parts of the world and, '*include good Christians, Moslems and 'heathens' from Africa and elsewhere.*'. By elsewhere, Swedenborg means exactly that. He explains: '*the human race is not from one earth alone, but from innumerable earths.*' He'd been told that there are a million populated planets in the Universe. This idea would have qualified Swedenborg's as insane in his time, but today's astronomers would regard a million as a perfectly reasonable, if not conservative, estimate. Unfortunately, Swedenborg got this figure from some '*wandering spirits*' from the planet Mercury, a claim that astronomers and anybody else today would have to judge as iffy.

So was Swedenborg mad? We can't know, but we must have our suspicions of any bloke who claims to spend his evenings chatting with dead people from Mercury. Yet in his own defence, Swedenborg might point out that in 2012 NASA announced they had found evidence of water and organic life on that deeply unpromising planet.

There are accounts of Swedenborg having psychic talent. He is said to have somehow sensed the murder of Tsar Peter III of Russia on the hour it happened, and to have known about a fire breaking out in Stockholm when he was 400 km away. They make for a stirring read, but of course neither of these nor any other story about Swedenborg's 'psychic powers' can be investigated now.

The greatest philosopher of his day, Immanuel Kant, was in two minds about Swedenborg. Hedging a bet, Kant described him as a, *'perhaps genuine visionary,'* and he stressed that Swedenborg's account of his travels in the spirit world were, *'not at all to be sneezed at'*. On the other hand, Kant felt that some aspects of Swedenborg's visions may be *'dismissed without hesitation'* and that at times he *'boldly speaks nonsense.'*

Swedenborg died in London on March 29th, 1772. Elizabeth Reynolds, who worked in his lodgings and was very fond of the old scientist, said that Swedenborg predicted the exact date of his death three weeks prior to the event. His biographer Cyriel Sigstedt quotes Elizabeth as saying that the prospect of his impending demise made Swedenborg, *'as pleased as if he were going to have a holiday and go to some merrymaking.'* It seems that if other people doubted the truth of Swedenborg's journeys in the after-world, he didn't. Nor did the man who – inspired in part by Swedenborg – brought the otherworld into the cultural life of England.

William Blake

Best known for the poem that begins, *'Tyger, tyger, burning bright,'* and for writing the words to the hymn *'Jerusalem'*, William Blake was an engraver by trade, and a highly talented painter. But it is for a separate reason that Blake is unique in English art.

238

There was probably never a time when Blake didn't experience visions. At around four years of age he saw what he took to be God's head peering through a window at home, and at nine he was walking in Peckham, near his South London home, when he saw, '*a tree filled with angels, bright angelic wings bespangling every bough like stars.*' Shortly after that he saw an Old Testament prophet (Ezekiel) and was visited by God himself. Plainly he was an odd kid. Believing that he was making this stuff up, his mum would beat William whenever he mentioned running into a Biblical character. This remedy failed: Blake's visions continued up to his dying day. As well as religious figures, Blake 'saw' the spirits of the dead, including the French writer Voltaire, the great Welsh king Owen Glendower, the Scots rebel William (Brave Heart) Wallace and a succession of English kings. Blake would hurriedly sketch their portraits as they appeared before his eyes.

Since he believed his visions to be absolutely genuine, the existence of another world was a straight-up fact to Blake. After years of living with William and his post-terrestrial chums, his wife Catherine even began to have visions of her own, on one occasion seeing a parade of spirits walk into the Thames.

Several of Blake's paintings are stupendous: *Prometheus Bound*, *The Great Red Dragon*, *Angels Rolling Away the Stone from the Sepulchre* and *The Ancient of Days*; but it is in his writing and his conversations that Blake is at his most startling, unique and – to some – crazy. He didn't try to play down his visions. Instead he would respond very candidly to anyone who asked about them. In January 1802 he wrote to his friend Thomas Butts:

> *I am not ashamed, afraid, or averse to tell you what ought to be told: That I am under the direction of Messengers from Heaven*

It was these heavenly *Messengers* – angels – that Blake tended to see most often. They were happy to chat with him about life, religion and art. The archangel Gabriel, for instance, told him that Michelangelo could paint a very tidy angel. When asked by Blake for proof that he was indeed the archangel, and not some malevolent spirit, Gabriel raised the roof of Blake's house, floated up in front of the sun, and shifted the entire universe. That settled the matter as far as Blake was concerned.

Once he got to know them, Blake came to the opinion that angels weren't all that. In fact, they could be dull and big-headed: '*I have always found that Angels have the vanity to speak of themselves as the only wise* [beings].' Blake went further, blaming angels for a lot of suffering in the world: '*Is not every infant that dies of disease in effect murdered by an Angel?*'

In his earlier years Blake was influenced by the teachings of Emanuel Swedenborg, particularly his accounts of his encounters with angels. But once Blake had met a few of these airborne spirits himself, he revised his opinion of the great scientist. Swedenborg had only chatted with the teacher's pets, the good angels of heaven, and not with the badass angels of hell:

> *Swedenborg has not written one new truth…he conversed with Angels who are all religious, and conversed not with Devils who all hate religion.*

Blake was a rebel and he liked a rebel angel, or a Devil as he called them. He describes being around when an angel and a fiery devil argued over religion. The angel embraced the flaming devil and turned into the prophet Elijah from the Old Testament. Blake concludes the anecdote by saying,

> *This Angel, who is now become a Devil, is my particular friend; we often read the Bible together in its infernal or diabolical sense, which the world shall have if they behave well.*

Well what the hell is going on here? Does Blake seriously expect us to believe that he has kept the company of unearthly beings, and that these creatures swap identities and sit down with him to read the Bible? Let's face it, he has imagined the whole thing. Blake's answer to this would be simply to agree. To Blake, imagination is ultimately all there is:

> *Imagination is the real and eternal world of which this vegetable universe is but a faint shadow*

To back this up, Blake points out that every part of our world: furniture, a house, transportation, shoes, first had to be invented, imagined, before they could exist as physical objects: '*What is now proved was once only imagined.*'

The real day-to-day, bus-is-late-again, what's-for-dinner world is, to Blake, not very real at all. He calls it a '*vegetable universe*', a sort of screen or projection that manages to convince us that it is both truly and exclusively real. As far as Blake is concerned, if we believe that, then we are wrong on both counts. We need to open up, and see things as they really are:

> *If the doors of perception were cleansed,*
> *Everything would appear to man as it is, infinite.*

But, what about these angels and dead people? How real are they then William? '*A Spirit and a Vision are not, as the modern philosophy supposes, a cloudy vapour or a nothing: they are organized and minutely articulated beyond all that the mortal and perishing nature can produce*'. So, they are more real than reality. We'll return to this characteristic later.

As if hanging out with beings from another dimension weren't nutty enough, one of Blake's friends, Allan Cunningham, recounts William telling him that he'd been witness to a funeral of the Little People:

> *I saw a procession of creatures of the size and colour of green and grey grasshoppers, bearing a body laid out on a rose leaf, which they buried with songs, and then disappeared. It was a fairy funeral.*

This kind of talk meant Blake had to be crazy. A newspaper report of an exhibition at London's Royal Academy in May 1785 said that Blake, '*appears like some lunatic, just escaped*'. And in 1809, an art critic described Blake's paintings as the work of, '*an unfortunate lunatic,*' as if there could be a fortunate one. Not everyone was as cruel: a vicar by the name of John

Martin had his doubts about Blake's sanity, but said, that if Blake were cracked, '*His is a crack that lets in the light.*'

A young artist called Seymour Kirkup met Blake late in William's life. At the time Kirkup couldn't swallow any of Blake's talk of spirits. But because, to quote him, Blake was one of the '*most upright, and most sincere men I ever knew*', Kirkup decided that he was a madman rather than a liar. Fifty years later Kirkup, who by this time had had some unusual experiences of his own, softened his opinion, reckoning that Blake's visions were '*possible, tho not certain*'.

Many who knew Blake best were certain, however, that he was perfectly sane. Edward Calvert, an artist who became a friend of Blake, said '*I saw nothing but sanity…saw nothing mad in his conduct, actions or character*', and another good friend, John Linnell, thought that Blake was anything but mad: '*I never in all my conversations with him could for a moment feel there was the least justice in calling him insane.*'

Blake didn't believe himself to be mad, but at times he was troubled by the strain of having to live in two worlds, the solid one we know all-too well, and the Blakey world of visions:

> *I have indeed fought through a Hell of terrors and horrors (which none could know but myself) in a divided existence.*

The problem for Blake was that his numinous world was actually the true one, and this physical realm an altogether less solid place, crowded with strange creatures who kept telling him he was off his head: '*I know that This World Is a World of imagination & Vision. I see everything I paint In This World, but everybody does not see alike.*' To Blake, imagination comes from the outside, from the heavens above. As evidence of this, he wrote in a letter to his friend Thomas Butts about his experience of automatic writing: '*I have written this Poem* [the Four Zoas] *from immediate Dictation, twelve or sometimes twenty or thirty lines at a time, without Premeditation and even against my Will*'. Milton had similar experiences when writing *Paradise Lost*. Shakespeare also had this kind of spontaneous creativity; his close friend and fellow playwright Ben Johnson said, '*I remember the players have often mentioned it as an honor to Shakespeare, that in his writing, whatsoever he penned, he never blotted out a line*'. The work flowed through Will's pen, uninterrupted lucid and complete. It's not exactly the same with Blake's *Four Zoas*, which on the whole is a dense and confusing poem, although it does contain flashes of absolute brilliance. One of these instances of inspiration features a female deity called Eno.

> *Eno, a daughter of Beulah took a Moment of Time*
> *And drew it out to Seven thousand years...*
> *She also took an atom of space & opend its center*
> *Into Infinitude*

There are two ideas here more than 100 years ahead of their time. First, Blake says that time is not fixed: a second can be stretched out for thousands of years. This thought was ridiculous until well into the 20th Century when Stephen Hawking and others calculated that if a woman were to fall into a Black Hole, an observer would see her frozen at its edge, with time stood still. Blake would not have been surprised. He put it this way: '*I see the Past, Present & Future, existing all at once*'. We can of course disagree: tomorrow is never going to be last Wednesday, but we can come back to Blake's crazy world of time later (and earlier if you happen to be him). It took until 1970 for science to come in line with the second of Blake's idea, that atoms contain infinity. It did this with String Theory, which reasons that just about every part of an atom comprises or is produced by strings, strings that are infinitely thin.

Elsewhere in the *Four Zoas*, Blake has Tharmas say:

> '*I am like an atom*
> *A Nothing left in darkness yet I am an identity*
> *I wish & feel & weep & groan.*'

Again, Blake has anticipated modern scientific theory, which holds that an almost nothing appears to have awareness or consciousness.

While most of us in the west are content to regard Blake as very likeable and talented but mentally unwell, many Buddhists see him in a completely different light. For them, he is a *Samantabhadra*: a sacred figure who embodies aspects of Buddha on earth. The Buddhist education site dharmanet.org says, '*Perhaps no figure in English literature more fully exemplifies the archetypal qualities of Samantabhadra than the British visionary poet and painter William Blake*'. In *the Tibetan Book of Living & Dying*, the llama and scholar Sogyal Rinpoche asserts that Blake was able to perceive a reality the rest of us will only see when we leave this life, when,

> *All our old concepts of the world or matter or even ourselves are purified and dissolved, and an entirely new, what you could call 'heavenly' field of vision and perception opens up. As Blake says:*
> *'If the doors of perception were cleansed,*
> *Everything would appear to man as it is, infinite.'*

I'm not too much for poetry, so I'm going to be wrong, but for me the greatest four lines in an English poem are Blake's:

> *To see a World in a Grain of Sand*
> *And a Heaven in a Wild Flower*
> *Hold Infinity in the palm of your hand*
> *And Eternity in an hour.*

To Blake, we don't need a telescope to catch a glimpse of infinity; we can find it by simply gazing at our upturned palm, as a single grain of sand holds everything. It does hold an incredible number of (about 100 quintillion) atoms, and as we shall see, every atom is a world of its own. And so Blake, like Julian of Norwich with her hazel nut, somehow calculated that the vastness of everything could be found in the smallest of anything. A wild flower growing through the patio will have some of us reaching for the weed-killer, but to Blake that same flower brings an electric thrill of wonder.

The way he sees it, we don't have to wish for an afterlife of heaven and ecstasy and joy: we can have it all now. In addition to saying that infinity is there for all of us to see, Blake is sure that our minds can reach far beyond our eyesight: '*One thought fills immensity.*' We're put in mind too of Swedenborg's warning that we our thoughts and affections really extend beyond ourselves.

One hundred years later, Swami Vivekananda an Indian monk and scholar, would say something very similar: '*Thoughts live; they travel far*'. In 1896, Vivekananda sailed into Southampton with the intention of introducing the English to Hindu philosophy. Funny, young, charming and smart, the press and the public were entranced by him. Not that Vivekananda pulled any punches; he told the Sunday Times that the English, '*have many prejudices that need to be broken through*'. Although there is no evidence that he knew of Blake's work, Vivekananda once said as a neat coincidence, '*If we know one grain of sand, we understand the secret of the whole universe.*' While it's likely he would have made an exception in William's case, Vivekananda was pretty damning about spiritualty in England:

> *I am sorry to see in the West how much they make of death; always trying to catch a little life. 'Give us life after death! Give us life!' They are so happy if anybody tells them that they are going to live afterwards!*

So, that's settled then: we're all headed for an afterlife. No, we're not, says Vivekananda: '*It is child's talk that a man dies and goes to heaven.*'
Oh, where are we going then? Vivekananda's answer is that we have just asked a stupid question. We can't go anywhere because we never die, and the reason we never die is that we were never born in the first place. Numerous people these days can produce video evidence to prove they were, but even that wouldn't sway Vivekananda. He explains: '*your body, your house, the people and the world are all absolutely unreal like a dream*'. At

this point Blake might have slapped him on the back and said, '*That's just what I've been trying to tell them Viv.*'

To Vivekananda, we are far too hung up on individuality. Reality proves to be the opposite: we are all one. Everyone is everyone else. So, I shouldn't worry if I die, because we never all die. I find it difficult to be so generous spirited: why should it be me that takes one for the team? Not that I want to live forever: I love spaghetti, but I can imagine being sick of bolognaise after a quarter million years or so. No, I'm happy to die really, but I don't like to think that when I'm gone, I'll never see a loved one again. Perhaps I should just get over it.

So if the affable Swami turns out to be right, we are all nothing and everything's pointless. But we're wrong again apparently: Vivekananda's angle is that although the world is an illusion, like a giant David Blaine or Dynamo trick, there is some genuine core to us all: atman. Atman is like some universal mind. That's where we all belong. Together. So where's that then Viv? Here, apparently: '*All the souls that have been, are, and will be, are on one geometrical point.*' I suppose we are back now at Julian of Norwich's '*I saw God in a Point,*' and we'd probably be helped by wiping clean Blake's double-glazed doors of perception: everything is right in front of us, if only we could see it. Of course, there's no material evidence for this and we can choose to believe none of it. Call ourselves atheists. But Vivekananda is absolutely fine with that: '*We are all atheists; let us confess it,*' he once wrote.

So here's a baffling character to turn up in Victorian England: a holy man who says that everyone, himself included, is an atheist, and that none of us really exist anyway. And they thought Blake was certifiable. I like to think that it was as his boat sailed out of Portsmouth for home that Vivekananda wrote another of his memorable lines: '*I care not even for nature's laws. Death is a joke to me*'. India treats its gurus like England its sports stars, and Vivekananda received a hero's welcome when he disembarked at Bombay. He died aged just 39; I hope he saw the funny side of it. Influenced by Vivekananda and other Eastern sages, Londoner Annie Wood Besant said with absolute confidence, *'There is no such thing as Death at all.'* This restricts me from stating with absolute confidence that she's dead, but no-one has seen her around since September 1933.

And what happened to Blake? His friend George Richmond was at Blake's bedside when he took his final breath in 1827. He wrote straight away to tell another friend, Samuel Palmer, that Blake, *'Died in a most glorious manner…. Just before he died His Countenance became fair. His eyes Brightened and He burst out into Singing of the things he saw in Heaven.'*

Happily, we are still in an age of visionaries. Patricia de Menezes converted to Catholicism so she could marry. In 1985, at the age of 45 Patricia started seeing the Virgin Mary and, on occasions, Jesus, assorted angels and Mary's husband Joseph. They appeared to her in a range of places, but most often in the pine tree by her home in, incongruously, Surbiton. Over the thirty years since her first vision, Patricia has attracted a large following of believers who have formed a church called the *Family of Divine Innocence.* Her son Subash has commented that,

> *I didn't really want anything to do with it, to tell you the truth. I'd drifted away from the Church, and all of this was far too strange for my liking…My mother asked the Lord, 'Why come here to Surbiton? Why choose me? Why not come to some poor person up in the hills in Bangladesh?' Our Lord said, 'This country, this place, is poorer spiritually than Bangladesh.' I knew my mother couldn't make up something like that. It was beyond her.*

Mrs de Menezes applied for her visions to be officially recognised by the Vatican, but the request was rejected on the grounds that her quotes from Jesus included inappropriate words and phrases and featured *'intemperate language'* in attacks on the Catholic Church.

The rational explanation for all these visions is that the brain of the person 'seeing' the otherworldly being has malfunctioned in specific zones located either side of their head, just above each ear. We will look into the role of these areas, known as the temporal lobes, shortly.

Paranormal England

5 Worst Vegetables: New Potatoes

New potatoes? What was wrong with the old ones? What is this, some kind of upgrade?

Jack Marteau, Blog 2009

The skies over medieval England teemed with spirits: angels, saints, devils and at least one god. It was heresy then to state none of these beings existed. Conversely, now that the country has been found empty of spirts, it is a kind of modern heresy to say that supernatural beings prevail. The English have two predominant senses: humour and pride. We control our fellow citizens by using the first against the second. Taking the piss. The English have comfortably enough arrogance to withstand being disliked – at the height of the Empire up to one third of the planet had the hump with us, and we really didn't give a fig – but the one thing we English have never been able to endure is to be laughed at. Our pride can't take the derision. Anyone broaching the subject of the supernatural runs this risk. Talk of non-material worlds is taboo, and is usually silenced by mocking responses such as, '*And were there seventeen pixies and a giant space-fairy next to the bloke?*' I've been guilty of this myself, in this book. What can I say? I'm English. So, with the risk of social humiliation in mind, let's delve into the forbidden land of the spooky.

Premonition

In an interview with researcher Keith Hearne in 1981, Lesley Brennan, a 31-year-old woman from Cleethorpes, Humberside described a vivid experience she'd had seven years earlier:

> *I was watching television on Saturday 1st June 1974, at early lunch-time, when I saw the word 'Newsflash' appear on the screen. A voice*

said that a serious accident, involving several deaths had occurred at Flixborough. I was alone at the time. Two friends [Peter East and his girlfriend, both aged 23 at the time] who were living with me, came in a little later (between noon and 2 p.m.) and I mentioned the news to them. The next day we realised that the accident did not happen until several hours after I saw the Newsflash. I had no links with Flixborough and knew no one who worked at the plant.

The explosion happened, without warning at the Flixborough chemical plant of Nypro (UK) Ltd. The blast was enormous, equivalent to 30 tons of TNT. Twenty-eight people died, 70 were seriously injured. 1,821 houses were damaged, some of which were three miles from the blast. The disaster happened at 4.53 pm, hours after Lesley Brennan had 'seen' the newsflash. Lesley and her two housemates scoffed at the TV News that night for getting the time of the explosion so utterly wrong. It was only upon reading the Sunday paper, with its report of dozens of broken clocks in Flixborough village frozen at seven minutes to five, that they realised something very strange had happened to time in their own home.

Keith Hearne checked with all four TV companies that had been broadcasting in Cleethorpes in 1974; none had issued any newsflash prior to 5 p.m. Hearne then contacted Lesley's two former house mates, to see if they supported her story. They gave a joint signed statement:

> *We confirm that we have seen the statement made by Lesley Brennan concerning her ostensible precognition of the 1974 Flixborough disaster and that she did communicate to us the news of the accident at lunchtime on Saturday 1st June 1974*

It's possible that the three concocted the story between them, but if so, it seems strange that they would do this for no apparent gain.

Or maybe Lesley dropped off in front of a boring Saturday lunchtime programme, and dreamt the Newsflash? History is dotted with stories of premonitions occurring in dreams. In February 1883 a 41-year-old woman,

Mrs Burton from Shrewsbury, wrote to the Society for Psychical Research, saying: '*Ever since I was twenty-one the following dream has occurred with certain varieties: in my sleep I see suddenly a naked infant lying in or falling in a bath.*' if she saw only the baby, then she somehow knew that a death would happen within the coming 48 hours. If a person she recognised were standing next to the infant, she then knew which family was about to be bereaved.

Edward Gurney of the Society asked Mrs Burton for examples. She wrote back that on 29th January 1873 she had dreamt of the baby in the bath. The following morning, she warned her husband that someone they knew would die within a few hours. He laughed, but later in the day they got news that a close friend's son had died. Mrs Burton stated they hadn't known he'd been ill. Mrs Burton gave three other examples of dreams that predicted deaths, along with dates, all of which Gurney validated via death registry records. In her most up-to-date dream, Mrs Burton herself stood '*in deep mourning*' next to the baby in the bath. She knew this meant it was curtains for Mr Burton. She doesn't say if she told her husband, but if she had it's doubtful he'd have laughed this time round. Anyway, he was dead within a couple of days. They say every cloud has a silver lining: once Mr Burton had taken his last breath, Mrs Burton didn't have any further nightmare premonitions. Or perhaps just one more, the dream that presaged her own demise.

Many of us will have come across stories of people who, in the hours before a terrible event, had a dreadful sense that something awful was about to happen. The Scarborough-born writer Susan Hill wrote about exactly this experience in her novel, *In the Springtime of the Year*. Ruth, the book's central character, is hanging out the washing when, '*she felt as if she had been struck in the face, but it was not pain, it was a wave of terror, rising, breaking and pouring down over her...It was the first time in her life that she had known anything like it.*' Later that day David Colt, her husband's workmate, calls at the house without warning:

Ruth saw him. Saw his face. Knew.
'A tree fell...it killed him. He's dead'
Everything within her fell into place and she was still. She accepted it at once, and understood, remembering that she had known, known the moment it happened.

We can all have morbid thoughts about a loved one who is late home: we imagine a car crash, or an incident at work. As soon as she or he walks in through the door we relax, and our black fantasy evaporates, gone and never to be recalled. But if something terrible were to happen, we will feel that we had known for certain that tragedy was about to strike. The researcher Caroline Watt calls this *'selective recall'*: we may have feared the worst a hundred times before, but the only occasion we might truly remember is the one we have immediately before a terrible event. It's not necessarily a premonition; it's a coincidence. But there's another kind of premonition. A stranger one.

On Thursday 3rd December 2009 Debbie, my wife, was visiting a friend:

I was chatting with Liz for quite a while, and I was telling her Rose [our daughter] *was doing really well and Jack was doing really well in Italy, I'd just had my 50th, and I said to her, 'I think it's the happiest I've ever felt.' It just came out in conversation.*

In all her adult life, Debbie had never been moved to say that before. She went to bed and at one in the morning she was awoken by the landline: *'I rushed downstairs and it was Rosie saying, 'Oh mum, Ross has phoned. Jack's been hit by a car.'...then I don't remember much.'*

This experience of being supremely happy only hours before a tragedy is something Susan Hill's character Ruth went through immediately before her husband's fatal accident: *'as she walked, she had felt a great happiness spurt within her...it was as though she had been re-born into some new world...she was giddy with this happiness. She had to remind herself that nothing had really happened.'*

252

Curious that, like Debbie, a character in her novel Springtime had felt extremely elated just before a terrible event, I contacted Susan Hill and asked her if she had any personal reason for creating this part of the story. Her reply surprised me:

> 'Springtime' was written a year after the man I was to marry died suddenly. I had been away for a few weeks writing a book in a house by the sea. The day he died, I was packing up and clearing, having finished my book, and went out for a walk on the shore. It was a cold but bright sunny beautiful day and I had that strange sense of absolute happiness and almost exhilaration...of course I was glad to be going home and seeing David but it was more than that. I had so many experiences over that time and no matter who might try to dismiss them as 'heightened emotion' etc. I know the difference between things you wish for and are in a state to 'conjure up' and things that happen.

I wrote to PMH Atwater, an international authority on experiences around death, to ask if she had come across cases of people feeling elated immediately before a tragedy:

> Oh, my goodness, Dave. That is right on for the majority of people...relatives or friends who are close to the individual...often pick up something is about to happen...the closer to death the individual is, the more those close to the individual will in some way pick it up.

And another common pattern has emerged from PMH's research:

> In the weeks before, usually 6 to 8 weeks in advance, the individual about to die starts acting differently – as if getting their affairs in order is now very important: speaking to relatives and friends in more intimate ways, seeing things or going places that are important to him or her. This behavior change can become almost an obsession. . . until about 2 to 3 days before death. Then he or she

becomes calm, bright, happy, wide awake and at peace – almost as
if "all is well" and everything is okay. Death usually occurs fairly
quickly after that.

PMH's words rang through me. Pieces assembled themselves into a sudden coherence. Before he left for Italy, Jack had taken a tour to London, Manchester, Belfast and Dublin, visiting all his friends and his sister Rosie. This was unlike him; Jack lived by others coming to him. He stopped off in Salisbury to meet with Callum, an old school mate. They had fallen out heavily years earlier. Jack's visit healed the rift. In videos taken three days before his death, Jack is relaxed, happy and very funny; a completed man radiating easy joy. Ross, his friend and flatmate, was with Jack throughout his last weeks of life. A true feet-on-the-ground Yorkshireman, the day after Jack's death Ross told us that throughout those weeks, '*He had an aura about him.*'

In June 2017 Deb and I visit Marge and Chris in Beckenham. They've been together forty years, and we've been their friends for almost that long. Marge has stage 4 cancer that has penetrated her bones; fully emaciated and in deep pain, she is near the end. A few nights previously, Marge had a vivid dream about Jack. '*He said to me, "Don't worry about Chris – he'll be OK; and Deb and Dave are doing better now"."* Marge feels strongly this was a genuine visit from Jack. She dies ten days later. Marge had nearly died from meningitis as a kid, and this near-death experience left her with some psychic abilities. It's been tough for him, but as I write this, Chris has been OK following Marge's death. And Deb and I are indeed been doing better.

Around 1880 John Dunne dreamt that he was travelling through the skies inside what looked to be a sort of flying canoe. It was just a ridiculous fantasy: the aeroplane wouldn't be invented until 1903. But the dream was so powerful it stayed with John well into his adult years. He grew up to become an engineer and inventor, and in 1910 even built his own aircraft, and took it for a test flight. Its wings were sloped back in a v shape, and its

254

engine and propeller were mounted at the back of the plane. Sat out front, John opened the throttle. The thing gathered speed and climbed into the air. With nothing before him except the open skies, John looked down at the flimsy wood-and-canvas nose cone surrounding his legs and suddenly realised he was flying in a canoe-like craft, just like the one he'd seen in his dreams, thirty years before.

This wasn't the only dream John had that subsequently seemed to come true. In 1902 he was serving in the British army in South Africa. In the spring of that year he had a particularly vivid and traumatic nightmare about a catastrophic volcanic explosion on a French-speaking island. Just before he awoke, John found himself pleading with a French official to send help to the island, shouting, '*Listen, four thousand people will be killed.*' This number had come up repeatedly throughout the dream. With the next delivery of papers came the news that Mount Pelee had exploded on the French-speaking island of Martinique. In just three minutes, the island's capital, St Pierre, had been wiped out by a fireball. It was one of the deadliest volcanic events in human history. The Daily Telegraph put the death toll at 40,000, not the 4,000 that was such a feature of John Dunne's dream; somewhere he'd lost a zero, but taken as a whole the similarities between his dream and the real-life event were striking.

Dunne was convinced that these two dreams, (a future view from his own cock-pit, and the unfolding catastrophe on Martinique), were premonitions. Being an engineer, he tried to figure out the mechanism by which his glimpses of the future might have been produced. He eventually came up with a theory that it's not time that moves, it's us. We move through time. And if time is indeed static, then (according to Dunne), past, present and future must all exist simultaneously. This allows us to jump across time and experience premonition. I don't know: the Incas used to believe this, and they don't seem to have much of a future lately. Dunne set out his theory in a book, *An Experiment with Time*, which featured baffling diagrams of lines and arrows going off in all directions. The bottom line for Dunne is that because we can (on rare occasions, such as during his two dreams) inhabit completely different times, we are capable of being outside of time. Independent of it. And we can therefore, according to Dunne, exist across all time; we can be immortal. We just have to die to achieve this.

The next story reads like a lost episode of Downton Abbey. It involves a Duchess called Mary Hamilton, a man by the name of Alfred Cooper and a Lord 'L'. I have been unable to discover his surname. In a letter to the paranormal investigator Frederic Myers dated 6ᵗʰ June 1888, Alfred Cooper wrote that he visited Mary Hamilton two weeks before the death of the man he calls Lord L. At this meeting Mary told Alfred:

> *'I went to bed, but after being in bed a short time, I was not exactly asleep, but thought I saw a scene as if from a play before me. The actors in it were Lord L———, in a chair, as if in a fit, with a man standing over him with a red beard. He was by the side of a bath, over which bath a red lamp was distinctly shown.'*

Cooper told Mary that this Lord L had been a bit rough lately, but he was sure it was nothing serious. Two weeks later Lord L died. Cooper was with him that day and described the scene:

> *There were two male nurses attending on him; one had been taken ill. But when I saw the other, the dream of the Duchess was exactly represented. He was standing near a bath over the Earl and, strange to say, his beard was red. There was the bath with the red lamp over it…It is a most remarkable thing.*

Cooper added that Mary had not heard that Lord L was ill. '*She knew she was not asleep, for she opened her eyes to get rid of the vision and, shutting them, saw the same thing again.*'
Mary Hamilton countersigned the letter.

Mary seems to have been more amused than upset by her vision of Lord L's death scene, but some premonitions are just plain horrible. In his autobiography, *The Long Banana Skin*, the English comedian and writer Michael Bentine described how in the 1930s he and other patients had mistakenly been given an injection of typhoid. One of the men died instantly, and Michael was left in a coma for six weeks. He claimed that when he regained consciousness he was left with a particular and unwanted psychic power: the ability to foresee the death of others. Michael stated that while he was in the Royal Air Force during the Second World War, he could 'see' which of his comrades were about to live or die. When he saw a skull super-imposed over their face, he knew they would not return from their next mission. In later life he had the horror of seeing a skull projected onto the face of his own son, who died shortly afterwards in a plane crash.

Out of Body Experiences

In 1961 Robert Crookall from Dursley in Gloucestershire published over 150 reports he had collected of out-of-body experiences. Here are my favourite three:

In February 1954 Horace Wheatley fell into a coma, during which he found himself *'floating in an atmosphere of peace and serenity.'* Writing from his bed at the Royal Sussex Hospital, Brighton just days later, Horace reports that while he was in this marvellous state,

> *a local government officer I knew quite well came forward to meet me. He greeted me. 'Welcome Wheatley,' he said, and then continued, 'I shall have to see you later'.*

It's reassuring that although they knew each other 'quite well', and were apparently both dead, the man from the council didn't stoop to any first-name nonsense. Horace (if I may call him that), ends his story on this dramatic note:

Now the interesting point about this 'interview' is that at the time I did not know that this friend had 'passed on'. I was told it afterwards by my wife.

Strictly speaking, this is a near-death experience, but as the term didn't exist before 1975, out-of-body experience will do.

Writing in 1931, Frank Hives said that he had been having out-of-the-body experiences for more than twenty years. These journeys happened when he was asleep, or (once), when he was ill. In 1908 Frank was working for the British empire in Nigeria and had been out of contact with England or elsewhere for several weeks. *'So far as I knew, my brother was in New Zealand where he had been settled.... He had not been in my thoughts, for we had little in common.'* Frank went to bed and as he fell asleep, he, *'felt myself gliding away. Then, suddenly, I stood in a field, which I recognized. It was in the meadow adjoining the churchyard at Breamore, in Hampshire.'*

There was snow on the ground and looking down Frank noticed that he was dressed for the tropics in shorts and a thin shirt, yet he felt no cold. He then, *'glided through the thick hedge without feeling that it was there.'* Moving into the churchyard, Frank noticed that he left no footprints in the snow. Beneath a yew tree stood

> *seven or eight people, every one of whom I knew well. I moved a little nearer so that I was close to my sister who was in one of the groups. I spoke to her but she took no notice; nor did any of the others.*

Looking down, Frank saw a coffin with a metal plate bearing his brother's name and date of his birth. *'I knew that he was dead,'* he recalled. The next morning Frank told his fellow officers about his experience:

> *I wrote a description and made a plan of what I had seen. The officers signed both. A month later all the details were confirmed in a letter from my sister in England.*

Frank's brother had returned to England from New Zealand unexpectedly, contracted pneumonia and died within a fortnight at his sister's house in Hampshire. He was buried in Breamore churchyard on the day Frank had his 'experience' (he did not regard it as a dream).

> *Several months later I returned to England and went to stay at Breamore. There I visited the churchyard with my sister and two of the others who had been in the group...as we came around the church I saw the grave, over which the grass had by then grown. It was not at that time marked by a headstone, but I went straight to it and indicated that it was my brother's. And I was quite correct.*

It's a great story, but with everyone involved as dead as the lamp-oil trade, we unfortunately have no way of checking its veracity.

The third case comes from Laura Brisson, who in 1950 recalled something that happened in her youth:

> *In 1918 I received word that my favourite cousin had been killed in a motor accident. I was unable to leave home, and an old friend attended the funeral instead. That night I fell asleep thinking of my cousin. I awoke to find myself lying in a horizontal position about one foot above my body which I could see on the bed below me.*

Laura '*floated* straight out of the house, through the locked front door.

> *Then, in a flash, I found myself standing upright in my cousin's home eighty-six miles from my home. I was in the dining-room and afterwards described the exact position of a night-lamp on the table. I also saw the foot of my cousin's casket, remembered the colour (a grey velour), and also told the exact place in the living-room where he was laid out. I entered a bedroom where my friend was sleeping, approached her, and, intending to awaken her, pulled her arm. Then I remembered that I must be dead and it would startle her if she saw me. So I started to turn away from the bed. Suddenly she*

opened her eyes and saw me. On the instant I found myself back in my room, lying above my body in the horizontal position. It seemed ages before I could force myself back inside it. There seemed to be an opening in the chest through which I entered. It was a most unpleasant experience, as my body felt cold and rigid. When my friend returned from the funeral, she told how she had felt me pull at her arm, awakened, recognized me, and then saw me vanish.

Telepathy

> Sickness will surely take the mind
> Where minds can't usually go
>
> Pete Townsend, Amazing Journey

Head injuries or serious illnesses are more common among people with claimed psychic abilities. Additionally, psychics are more likely to be female, and to have suffered a significant emotional trauma in childhood, often the death of a parent. There's some MRI scan evidence that individuals who believe they have psychic abilities have significantly reduced activity in their brains when they attempt to exercise their channelling powers. This might mean that they are entering the same brain state that is occupied by those who meditate frequently, or that they have some brain malfunction that causes them to see or hear things that aren't there, or (as believers may claim) they are shutting down standard mental activity to make way for signals coming from 'outside'.

No-one has been able to prove the existence of psychic abilities under strict laboratory conditions. To an extent this isn't surprising: our abilities and instincts contribute to our survival as a species. As scientific tests measure the capacity to predict events that have no bearing on survival, such as which symbol is to appear next on a computer screen, or if pictures of tractors or spoons can be mentally transmitted to someone in another room, it is argued that no psychic power is likely to manifest in such circumstances. If

260

telepathy truly exists, it is most likely to show itself *in extremis,* and between people with a very close connection. And the closest any of us can get is to have come from the same egg and to have shared the same womb. To be an identical twin. So, can twins read each other's moods when they are physically separated? In other words, does telepathy really exist?

Identical twins Daphne Goodship and Barbara Herbert were separated at birth in July 1939. Given up for adoption, they spent most of their childhoods unaware they had a twin. Daphne grew up in West Yorkshire and Barbara in Dover. In her adult years Daphne learnt that she had a twin sister, and in 1979, as the result of significant detective work, she and Barbara met for the first time, aged forty. Both women arrived at their reunion in London wearing a beige dress and a brown velvet jacket.

Barbara had been evacuated to the small Hampshire village of Silchester during the Second World War; Daphne moved there later, unaware that it had been home to her sister. Unknown to Daphne, Barbara's maiden name was Sandal; Daphne had moved to Sandal (in West Yorkshire). Both had fallen downstairs at the age of 15. These accidents left them both with a weak ankle. Both were aged sixteen when they met their respective future husbands at town hall dances. Both men worked for the local council at the time, as did Barbara and Daphne. The author Peter Watson listed 31 things that the women had in common, including love of certain food and drinks, identical hand gestures and facial expressions, shared fears of heights and blood, almost identical taste in books and magazines, and a terrible sense of direction.

In another odd coincidence, when interviewed separately by Thomas Bouchard, a researcher into identical twins, Daphne and Barbara reported the same childhood aim, '*We both said we wanted to be opera singers and neither of us can sing a note,*' said Barbara. While carbon-copy gestures and a shared taste in food can be explained by their identical DNA, the reasons why they held the same ambition or came to live in the same small village would seem to lie outside of genetics. But rather than leaping to any conclusions, let's look for more instances of identical twins acting in identical ways.

Identical twins Dorothy Lowe and Bridget Harrison were separated only weeks after their birth in 1945. Dorothy settled in Burnley, and Bridget in Leicester. Until 1979 neither woman knew they were a twin. When they met, they discovered some very interesting coincidences. Dorothy had named her son Richard Andrew; Bridget had named her son Andrew Richard. Dorothy had called her daughter Catherine Louise and Bridget had named her daughter Karen Louise (she had wanted to call her daughter Catherine but switched to Karen in response to a request from a family member.) The strangest coincidence involved the keeping of a diary. For the year 1960, and only for that year, both girls (then aged fourteen) bought a diary. The diaries were the same make and same colour. They went on to fill in the same days, leaving the same days blank. Again, some of these coincidences could be the result of genetics. Perhaps Bridget and Dorothy were both drawn to the sounds made by the names Richard, Andrew, Louise and Catherine as a form of shared musical taste. And, as with Daphne and Barbara's choice of brown and beige, it's likely that DNA could influence the colour of the diary they each decided to buy. It is, though, quite a long shot to say that genetics could tell any of us which day we should write in a diary and which day to leave blank.

The four-time Olympic champion Mo Farah has a twin brother, Hassan. Although they live thousands are miles apart, they each sense when their twin is in difficulty:

> *It's hard to explain to someone who doesn't have a twin, but whenever Hassan is upset, or not feeling well, I'll somehow sense it. The same is true for Hassan when it comes to sensing how I feel. He'll just know when something isn't right with me. Then he'll pick up the phone and call me. Or I'll call him.*

Identical twins Christine and Louise Miller from London experience each other's emotions, and often have the same dream at night. Their embryo split later than normal, which puts them into a super-identical category. Members of this exclusive club are more likely than other identical twins to report spooky types of connections.

Twins Irene Reid and Jeanette Hamilton were born in Glasgow April 1944 and separated just a few weeks later. They did not come into contact again until 1977: Jeanette was living in Paisley and Irene in Leicestershire. Both were employed selling cosmetics, and both were cub pack leaders. Jeanette said,

> *Irene and I both asked for the same Christmas present, a school desk and chair, when we were six. And when we got the presents we both asked: 'Is that all I am getting?'*

Among several other similarities, Irene and Jeanette had scars on the same part of their bodies from childhood accidents. Jeanette had a wasted muscle in her right hip. Although this problem never caused Jeanette any pain, Irene suffered throughout her life from a pain that ran from her healthy right hip down to her knee. No medical cause was ever found for this.

Awareness of a twin's pain or discomfort seems to manifest in the physically fit twin as a genuine sensation rather than a psychic thought. The twin 'feels' their sibling's pain. Other sensations may also become involved. Johnny and Jimmy Cramp were born in 1955. At the age of three, when Jimmy was tickled, his brother Johnny would laugh. In November 1958 Kenneth Main from Gateshead was struck down by chest pain at the hour his identical twin Keith was undergoing heart surgery. Kenneth suffered similar pains on the day Keith's stiches were taken out; Kenneth's discomfort was so severe that his parents took him to the doctors, but no cause for the pain could be found.

Cases of this type are nothing new. In a diary entry dated 7th April 1781, John Wesley, the founder of Methodism, mentions a pair of twin sisters.

Despite their living apart, Wesley noted that, '*if either of them is ill, or particularly affected at any time, the other is so likewise.*' Wesley also commented that the women have identical dreams on the same nights.

In 2004 the Department of Twin Research, based in London, asked 5,512 twins if they had an ability to know what is happening to their twin brother or sister when they are apart. One in five of the identical twins said yes. Wanting to know more, a team of researchers led by Goran Brusewitz interviewed 301 of these twins about their telepathy-like experiences, strange coincidences, shared dreams and swapping of aches and pains. They found that people having one or more of these strange experiences were likely to have been very close to their twin either in childhood or in their adult years, and that twins who share the same dreams were very likely to have had other telepathy-like experiences. Almost half of twins who reported a telepathic experience said that it had occured during a time of pain, illness or injury.

The Bee Gees twin brothers Maurice and Robin experienced several telepathy-like experiences. Maurice recalled Robin having a bike accident:

> *He was riding a bicycle and he had a crash. I didn't; I was at home, but I ended up aching and I wondered what the hell I was aching for. Robin came back and he had bruises in exactly the same places I had mine.*
>
> *When Robin was in the Hither Green train disaster, he was late for a press conference and I said, 'There is something wrong. Something has happened to Robin.' He pulled six people out of a carriage...He laid them on the lawn, and they were all dead. I knew he had been through a strenuous thing—my arms were aching.*

The British author Guy Playfair also interviewed hundreds of the London twins, and published the results in his book *Twin Telepathy.* These are some of the experiences that the twins related to him:

- 'As a child at school I cut my hand badly. Across the room, and completely unaware of what I was doing, my sister reacted to the pain and I thought it was she who had injured herself. It was only when I saw blood I realized it was me. The class and the teacher all remember it — we were about 7 years old'
- 'As teenagers my sister had an operation. I passed out in class and told my mum the time. It matched up with my sister getting her anaesthetic but was earlier than scheduled so I couldn't have 'known'.'
- 'I recall an incident when as a child I injured myself and my sister felt the pain. On another occasion, again as children, when I was under a general anaesthetic, I understand she felt very drowsy'

Playfair gave a shocking reason for his interest in 'twin telepathy':

> I happened to meet a man who had been with his father at the moment his father's twin brother was shot dead 20 miles away. Had he reacted in any way, I wondered? He had indeed. As the son told me: 'We were getting ready to go to my sister's school play, and I was standing in the drawing-room with my father. Suddenly, for no apparent reason, he slumped down into a chair. He looked dazed. I was terrified and thought he had suffered a heart attack. A few minutes later he recovered, the phone rang, and it was the police'.

So in looking at the experiences of twins, it would be fair to say there is poor evidence for telepathy in tests where there is no real crisis. As a rule, for instance, a twin can't guess what playing card her sister/brother is holding behind the screen. But where injury or other physical danger is involved, there is decent evidence of telepathy between twins, something that runs hard against our current understanding of universal physical laws.

The shared dreaming reported by some twins hints at an invisible weaving together of minds, as if brains can become entangled. Although this may be an idea too far for many of us, it is given some support by the fact that identical twins develop from the same fertilised egg, and therefore the same cells that make up that egg and therefore the same tiny molecules that go to make up those cells. We will take a close look shortly at very tiny things, specifically very tiny things that become entangled.

Everything Changes

Top 5 Sitcoms: The Office

I worked in an office for work experience but after 2 days of flagrant slacking they sent me down to the basement to work in filing. It was all dark and dingy and everyone was a bit funny looking and thick. 'I bet you fitted right in then J-Mart!!!' 'HAHAHAHA....yeah, kinda'.

Jack Marteau, Student Direct Magazine, 2009

As anyone who has suffered a sudden tragic bereavement will testify, anything can happen at any moment. The world may appear to be going largely to plan, but chaos is just a car skid, a failed blood vessel or an odd lump away. Life is changed forever in an instant. In 1818, 22-year-old John Keats wrote to his younger brothers George and Tom, '*There is nothing stable in the world; uproar's your only music.*' He was as correct as he had imagined: in three years both he and Tom would be dead.

Change is inevitable: even mountains, given enough time, will erode into dust. So, does nothing stay the same? Going back to Keats, he believed that at least one thing goes on forever: beauty.

> *A thing of beauty is a joy for ever:*
> *Its loveliness increases; it will never*
> *Pass into nothingness*

For Keats, all is secondary to beauty, because beauty outlives all else. It can never die. Writing to his brothers again, Keats says, '*with a great poet*' (he didn't mean himself, but he's right up there) '*the sense of Beauty overcomes every other consideration, or rather obliterates all consideration.*' Keats doesn't claim to have invented this idea. It goes back to the ancient Greeks, and Plato's belief that there are some absolutes in life, things that never change or die. The big ones among these are truth, justice...and beauty. If these things are immortal, says Plato, then the closer we live by them, the more immortal we become. In its way, this idea adds up to a religion, but without the customary gods and demons.

The question remains, what did Keats (and Plato) mean by 'beauty'? Does a beautiful eyebrow count? Hard to say, but Keats gives us an emphatic if circular definition in *Ode to a Grecian Urn:*

> *'Beauty is truth, truth beauty,'*

And truth is permanent. Keats even goes further. He says, *'What the Imagination seizes as Beauty must be truth — whether it existed before or not.'* So something like a beautiful thought or idea is permanent too, despite it having no physical reality. This is getting a bit deep now, so let's escape to shallower waters, to return if we get to feel more clever.

Fellow poet Percy Shelley was deeply upset when John Keats died. He wrote the poem *Adonais* to express this sorrow and to declare what he believed had become of his friend following his death:

> *He is made one with Nature: there is heard*
> *His voice in all her music, from the moan*
> *Of thunder, to the song of night's sweet bird;*
> *He is a presence to be felt and known*
> *In darkness and in light, from herb and stone*

It's a lovely idea, that Keats has been recycled throughout the natural world, but if Shelley were struck by lightning or buried in a rock fall, he might not thank his dear friend for any part he played in the incident. Shelley had an answer to this too: Nature must renew itself; it's Elton John's good old *Circle of Life.* You, me, everybody must accept the losses of today for the gains of tomorrow. Shelley distils this belief to, *'If Winter comes, can Spring be far behind?'* From destruction comes new life. In Shelley's words, Nature (with a capital N) is both *'Destroyer and preserver'.* Shelley was fascinated by India and it's very likely he took this idea from the Hindu deity Shiva Nataraja's cosmic dance that simultaneously destroys and creates the universe in a whirl of two legs and several arms. Shelley had opportunities to fire-test his belief in the value of destruction: his first wife took her own life (after Shelley had left her), and he and his second wife Mary lost three of their children. There's a serving of poetic irony in Percy's own death: his boat capsized, and he was taken by Nature's great force and asset, the sea.

In *The Prelude*, William Wordsworth writes of a sense he has that everything is alive

> *To every natural form, rock, fruits, or flower, Even the loose stones that cover the highway, I gave a moral life: I saw them feel*

It seems reasonable that if something is alive, it might have some kind of feelings, but when it comes to gravel Wordsworth seems to have gone too far for most of us; perhaps he should have stopped at daffodils. And even there, he believes, '*every flower enjoys the air it breathes.*' it's tempting just to think, 'What a prat.' But to be fair to Wordsworth, this is how he feels: that all of planet earth is alive. I have to be brave here and support him: as I mentioned earlier, at the age of 40 I suddenly started seeing auras: a glowing light outlining people's head and shoulders, a yellow/white fringe that extends four inches or so around their outline. Although I'd heard about auras, I'd never particularly believed in them nor ever wished to see one. Things got weirder when I noticed that trees had them too, and even non-living things like items of furniture. So, as much as it embarrasses me, I have to say that I think Wordsworth is right when he says that rocks have emotions. My settee is looking a bit depressed.

Wordsworth and his 19th Century rhyming buddies would have been delighted by the Gaia theory developed by Brixton scientist James Lovelock in the 1960s. Lovelock says the earth is a single system, a living organism of sorts that adapts to maintain life on the planet. We are part of that life, but if we get too numerous or misuse the planet, we might find that Gaia (the earth) decides she'd be better off without us. The scientific community scoffed at Gaia theory fifty years ago, but the development of climate science related to global warming has meant no-one is mocking Lovelock now. To an extent, and definitely against James Lovelock's wishes, his Gaia idea is being turned into a kind of modern pagan religion, with people coming to see the earth as a wise but vulnerable being. A fragile goddess. But instead of offering a slaughtered lamb or valuable jewellery to please her, they choose to sacrifice their large-engine car or the long-haul flight they'd been fancying. Some critics of Gaia theory argue that the earth can't be a living organism because it cannot reproduce. A cute counter to this objection points out that humanity is planning to colonise Mars and probably other planets too, creating new Earths in the process. Viewed this way, we are the spores of Gaia. It's nice to have a purpose.

If Keats really was transformed into a bolt of lightning, there's an equal chance that most of us can change into an insect. 2,400 years ago the Zen master Zhuangzi wrote, *'Once upon a time, I dreamt I was a butterfly…Now I do not know whether I was then a man dreaming I was a butterfly, or whether I am now a butterfly, dreaming I am a man.'* Most people would say, you're a man you div: butterflies can't write. But William Blake could see what Zhuangzi was driving at. He gets all Zen-like in his poem *The Fly*:

> *Am not I*
> *A fly like thee?*
> *Or art not thou*
> *A man like me?*

He was up all night writing that one. But do things have to be either one thing or the other? Can't they be both? Blake sees this is an option too. To his mind, everything is everything else: *'I have said to the Worm: Thou art my mother & my sister.'*

Robert Browning, another 19th century poet (how many were there back then?) sees *'God in the star, in the stone, in the flesh, in the soul and the clod.'* This thought appears to have been influenced by a line in the Hindu

Bhagavad Gita: 'a clod of dirt, a stone, and gold are the same.' It had been written two thousand years earlier but must have spoken to Browning.

Keats has a similar thought, that everything is everything else:

> *we stept into a sort of oneness, and our state Is like a floating spirit's*

With their notions that dead friends might be recycled as herbs, or that gravel has feelings too, 19th century artists were starting to encroach on the dominion of science. There'd been a turf war going on for some time: Isaac Newton, for instance, argued that mathematicians were best placed to explain and describe colour. This sort of thinking drove Blake and other poets and artists nuts: How can a beautiful crimson rose be reduced to a sequence of numbers and squiggles? But this is the unromantic path that has led to digital photography, which converts a flower into a viable code. Even our own DNA has been broken down into a list of alpha-numerics. Newton saw no point in art, dismissing sculpture as simply the making of '*stone dolls*', and calling poetry, '*ingenious nonsense.*' Keats fought back for poems, having a dig at science, which he calls '*philosophy*':

> *Philosophy will clip an Angel's wings,*
> *Conquer all mysteries by rule and line,*
> *Empty the haunted air, and gnomèd mine—*
> *Unweave a rainbow*

Thanks to science, we now know that mines aren't inhabited by gnomes, but Keats needn't have worried overmuch about scientists killing all the magic in the world, because as we shall see in the next chapter, science now seems to have found evidence that supports the biggest idea of the Romantic poets, that a life force, even a mind, can be found in everything.

Top 5 Time Travel Movies: Back to the Future (1985)

Best movie ever. They should stop trying to make better films. I hope time travel is never actually invented, because someone might do something that stops this film getting made.

Jack Marteau   Student Direct Magazine 2009

If we are to gain a deeper understanding of death, we need to work out what we mean by its opposite, life. There are obvious definitions, involving growth or reproduction, but what is a life, what is existence? What is reality? The area of science that can probably offer the best chance of answering these questions is physics. Unfortunately, this means things have to get considerably more complicated now. If you reach a state of total confusion during this chapter, please feel free to skip to the next. I wish I could.

In using physics to figure out existence, it's worth bearing this comforting thought in mind: everything we thought we knew about existence might comfortably be wrong. But there are, however, two things we can say with some confidence about existence: We know almost nothing. We are almost nothing.

There was a common belief towards the end of the Victorian era that all the major discoveries in physics had already been made. At that point the English were satisfied that everything that looked solid enough, including ourselves, was indeed solid. But all of this was changed forever in the first half of the 20th century with the study of the atom, which led to the bizarre but serious conclusion that reality itself may depend on us being around to bring it into existence. Our first hint that this world may not be as real as every ounce of common sense tells us it must be, came three hundred years ago, via clergyman and philosopher Bishop George Berkeley. Berkeley wrote, '*all those bodies which compose the mighty frame of the world, have not any subsistence without a mind.*'

This sort of thinking can be traced back 2,400 years, when a Greek philosopher called Gorgias made the bold statement that nothing truly exists, not even Joey Essex. The Greeks loved coming up with way-out ideas and then debating how true or false they might be. We English prefer not to bother. When someone like Berkley claims it's doubtful that even something as solid as a table really exists, we're likely just to mutter, '*Of course it does, otherwise our dinner would fall off,*' and immediately go off to do something useful instead, like painting a shed. Dr Samuel Johnson, the funniest Englishman alive during Berkley's lifetime, thought the idea there's no such thing as a solid object was straight-up rubbish. Famously, he gave a large rock a full-blooded kick and as his foot rebounded in pain, said, '*I refute it thus.*'

But it turns out that Berkley may have been onto something. Because they are built from atoms, Samuel Johnson's sore foot, the rock and every other solid object are almost nothing but empty space. As we were told at school. an atom is a little like a sphere, with a tiny nucleus right in the centre, an outside skin of electrons, and a huge lot of nothing in-between. To give us an idea of how much nothing this involves, if we imagine that an atom is the size of St Paul's cathedral, the nucleus at its core would be no bigger than a grain of sand. The walls, floor and roof that represent the cloud of electrons that orbit the nucleus would be as fine as mist, more than 1,000 times thinner than the nucleus. As our bodies are made entirely from atoms, we are therefore at least 99.999999999999% nothing. The reason why Samuel Johnson's foot didn't pass straight through the rock was not because either the rock or his foot were solid, but because atoms that make up Dr Johnson's foot and the atoms in the rock acted like the wrong ends of two magnets, refusing to be pressed together (this repulsion is due to all electrons having a negative electrical charge). This same electron charge allows us to sit supported on a chair. Without this force, we'd pass straight through the chair, and the chair would pass straight through us: a nice mess.

Anyway, seeing as no more than 0.000000000001% of us is solid stuff, (and probably far less, if we allow for the gaps between atoms), how is it we feel far more significant than that? Is it just ego? In fact, we are significantly more significant than that. Because atoms contain a huge amount of energy, (as demonstrated by nuclear power stations or atomic weapons), we are a massive bundle of energy. Hard to imagine when we look around at one another dozing in front of the telly, but each of us is composed of more energy than the combined output of all power stations in the country across an entire year, (around seven hundred quintillion joules).

We were already waking up to the strange fact that we are almost nothing but energy in 1872, when the scientist and engineer William Thomson said, *'motion is the very essence of what has hitherto been called matter.'* In other words, matter, the brick and mortar of life, is basically energy. Einstein set this thought in scientific stone with his famous equation $e=mc^2$ ('e' being energy and 'm' being mass or matter. 'C' is the speed of light, but you'd have to ask him why that's in there. Same goes for the '2'). Essentially, the speed of light squared is a huge number, so the equation tells us that even a minute quantity of matter (Blake's grain of sand, for instance) can be converted into a vast amount of energy.

But Einstein went deeper and further. Speaking at Nottingham University on 6th June 1930, Albert told the audience, *'We have now come to the conclusion that space is the primary thing and matter only secondary.'* This is a very exciting thought. As anyone with a telescope will tell us, space looks to be very empty, and certainly see-through. There's far more nothing than something out there. If Einstein is right, all that nothing is really something. Something very significant. The invisible is more important than the visible. The empty world is more important than the solid one. All conscious activity is invisible, so assuming again Einstein is correct, thoughts may be more important than Neptune or Saturn. Or Earth. The English scientist

James Jeans, also writing in 1930, saw things this way: *'the universe begins to look more like a great thought, than a great machine.'*

Towards the end of his life Shakespeare had been coming to similar conclusions. In what is believed to be his last solo play, *The Tempest*, Prospero is certain we are no more solid than dreams, our whole lives contained within a bout of sleep: *'We are such stuff as dreams are made on; and our little life is rounded with a sleep.'* In the imagination of an ageing Shakespeare, our dreams as well as our thoughts are as real as the solid world we live in, and he wonders if we may be no more than characters or *'shadows'* in some other being's dream.

Getting back to the importance of the invisible, the entire matter of the known universe, the billions upon billions of stars, gas clouds, planets and sundry rocks, add up to 5% of what we know is really out there. The rest is an invisible riddle that we call dark energy and dark matter. Clever people know this dark stuff is out there, because they have measured individual galaxies being squeezed together and the universe as a whole being stretched apart by unseen forces. It is dark matter doing the squeezing and dark energy doing the stretching. Unfortunately, no-one is clever enough to say what any of this dark stuff is. Never mind. Let's just be happy to say that 95% of the universe is a complete mystery to us. So, how much of the known universe, that 5%, have we absolutely figured out? Despite the incredible achievements of the ancient Egyptians, the Greeks, the astronomers of Islam, India and China, Copernicus, Galileo, Newton and others, the answer is not so much. In the first half of the 20th century Einstein's best estimate was that we know less than *'one thousandth of one percent of what nature has revealed to us.'* It's reassuring that we know almost nothing. We can keep an open mind, while being careful not to assume that every mysterious light in the sky comes from a flying saucer piloted by the tooth fairy.

Moving forward a century or so from Bishop Berkley and his 'tables and chairs only exist in the mind' idea, we arrive in Somerset in 1802 and a man by the name of Thomas Young. At that time, it was believed that a light beam was made up of a stream of particles, like a string of microscopic pearls. Young tested this idea by shining a beam of sunlight at a timber board with two slits cut through it. The slits were side-by-side, identical and extremely narrow (each the width of a human hair). The beam of light shone through these two slits and hit a plain black screen he had put up behind it. The beam hit this screen not (as everyone would expect) in just two places, but in several spots, spaced at regular points across the width of the screen. It also left some parts of the screen unlit. The screen had become striped, like a zebra's coat. Young repeated the experiment, but this time using a shallow tray of water, split into two by a dividing wall. This wall also had two similar narrow slits cut through it. Young pushed the water in a wave towards the dividing wall. As it passed through the slits in that wall, the wave turned into a series of ripples. These ripples progressed to hit the far side of the tray at the same points as the sunlight had hit the screen. So light is a wave, not a particle!

Super-positioning

It turns out that Young was three-quarters right. Repeating his experiment today with modern equipment, we discover that light can be a wave or a particle, depending on who is around at the time. When a single particle of light is fired at both slits AND someone watches both slits carefully, the light only goes through one of them, so at that moment it is a particle and not a wave. But as soon as someone stops watching, the light goes back to passing through both slits at the same time. A particle, like a person, can never be in two places at the same time, but a wave can: we can watch the same wave moving and breaking across the entire width of a beach.

The self-same thing happens with another tiny particle, the electron. If it is fired at a wall with two slits, the electron goes through both slits at the same time and makes Young's zebra-coat pattern on the screen behind, but if someone watches the slits, it innocently passes through just one of them, like a smuggler whistling as he walks through an airport Nothing to Declare gate.

This early 20th century discovery has had a massive impact on the way we understand existence. Light beams and electrons are two of the most important building blocks of reality. Without light nothing can exist, and without electrons there can be no atoms, no molecules, no minerals, plants, animals, air; no us.

Although he didn't know it, Thomas Young had stumbled upon a vital part of what is now known as Quantum Physics. Quantum physics can be translated as the strange things that happen with very, very small things. Particles turning into waves is known as super-positioning, because when they are waves, they seem to go anywhere and everywhere at the same time. They're not in one position or another, but they may be in any position. So they're in super-position, that is until we look at them again, and they're particles, in just one position, and not in super-position any more. What could be simpler than that?

For the past 100 years brilliant scientists from around the world have tried without success to fathom out why and how atomic particles change when someone looks at them. There are two main possible explanations. Either:
1. the person who is looking at the slits somehow causes a wave of light or electron wave to become a single particle, just by looking at it, or
2. The light or electron know they are being looked at, and so they decide to appear in one place.

Explanation number one is pretty crazy. If it's found to be true, it means that to some extent we build reality. It can't work on a bigger scale: a shoal of mackerel doesn't condense into a single fish when we turn to look at it, but for some reason this sort of thing happens in the world of the extremely small. And consciousness – aliveness – is so small that no-one's spotted it yet.

Explanation number two, that tiny particles somehow know they are being looked at, is even crazier. If it's true, then the tiniest, most common objects in the universe are conscious, are aware.

So is this such a big deal? Is it worth reading the rest of this nightmare chapter? Well, the deal is big because it opens the door to some fascinating possibilities. To understand what these might be, we should look to the second (and thankfully last) strange property of quantum physics: entanglement.

Entanglement

We know there is this strange thing going on where an electron or a light particle is vibrating around everywhere and anywhere (in 'super-position') until we look at it. Next, there is an arrangement where two or more particles have blended together. It seems to be something to do with their wave patterns merging. Anyway, they become joined up, and are said to be 'entangled.' Whatever then happens to one of these particles will affect the other. If these twin entangled particles are then carefully teased apart from one another and taken in different direction, they will still influence each other, even from opposite ends of a city, or a mid-sized nation.

How do we know that they influence each other when they are miles apart? The answer comes from the fact that particles spin in a certain direction. Electrons, for instance, either spin upwards, or spin downwards. I don't know why, they just do. It's a fifty-fifty chance that an electron will be 'spin up', and the same odds that it will be 'spin down'. Once one of these tangled up electrons is passed through a magnet to discover its spin (let's say it turns out to be 'spin up'), then its partner electron will instantly become spin down. The odds of the second electron being spin down would have been 50/50, but because it is entangled, and its partner is spin up, it is 100% guaranteed to become spin down. This happens instantly, even if the two particles are located miles apart. The current world record for particles being apart but still entangled is 1,200km.

So how do they do it? People wondered if the particle that's first to go under the detection magnet sends some signal to the other one, telling it what spin direction to take. It turns out that this is impossible. The change happens instantaneously. It has been calculated that this means the first particle would need to send a message to its partner at 10,000 times the speed of light, and nothing can travel faster than the speed of light, so that's not the reason. Although they may be at separate ends of the country, these particles are somehow still connected, and most physicists now believe that there has to be another, undiscovered dimension that provides the bridge between the two particles.

Quantum scientists have a name for the place where these two separated particles contact one another. They call it nonlocality. Non-locality really means 'not any place we know of'. It's almost a shrug of the shoulders. These particles are definitely connected, but not in any three-dimensional space. They are connected in non-space. But it gets stranger. Just as particles can be connected in non-space, it turns out they can be connected in non-time too. An Israeli called Eli Megidish and five workmates managed to entangle two light particles even though they'd never existed at the same time (the first light particle was already dead by the time its partner was created).

So quantum physics has now taught us that just as space exists, so too does non-space. And just as time exists, so too does non-time. Things can be hundreds of miles apart and not apart at all. Things can exist at different times, and yet be physically joined together. And perhaps it has also told us that the tiniest nuts and bolts of the universe – particles – seem to know what's going on. It turns out that reality, existence, is very odd. Shockingly odd.

Is Everything Alive?

More than just bobbing up and down like ocean waves, electrons and light particles vibrate, as if they have some life force within them. As the universe

279

is filled with light and electrons, this would mean that everything might, in some sense, be alive. Sounds improbable, I agree. A scientist from Nottinghamshire, Rupert Sheldrake sees this vibration (or 'oscillation') at every level of matter *'Atoms, molecules, crystals, organelles, cells, tissues, organs and organisms are all made up of parts in ceaseless oscillation, and all have their own characteristic patterns of vibration and internal rhythm'.* In a way, they've all got their own dance. As physics has discovered that matter is energy, we should expect it to vibrate. It would be more of a surprise if it didn't fidget a bit. Everything, therefore, is lively, but does that mean that everything is alive? Robots are pretty lively, but do they have a life?

Roger Penrose is a mathematician from Essex who has spent some time wondering if computerised robots can ever come completely to life, to think, feel and act the way humans do. This Artificial Intelligence question is a worrying modern-day problem: we already have enough dangerous clowns on the planet without someone building extra mechanical ones. But Penrose is an optimist: he believes that while we can rely on computers to compute, they will never be able to understand things the way we do. He thinks there's something inside us that gets/feels/understands existence in a way that no computer ever could. And Penrose thinks that this something happens at this microscopic quantum level. After all, if tiny electrons and light particles seem to know when something's going on, why shouldn't our own atomic components? We are, when all's said and done, held together by electrons. In the 1990s he started work with Steve Hameroff from Arizona to develop the idea that this sense of existence we humans possess comes from deep inside our individual brain cells, in things called microtubules. Microtubules are, as the name suggest, tiny tubes. They link together like internal scaffolding poles, giving structure to a cell. According to Penrose and Hameroff, as well as acting as miniature skeletons, these microtubules also send and receive information, using the same vibrating now-you-see-us, now-you-don't actions of electrons. In other words, through super-positioning. Our brains, according to Penrose and Hameroff, can enter quantum states.

This idea has made Penrose and Hameroff a laughing stock in the worlds of physics and biology. A sort of scientific Ant and Dec. Almost everyone else in a white coat prefers to believe that consciousness, knowing that we are alive, is a result of our eighty-five billion brain cells combining all their processing power to make a person smart enough to work out that she's called Katie and it's Wednesday. If, like a cat, we had 300 million brain cells, we'd maybe still know our name was Katie, but we wouldn't have a clue about days of the week. If we were a mouse, we'd have around 75 million brain cells, and we couldn't know if we had a name. If we had no brain cells whatsoever, as is the case with slime mold, (Physarum polycephalum), then we'd expect to be dimmer than a potato. How smart does slime need to be anyway?

But, as Penrose and Hameroff would be more than happy to point out, slime mold is very bright. She/he can find the right things to eat, slide away from danger and, when times are hard, reproduce, a blend of skills that can challenge the best of us. But it turns out that slime mold can also find its way around a maze, is capable of designing rail and road networks, and has even helped Airbus design airplane partitions that are every bit as strong but only half the weight of those in current use. I promise you, all of this is true. There's even a musician in Plymouth, Eduardo Miranda, who is duetting with slime mold to produce improvised compositions. And more than this, slime mold likes to party: when Andrew Adamatzky from the University of the West of England offered it a choice between its favourite food (dried oats and honey) and a drug (valerian tablets), the slime mold stuck out a couple of slow-moving arms and encircled the pills in a 'This is my stash!' embrace.

So, not only does slime mold seem to have a mind, it likes to get out of that mind now and then. How does slime mold pull all this off without owning so much as a single brain cell? Microtubules of course, say Ant and Dec. It's an implausible explanation: for the last hundred years just about everyone with a clue as to what a quantum state might be has been certain that the human body is no place for it to occur. It's too warm and wet. But over in Japan a man called Anirban Bandyopadhyay had been reading about Penrose and Hameroff's idea, and decided to put it to the test. He attached electrodes to microtubules, and even put one of the planet's tiniest probes inside one, and in 2013 he and his scientific team announced that they had detected quantum state activity (i.e. vibrating super-position-y, entanglement-y stuff) in the microtubules of living cells. Penrose and Hameroff felt pretty smug at this point, and the rest of the physics community went off muttering to themselves.

So what does all that tell us? First, that our brains might be able to enter a quantum state, allowing us to employ the quantum tricks we've just looked at: super-positioning and entanglement. Entanglement doesn't last long at all: usually a split second, although the current record is one hour, so if there is some contact that can be made between a tiny part of us and some other particle out there in non-space and non-time, then that contact would be over pretty quickly. For now, let's just keep this whole quantum mind thing up our non-sleeves and return to it when we come to look at personal accounts from persons who have been very close to death.

Going back to the potato. It's not as dim as it seems either. It can juggle light-waves to split water into hydrogen and oxygen. We would love to do this with anything near its level of efficiency, as free hydrogen from sunlight would solve a fat chunk of our energy and carbon emissions problems overnight, but we are not smart enough to replicate the plant's talent, despite it having (like slime mold) no brain cells at all.

But let's not abandon the human brain just because it's been outwitted by a potato. It is still an incredible piece of equipment: an organ so clever it even presumes to study itself. It's hard to imagine a kidney trying that.

The Brain

The human brain is very energy-hungry; it burns up a quarter of all the calories we consume, supporting the idea that our thoughts are a form of energy. And so too are the brains that produced those thoughts. And if thoughts and brains are essentially forms of energy, then thoughts are just as real as brains. Just as songs are produced by the vocal cords, thoughts are produced by consciousness. We can, therefore, reason that consciousness is energy. Which would mean that consciousness is every bit as real as the earth, the moon and the sun. Sounds daft, but that's where some schools of physics lead us. We talk about people having warm, or bubbly, or forceful personalities. All of these words relate closely to energy. A next step would be to wonder if personality isn't a form of energy too. It's produced by or, at the very least, held within the brain, so this seems like a reasonable thought. As energy cannot be destroyed (this is known as the law of conservation of energy), this would suggest that personality cannot simply vanish when a person dies: if the human personality is a type of energy, it must turn into something else. Science suggests, unfortunately, that that 'something else' may just be fresh compost. Never mind, let's carry on.

As we've found, the brain contains some 85 billion nerve cells or neurons. Each neuron has, on average, direct connection to 10,000 other neurons, so the brain's capacity to communicate information is very substantial. The brain's main tasks are to piece together reality and to help us survive. This work is shared between many separate areas of the brain, in a lightning-fast shuttle of chemical and electrical signals. The use of medical imaging machines such as MRI scanners has allowed us to reach a deeper understanding of the workings of the brain, but how far have we come to actually locating *us*, the part of our brain that makes us a true individual, different from every other person on earth? There are some brain regions that have been found to be larger among people with certain characteristics: very sociable people tend, for instance, to have a bigger medial orbit frontal cortex (a part of the brain located behind and just above the eyes). The lateral prefrontal cortex, an area just behind the forehead, tends to be larger among hard workers. These suggest characteristics, or personality traits, but as there are probably a billion homo sapiens alive today who are outgoing grafting types, we have to say that brain studies haven't got us very close to finding our individual selves.

Who are we anyway? If we are just highly evolved meat, a bunch of brain cells coming together and forming a Millie or Jim, how is it that we can be so annoying sometimes? We even get on our own nerves. And when this happens, who is it exactly that is getting so annoyed at us? We can argue that it is our mind, our personality, but what is this 'mind'? Is it just the brain in action?

Perhaps we're looking in the wrong place. Many cultures have developed a belief that we are located in the heart rather than the brain. This idea is given some strength by our tendency to clutch ourselves around the chest when we are in shock or deep sorrow, or to experience actual heartache when we lose a loved one. The heart has around 40,000 neurons of its own, and some scientists believe it is so intelligent that it generates decisions of its own (obliging us to choose between our heads or our hearts). We talk about gut feelings, and this is with good reason too: 95% of our stock of serotonin, a key chemical in the communication of emotion, is located in our bowels. So perhaps IBS is simply our body trying to tell us something. We'll be listening to our elbows next.

Even if we can't be sure that the brain is the absolute centre of us, we know that it's the organ we use to express ourselves: without a brain we couldn't say what we feel, or 'speak' with our eyes. That said, we can deceive others with earnest looks and outright lies, while other parts of us, particularly our posture, sweaty hands or restless feet, tend to tell the truth. This is why police officers are trained to observe body language, and lie detectors are attached to the skin rather than the vocal cords.

So, we can say that by its structure and working, the brain reflects some of its owner's personality, but we don't know where it keeps this personality; it helps us express and experience some of our emotions, but the brain is not necessarily the place where these emotions well up; it is the location for thinking, but it appears that not all thinking happens in the brain. Well, what about consciousness, the very spark of life, surely the brain is the wellspring of that?

Consciousness: the sense that we exist

Most neuro-scientists here in England would agree that consciousness comes from the brain. The brain creates it. Clearly. But when we ask ourselves the question, How does the brain do this; what is the mechanism?, things turn opaque. The simple answer is that no-one knows. The distinguished brain scientist Susan Greenfield from London feels that there's no 'centre' for consciousness. She also feels that consciousness is impossible to define: it's not something we do, it just is a something. An awareness of existence. Was that a definition? Probably not.

If brain cells produce consciousness, who or what is telling them to do that? If we want to concentrate on something such as reading a book or wondering how our daughter is doing at school today, the parts of our brains that are required to do this work jump into action (the visual and word recognition centres when reading a book, and the empathic and imaginative brain regions for thinking of our daughter). In these two examples, we, our minds, seem to have prodded our brain cells into action, rather than the other way around.

This feels like the right order of things, that we are in charge of our brains. It plays into our sense of importance and free will. If we are not in control of our brains, how can we hope to be in control of our lives? Well, there may be some bad news for us on that front. In 2008, a team of researchers gave some people a button to press and rolled them into a brain scanner.

285

Each volunteer was asked to make a choice to press the button with either their right or left hand, and to go ahead and press that button the instant they had made their choice. By monitoring the volunteers' brain activity on a screen, the researchers were able to tell which hand the participant would choose 7 SECONDS before the participant was aware of coming to a decision. While the volunteers were still thinking hard about which hand to use, their unconscious mind had already decided. '*By the time consciousness kicks in, most of the work has already been done*,' said John-Dylan Haynes, a member of the research team.

So, if someone asks us what we want to do at the weekend, we might fill a kettle, put it on, and get a couple of cups out while we carefully consider over our options. But in reality, we had already made up our minds before we'd reached for the tap. It's just that our brains hadn't told us. So if *we* make a decision before *we* know about it, who exactly are *we*? Our brain's next-door neighbour? Or the lodger? The psychologist Roy Baumeister calculated that we only have a truly conscious say in 5% of our actions. The remaining 95% of our behaviour is driven by our non-conscious minds. Did we even decide we wanted that cup of tea?

Jonathan Evans, psychology professor at the university of Plymouth, believes we have two minds, one very old and other new. Our older mind is the one that has helped us survive since we were fish or even bacteria. It works very fast, makes snap decisions and carries a fund of ready emotions: fear, anger, disgust and desire. The new mind has turned up relatively recently and is therefore distinctly human. It ponders subjects, asks itself questions about them, and uses stored knowledge to come to reasoned conclusions. It is capable of experiencing more subtle emotions such as regret, contemplation and disappointment.

Our old mind sees someone and forms an instant opinion of them, '*I didn't like him from the moment I clapped eyes on him*' or '*It was love at first sight.*' The old mind doesn't stop to ask why it dislikes someone or falls in love with someone else. Only later might its owner work out that they had

286

taken an instant dislike to someone because he looked just like a schoolteacher they'd hated. Similarly, love at first sight may be no more than attraction caused by the admired person's resemblance to an absent parent. Put simply, the old mind is prone to bias.

The new mind is slower and more rational. It's the new mind that thinks things through, sees the pitfalls of some of the old mind's rash choices, and uses reasoning to work out what's best. (*'I didn't like the look of him, but he's actually quite kind, so I'd judged him unfairly'* and *'I thought we were soulmates but looking back I realise I knew hardly anything about him'*). The great thing about the old mind is that it's permanently on duty, watching and listening for any sign of danger. Any strange noise at night will have the old brain shaking us out of our sleep to investigate. Because it demands so little energy and no conscious effort, we are often completely unaware of its endeavours. The new brain, however, requires quite a lot of heft, and so tends to stay off line, leaving the old brain to manage the shop. When asked if we want our sandwich made with white bread or brown, our old mind is happy to choose, sparing the new mind all the trouble of reflecting on relative levels of gluten, vitamin content, fibre and calorific value. But some tasks the new brain can't leave to its old neighbour. If we are asked, for instance, to mentally calculate 47 multiplied by 83, the old brain will refuse to get involved: this work is new brain territory, and it takes some mental puff for it to reach the correct answer.

Does this truly mean we have two minds, as opposed to one with two distinct ways of working? Evans puts it this way:

> *If I am having a conversation in a crowded room and someone across the room says my name, my attention will immediately switch to the other conversation, even though I was not consciously hearing it. So it was not 'I' who heard my name and it was not 'I' who decided to switch attention. So it cannot really be 'me' (the conscious self) who is in control!*

Evans' theory goes some way to explaining addictive behaviour, where our rational *new mind* self has resolved to quit gambling or drinking but is powerless to stop our more pleasure-driven *old mind* self from returning to these forbidden activities.

All the time we are awake and going about our daily lives, we can't know what our unconscious mind is thinking; we have to trust it has our own best interests at heart. A way to test if this is the case would be to get our unconscious mind to talk, and the only way to do this is to be hypnotised, affording our unconscious mind the opportunity to turn up and speak for itself. With this intention, the hypnotherapist Joe Keaton would often ask a deeply hypnotised volunteer what he or she felt about their daytime partner, the conscious mind. As it turns out, our unconscious mind doesn't think too much to us. Andrew Selby, who witnessed Keaton's hypnosis sessions, put it this way:

> *the person's unconscious ranged from stating that it had little time for its own conscious mind, to all but being highly derogatory about it.*

So basically, dear reader, our unconscious minds can be treacherous companions. An enemy within. Next time we ask ourselves, '*Why the hell did I do that?*', we might do well to remember that there are at two 'I's' involved, and the one that's probably to blame is keeping his/her head down and saying nothing.

Just as we begin to entertain the notion that we each have two minds, we may have to increase that number to four. Although most of our mental activities, planning a meal for instance, involve areas from right across the brain, a general pattern becomes clear from studies of how mental work is shared: the brain has two significantly different halves. The left half (or 'hemisphere') is often emotionally cool and decisive; the right hemisphere tends to be more relaxed and creative. The left is competitive and ambituous, looking to use its environment for personal gain, while the right side has a sense of humour and puts a high value on the natural world and our relationships with others. The left is excellent at analysing objects and systems, working out how they work, but the right side is able to see a wider picture. The right comes across as the more likeable side, but you couldn't trust it to organise something as simple as a bus ride into town. In short we, need both sides, sides that – as we shall find – often hold widely differing views.

The brain scientist Jill Bolte Taylor suffered a severe stroke that incapacitated the left half of her brain; for a while only the right side worked. And it turns out the right side of our brain doesn't have much idea of self:

> *I looked down at my arm and I realise that I can no longer define the boundaries of my body. I can't define where I begin and where I end, because the moleclues and the atoms of my arm blended with the molecules and atoms of the wall....I felt at one with all the energy that was, and it was beautiful there.*

All very lovely, but as the right side of the brain is very impractical, it neglected to tell her to call an ambulance. As a result, Jill almost died.

Like the narrow section of a walnut kernel that joins the two halves of the nut, the left and right sections of the brain are bridged by a slim tube of tissue called the Corpus Callosum. It is the major junction for the millions of signals that constantly shuttle between the two halves of our brain. As a desparate cure for some extreme types of epilepsy, surgeons will cut right through the Corpus Callosum. The operation almost completely separates the two halves of a patient's brain. This can bring comic results, with the alarmed patient finding herself in a full-blooded tug of war with herself when she reaches out for an item of clothing to put on, or for a piece of food. Each half of our brain has control of one arm, allowing a person who has had this radical operation to arm wrestle herself when the two sides disagree on what to wear or eat.

To complicate matters, speech is controlled by just one side of the brain, the left, giving it full control over whichever opinion is to be voiced. If the right brain disagrees strongly with what its next door neighbour is saying, it may resort to using the one hand it controls to smother the mouth and thereby gag the propaganda of its rival. Again, some people who have had their Corpus Callosum cut through have found themselves acting this way. They have even been known to fight with themselves for control of the car's steering wheel as a result of a divided opinion on where they should go; for this reason patients are advised not to drive for a while after the surgery, allowing the brain enough time to build new communication routes between its two sides.

Many of our everyday choices are the outcome of internal wrangles between the two halves of our brain, but because the organ is usually able to resolve these squabbles outside of our awareness, we can convince ourselves we have a single mind. We are single-minded. This idea falls apart, however, when we are forced to make tougher personal choices (Shall we go out with friends, or do our family duty? Do we share a piece of good luck, or keep the windfall to ourselves? Do we stay with our partner, or end the whole thing?) We fluctuate between the two ends of these dilemmas, either decision appearing to be the correct one depending on which half of our brain has the current upper hand. The right brain may, for instance, argue that persisting with a troubled marriage can only bring futher unhappiness to both parties, while the left brain urges, '*Keep in the relationship: divorce costs a fortune!*'

The above examples are confined to the conscious parts of our brain; if we add the unconscious work being done by both the right and left halves, then we have a total of four minds to satisfy. We can't know about any unconscious struggle our brain has with itself. We cannot be conscious of the unconscious. We only have clues. The fact that we can become sick when we are facing a big life problem suggests that there are storms raging at the bottom of our mental ocean. Distressing dreams also hint at major unconscious conflict. Dreaming, moreover, is a game that requires two unconscious players: somone to scripwrite our crazy nightly dramas, and another that has to live through each weird story. The fact that we are completely taken in by our dreams, experiencing terror, joy or panic as their plots unfold, suggests that two distinct minds are at work: one belonging to a playwrite and the other to the enforced audience member.

Admitting to ourselves we have four minds is difficult, not least because we can't be sure which of the four is doing the admitting, or indeed if there truly is an *ourself.* Rather than being a single, complete entity, might *ourself* simply be a marionette, acting out the compromises that have been agreed among the four constituent parts. A kind of walking, talking consensus? The Eastern notion that the whole 'self' idea is a delusion holds some credibility in this context.

But I don't truly feel that I'm several people. Deep down I have the strong sense that I am just the one single person, albeit a person who can have trouble making his mind up. Or making up his minds, as now seems to be the case. But still, I like to believe there is just one *me*, just one overall mind. I imagine most of us prefer this idea. Even people with Multiple Personality Disorder cook just the one evening meal. Does that mean that the absolute *me* is a synthesis of two, three or, as seems likely, four separate or partial *me's*? How does this fit with research that shows that we are unaware of 95% of our brain's activity, that the unconscious holds the whip hand? The answer would have to be that if there is one overall *me*, it is more likely to be an unconscious self. As much as I might declare, '*Look, I am me*,' there is a subterranean me that is quite content to say to itself, '*No, you're not, little fella.*' Swami Vivekananda, the Indian scholar who shook up Victorian England, would tell me I'm confused because I have been looking for me in all the wrong places: '*There is no such thing as freedom of the mind*', he said flatly, '*What do I care if the mind is controlled or uncontrolled! Let it run on. What of that! I am not the mind, let it go on!*'

The best handle science has on consciousness right now is the idea that it emerges from the collected work of brain cells. Can a single brain cell produce consciousness, a sense that we exist? Just about any brain scientist will say not. How about five neurons then, or five hundred? Again,the answer will be, 'Not enough'. So how many cells would be enough? No-one seems to know, but the majority of brain scientists would say there has to be a critical number. Some more radical scientists aren't happy with this. Their argument is that if it turns out that sixty billion neurons aren't enough for someone to know they exist, but at sixty billion and one neurons the light suddenly goes on, what was so special about that one additional brain cell? The answer is nothing, it's just another brain cell. And our best guess at the start of the paragraph was that a single brain cell cannot produce consciousness.

And so this very feasible idea that just as a telly can only produce a picture once it has had a vital number of components fitted, we require a critcal number of brain cells in order to become conscious, begins to look shakey. To add to the doubt, there have been documented examples of people with severly shrunken brains living normal independent lives. In 1980 Roger Lewin, a science writer, published details of a young man with advanced hydrocephalus (water on the brain). The man was under the care of a paeditrician in Sheffield, John Lorber. The patient's skull was almost completely filled with fluid, leaving him with just a sliver of brain tissue that amounted to between 5% and 10% of the mass of a healthy brain. Ordinarily this condition would leave the patient blind, unable to speak, and with almost no capacity to think. And yet the man had a measured IQ of 126 and graduated from Sheffield University with a first-class honours degree in mathematics. A similar case was reported by doctors in France in 2007, involving a married 44-year-old male patient whose skull was largely occupied by two huge pools of water. He was holding down an office job and had no health problem other than a mild weakness in one leg.

And as we've seen, slime mold does very nicely with no brain at all.

In 1898 the psychologist William James developed the theory that rather than generating all of its owner's conscious experiences, the brain transmits and receives consciousness, like a two-way radio:

> *there is a continuum of cosmic consciousness, against which our individuality builds but accidental fences, and into which our several minds plunge as into a mother-sea or reservoir.*

Is there? If we were to update James's idea, we would say the brain is like a personal computer. It can perform many marvellous functions when offline (monitoring our body, helping us move, surveying the local environment for any risks), but wider consciousness only kicks in when we are online. Opening a website does not mean the internet is inside a smart phone or computer, but at the same time our smart phone or pc form part of the internet. We are therefore located both inside our brains and everywhere else outside. It sounds like nonsense, but there could be something in it.

As we know, serious damage to our brain damages our consciousness. Doesn't this mean William James had to be wrong? We may still be able to experience consciousness (in other words, we may still be aware of our own existence), but we might be unable to give any sign of this. Locked-in syndrome, for example, involves someone with significant brain damage appearing to all intents and purposes 'gone', in a permanent vegetative state, incapable of movement or thought. Non-conscious. But modern techniques involving MRI scanners have found that some people with this condition are fully aware of their existence and desperate to communicate.

But what about personality changes that come about from a head injury; they must prove that we are, in essence, our brains? Serious head injury can result in a previously easy-going person turning, after their accident, into someone quick to anger. Or a lively and excitable person may become very unemotional and apathetic to life following brain injury. It's a tragedy for both the injured and those who have loved them. In severe cases their old self is, in many respects, gone. This is very strong evidence that the self, consciousness, us, exists completely inside the brain.

There are, however, some aspects to the human personality that seem to remain largely unchanged by serious head injury. Relatives of fifty-five people who had suffered severe head injuries in Scotland were asked about the changes they had seen in their loved one's personality one year on from their accident. The biggest changes involved mood; their injured relative had often shifted from being a relatively even-tempered person to someone far more irritable. They were also, in general, significantly unhappier, and far less enthusiastic about life. In fact, almost everything about their loved one had changed. Among the few exceptions were their '*kindness*', '*sensitivity*' and '*generosity*,' which in the injured patients remained very close to their pre-accident levels.

These qualities, kindness, sensitivity and generosity, might be regarded as the core of humanity. Over in Texas, Brent Masel, a neurologist who has spent much of his life working with people with serious head injuries says,

> *Your overall personality remains about the same. If you were a nasty guy before the injury, you're likely to be a nasty guy after. If you were a sweetheart before, basically you'll be a sweetheart after.*

But in studying and treating these injuries, Masel has come across a number of people who weren't too lovely prior to their injury, becoming improved in character:

> *I really haven't seen that many nuns — for lack of a better word — become aggressive, hostile people. It's more the other way around, and I don't know why.*

Bearing in mind that we are at the outer fringes of brain science here, there is some evidence to suggest that the deepest elements of personality, our true or inner selves, may survive a terrible brain injury. This in turn keeps William James' idea alive that our minds can be both inside and outside our body; kindness might not be traced to the tissues of the brain, or anywhere else in the body.

Nature of Reality, Existence

As mentioned earlier, most physicists now believe that everything solid can be regarded as essentially energy. We are as substantial as ghosts. If we could see properly, we could see through everything: each other, houses, mountains, politicians. We are almost-nothings, but almost-nothings that can feel overwhelming emotions: joy, passion, fury, sorrow. We feel; therefore we exist. We have minds. That's all we know, but it's a very good start. We know we exist because we feel that we exist, we experience existing. We know we are alive because we *feel* alive. We also know there are things outside of ourselves because we hear, smell and see them: grass, birds, buildings, the sky, we experience them all. Horses, sharks, cats, they all have minds because they experience us and each other. How about rocks and stones; do they have minds? Most scientists would say no, don't be stupid. But there are some clever people out there who are stupid enough to believe that they do.

The Oxford-born philosopher Galen Strawson, for instance, thinks that rocks and mountains might have minds. He explains why. According to Strawson, all we know is that we are made of something and that we have minds. So we can say that things that are made out of something can have minds. What we can't say for sure is that things made out of something don't have minds. We have no proof of that. We only have proof that there are things that have minds. So rocks and mountains may have minds. It looks as if Galen's just believing in magic here, a folk tale world of talking mountains or walking rocks. But he turns the tables by saying that if it's true that most of the world is dead, how come we can even feel, let alone think and speak? How can our minds have simply sprung up from the same 'dead' raw material that makes boulders and gravel? Isn't that, he asks, just magical thinking? Huh, he's not so stupid after all.

And as we've seen, even creatures without a single brain cell can be pretty smart: slime can even solve puzzles. So how far down the scale can things get while still having some sort of mind? All the way says Galen. And as we've also seen, if we take everything down to its most basic ingredients, we find that everything is built up from the same sub-atomic particles, and that these particles are just energy. This is not a new idea, that everything – you, me, fish, rocks – everything is just a twist of energy; a you-shaped twist of energy, a me-shaped twist, fish-shaped and rock-shaped twists of a single substance: energy. Galen just takes this one step further. If we are basically nothing more than energy, and we have minds, then energy must have a mind. Energy is a mind-stuff. And as the entire Universe is made of vast amounts of energy, this would have to mean that the Universe is one enormous mind. Back in 1927 Arthur Eddington, a scientist from Cumbria, had a very similar thought: *'the stuff of the world is mind-stuff'*. And if Galen and Arthur are right, when we die, we carry on, because even as compost, which was mentioned a few pages ago, we are still mind-stuff. So our minds live on, in the carbon, hydrogen, oxygen and whatever else you get when we break back down into the star remnants that went into making we earth people many ages ago. There are of course some problems with Arthur and Galen's ideas: if every tiny part of every atom is a form of consciousness, of mind-stuff, how can they come together to form one mind, rather than – say – seventeen trillion minds? And how about the deadest lump of rock at the furthest frozen-dark boundary of the universe? Is it part of consciousness too, albeit a pretty dim part? Until these questions get answered, the claim that consciousness is the essential ingredient of everything requires belief as well as reflection.

In his later years, Isaac Newton abandoned conventional science in favour of alchemy. He kept 175 books on the topic in his personal library. Despite its cranky reputation, Newton was irritated when people asked if he was trying to turn base metals into gold: *'Alchemy tradeth not with metals as ignorant vulgars think.'* But the Victorian scientist William Barrett stated that Newton had complained in various letters about how much time and money he had wasted on '*alchemical powders*' that were purported to turn lead into gold. In addition to this time lost being ripped off by mail order, Newton would work in his laboratory for weeks on end, hardly sleeping or eating. He needed to put the hours in, because he was searching for nothing less than the true substance of the universe. In 1669 he wrote of his objective, '*the vital agent diffused through everything in the earth is one and the same. And it is a mercurial spirit...which is dispersed through every space*'. Some scientists take this to mean that Newton didn't understand the basics of chemistry, (nobody knew of the existence of hydrogen or oxygen back then), but it seems just as likely he was looking deeper than the elements, into the atom itself, for the same mind-stuff that scientists Arthur Eddington and James Jeans had come to believe was the essence of everything.

At the same time as Newton was scouting around for his *vital agent*, writer and philosopher Margaret Cavendish was forcing her way into the boys' club of science. Margaret was no fan of the idea of atoms (she believed instead that things just keep getting smaller), but she argued that if atoms did indeed exist, then they had to have the wit to move and arrange themselves in the correct way to create the order of the natural world:

> *there can be no regular motion without knowledge, sense and reason; and therefore those that are for Atoms, had best to believe them to be self-moving, living and knowing bodies*

To Margaret it made sound scientific sense that matter at even the sub-atomic level should have a mental life. Motion, specifically ordered motion, is mind.

Animals

Years ago I met a man with a terrible secret. He had killed someone. They had got into an argument, the situation fell out of control and a knife appeared. The other man died. This had happened twenty years earlier, way before the advent DNA profiling, and the police had long-since closed the investigation. He'd got away with it. But the man was so troubled by what he'd done that he decided enough was enough: he was going to surrender himself and go to jail for life. And he did. I was shocked and confused by his decision. Why turn yourself in when no-one was ever going to come looking for you? The modern answer would be 'for peace of mind,' but how peaceful can one's mind be in Wormwood Scrubs? Although I had no real confidence that such a thing existed, I was left wondering if he'd turned himself in to save his own soul. I don't choose the term easily. '*Soul*', says Cole Moreton, '*is a word no English person can use without feeling uncomfortable*'. It's hard enough for us to type.

What's so special about me anyway that I should even consider having a soul? Come to that, what's so special about any people? In 1589 the Bishop of London John Aylmer, gave a categorical answer: '*God is English.*' Heartening news. We can all now put up with the weather, as we are assured preferential treatment come Judgment Day. But what about our pets? The English would be screwed if their cats, dogs, rabbits and horses were turned away at the pearly gates: we'd have to talk to each other. Are animals smart enough to have souls and therefore qualify for paradise? Can a budgie ever be kind? A dog generous? Let's look at the animal kingdom.

Much of what makes we humans unique and special is the size of our brain. There are, however, many species of whales, dolphins and porpoises with brains larger than our own. The adult bottlenose dolphin has a brain that weighs in at 1700 grams. The adult human brain tips the scales at 1450 grams. (The largest ape's brain belongs to the gorilla, at 750 grams). The largest brain on the planet belongs to the sperm whale; it is almost six times the size of our own. Whales and dolphins have owned brains as big or bigger than ours for the past fifteen million years. We only evolved sizeable brains around half a million years ago; cetaceans have therefore had sufficient hardware to calculate how best to live for thirty times as long as humankind.

Although killer whales and humpbacks don't get on, there are no whale, dolphin or porpoise wars. Dolphins and whales are generally much bigger than us, and so we humans have presumed they developed large brains in order to control their huge bulk. But research in the 1960s found that the brains of whale and dolphin have significant areas that are uninvolved in the captaining of their great bodies. Instead, these zones are freed up for 'silent' work. This silent work involves thinking, remembering, feeling, communicating...the sort of things we humans regard as human.

The radical American brain scientist John C Lilley believed that many species of cetaceans are, '*capable of extensions of computations into the past and into the future beyond the range of the human.*' Put simply, he was sure they're smarter than us. Their hearing, for instance, is ten times quicker and more efficient than ours, so at times we can appear slow-witted to them.

But are they compassionate? Do they have a 'soul' (that embarrassing word again)? Perhaps they do. Human compassion and kindness towards others often involve a sub-type of brain cells known as spindle neurons. These spindle cells are also found in higher apes such as chimpanzees and gorillas and are very common in the brains of humpback whales. I was lucky enough once to make eye contact with a humpback whale, and she/he looked at me with the easy confidence of someone that knows themselves to be anyone's equal. She/he came across as a person as much as a mammal.

In 1996 a female gorilla called Binti Jua demonstrated compassion and a sense of doing the right thing by rescuing a 3-year-old boy who had fallen into her enclosure at Brookline Zoo in Illinois. Binti Jua carried the unconscious child to a gate where staff could come and take him to safety. When an elephant dies, members of the herd will cover the dead animal with leaves and grass and keep a week-long vigil over its body. As a further sign of mourning and respect for the dead, elephants visit the bones of the departed for many years after their companions' deaths. In a sequence of experiments that seemed to demonstrate that animals can act with more humanity than some humans, laboratory monkeys and mice were both given

299

a straight choice between going hungry or pressing a lever that delivered them food but gave fellow incarcerated creatures an electric shock. Many of the monkeys and the mice chose to go without food. Consideration for others seems to extend to the insect kingdom: a recent experiment found that a calm woodlouse can reduce the agitation of its neighbouring woodlice. *'Even insects express anger, terror, jealousy and love,'* opined Charles Darwin.

How about plants then? Can they be nice? Daft as it sounds, there's evidence that they can. Suzanne Simard has spent much of her life studying trees, and she has discovered that a sturdy tree will use the root system it shares with fungi under the forest floor to send some of their spare food (i.e. carbon) to under-nourished trees living nearby. They'll even scrunch their roots up a bit, to allow a younger sapling space to grow. Some trees are very active in donating carbon to weaker neighbours, (Suzanne calls these *'mother trees'*) while other healthy trees are comparatively mean with their food; it seems that not only can trees be generous, they can also be selfish. Trees have no brain cells, spindle or regular, but we can see from Suzanne's work that they show signs of what some would call compassion, the bread and butter of a 'soul', if such a thing exists. At this rate, heaven's going to be full by the time we get to go there. At the very least, it will have a nice bit of woodland.

So we don't know how consciousness is constructed, we don't know how many brain cells it takes to produce or sustain it, and we're not even sure that the brain produces all of it. We are almost certain we are not the only animal to have a sense of right and wrong, and even members of the fungus and plant kingdoms seem aware of the needs of other organisms.

What we do know is that when the brain is shut down, whether via deep sleep or anaesthetic, we are un-consciousness. And we assume that an unconscious person can't perform many of the tasks that are second nature to a conscious individual: they are unable to observe, reflect, analyse or communicate. They can dream, but if the brain completely shuts down as it

300

does when death approaches, then their consciousness will dim and disappear. At the moment of death, according to our present knowledge of brain science, consciousness vanishes forever. For those of us who have lost a loved one, or are about to die ourselves, this can be a pretty depressing thought. It remains theory rather than fact: because no-one knows where conciousness comes from, we cannot be certain where it goes. Or even *that* it goes. But any theory about the possibility of any life after death requires decent evidence that consciousness can exist outside of the brain.

Does consciousness exist outside the brain?

The incredible success of the scientific method suggests we should be able to figure out just about anything, even life itself. But while work is advancing solidly, no doubt, on the best way to grow courgettes on Mars, science has failed to answer some of the most important questions of all: why we kill each other, why we kill ourselves, what is existence and what happens when it ends. Much of our own deeper nature seems beyond our reach, so it's likely we're expecting too much of science to provide absolute answers to all of life's mysteries.

In order to entertain the question of whether English life can continue after death, we must look at the evidence that consciousness can ever exist outside the body. The most relevant two subjects to investigate are:

- claims of encounters with the dead; and
- near-death experiences (NDEs)

Science can't give us solid yes or no answers here because neither near-death experience (NDE) nor encounters with ghosts can be properly tested: the brain of a person who has had a Near Death Experience will have returned to normal functioning by the time they can be examined. The same goes for ghost sightings, unless the person seeing the ghost happens to be lying in a brain scanner at the very moment the spook turns up. Because of these limitations, we must turn to individual accounts of personal experiences, and make our own minds up about these strange tales of the paranormal. We'll start with an English favourite: the ghost story.

Ghost Stories

I never really found ghosts that scary since they don't look that scary due to the fact that they're invisible. That's not to say I wasn't scared of everything else... the dark, heights, my own shadow.

Jack Marteau, Student Direct Magazine, 2008

England's crammed with ghosts. Hard to understand why, given the English tendency to be reasoned and unexcitable. But perhaps that's the answer: we need some mystery and thrill in our lives. Although ghost stories can be great fun, few of us take them seriously. But things were different before the industrial age: the absence of any street lighting meant the whole world was pitch black 50 per cent of the time. Any strange sight, sound or unexplained incident allowed the mind to conjure up images of dead souls, vengeful as well as benign, roaming the earth at night.

It's likely that the English had a solid belief in ghosts by the time Christianity arrived, but this would have presented no problem to the early church. Preachers were happy to regard ghosts as souls doing time in purgatory, sharing their misery with the living. They served as reminders of the importance to stay within the teachings of the church and keep to the path of righteousness.

While most ghosts were happy just to startle the living daylights out of everyday folk, some preferred to give people a good hiding. An account, written in the late 1100s by William of Newburgh, centred on a man who suspected his wife of adultery. The suspicious husband hid himself up in the rafters of their home to spy on her. Sure enough, she arrived with her lover, and as they fell into a lustful embrace the enraged husband lost his grip and fell from his perch. He died from his injuries and soon after his burial, this still-livid man rose from the dead and began terrorising the neighbourhood, exciting the attention of local dogs. He made a habit of beating up anyone he came upon or infecting them with a deadly illness from his foul, rotting body. Desperate to put a stop to these troubles, two local men dug up the man's corpse and burnt it to ashes. That fixed it: his ghost was never seen again.

During the 14th century James Tankerlay served as parish priest to the village of Kirby in Yorkshire. He wasn't the best priest in the world, on account of his keeping a mistress, breaking the golden Catholic rule of celibacy. Following his death, Tankerlay was seen roaming the local countryside at night, frightening the living. It all came to a head when he is said to have visited the home of his former mistress and somehow knocked out one of her eyes. Enough was enough, and the Abbot of Byland had Tankerlay's body dug up and thrown into a lake in Goremire. With that, the hauntings ended abruptly.

It was not just regular country-dwellers who believed in ghosts. In 1397 Richard II ordered the execution of the earl of Arundel on grounds of treason. The earl's head was duly chopped off, but sometime afterwards rumours reached Richard that the earl had been seen out and about, his head securely back on his shoulders. A few nightmares later, Richard had Arundel's tomb opened, to check that the earl's head was still separated from the rest of his body. But even this didn't calm the superstitious king, who then went on to hire a personal bodyguard to protect him from Arundel's ghost.

Today, most paranormal researchers regard ghosts as products of the mind, our imaginations generating images and sounds that combine to form characters that subsequently slip through the net of our unconscious brains and seemingly come to life in the waking world, right before our eyes. Shakespeare is happy for us to believe that ghosts can be both real and the products of imagination. Hamlet is out with two companions when he is approached by the ghost of his father. All three see the phantom as clear as day. Banquo's ghost gate-crashes a crowded dinner party, but he is seen by only one person: Macbeth. This is the modern take on ghosts, that they are creations of the brain, in this case the guilt-crazed mind of Macbeth, who'd had Banquo murdered only hours earlier. Macbeth has already had at least one hallucination, seeing a dagger hanging in front of him, but realised it was, '*A false creation, proceeding from the heat-oppressed brain.*' Banquo's ghost is likely to be just as unreal; at no point does it speak. But the ghost of Julius Caesar appears late at night and does speak, although only Brutus hears or sees anything, making it probable that the dead visitor is a figment of Brutus's guilty conscience.

Ghosts often turn up to settle a score in Shakespeare. The murderous Richard III falls asleep the night before the battle that will see him killed. The ghosts of nine family members and friends who Richard has had murdered appear in his dreams. Each, including his dead wife Anne and the two nephews he'd had killed in the Tower of London, take a turn to curse Richard's luck at the forthcoming battle. Richard wakes in a cold sweat, his big day thoroughly jinxed. It's easy to see Shakespeare as simply playing with the idea of ghosts, but women were being burned for witchcraft in England during his lifetime, and belief in the supernatural was so common that the anyone convicted of conjuring up spirits could face the gallows.

The Reformation took some of the steam out of the English belief in ghosts. Protestants had no time for the notion that dead souls serving time in purgatory might wander the earth for years on end. No, according to Protestants, when they die, a person goes straight to heaven or straight to hell, forever. There's no way the dead could re-visit this world. Although they continued to appear in Victorian literature (haunting *Wuthering Heights*, camping it up in *A Christmas Carol* and foreshadowing disaster in *The Signalman*), by the mid-19th century ghosts had become an increasingly rare sight. A notable exception, and the most puzzling account of an apparition in England, is the Cheltenham ghost. It's a long story, but an interesting one.

In Spring 1882 the Despard family moved into a big twenty-year-old house in Cheltenham, Gloucestershire. The house still stands on the corner of All

Saints Road and Pittville Circus Road and is now known as St Anne's. The Despard family comprised mum Harriet, who was an invalid, dad Frederick, (a retired army officer), four daughters and two sons. As was the case with just about every upper-middle-class Victorian home, a team of servants made up the household. Within a few weeks Freda Kinloch, (a daughter from Frederick's first marriage), and her husband also came to live at St Anne's.

In June 1883, just over a year after moving in, nineteen-year-old daughter Rosina Despard heard noises from outside her bedroom door. She guessed it was her poorly mother. Rosina took up her candle and opened the door:

> *I saw no one; but on going a few steps along the passage, I saw the figure of a tall lady, dressed in black, standing at the head of the stairs... The face was hidden by a handkerchief held in the right hand.*

She told no-one about what she'd seen, other than her close friend Catherine Campbell, to whom Rosina wrote a series of letters that included news of further ghostly goings-on in the house. This correspondence became the main source of the reported facts of the story. Neither Catherine nor Rosina ever published the letters, due according to Catherine to their personal nature. This is frustrating but makes some sense: it's possible they contained disclosures about their own or others' love lives.

Over the next two years Rosina saw the mysterious woman several times, sometimes in broad daylight:

> *The face was hidden in a handkerchief held in the right hand.... I saw the upper part of the left side of the forehead, and a little of the hair above. Her left hand was nearly hidden by her sleeve and a fold of her dress. As she held it down a portion of a widow's cuff was visible on both wrists.*

On 29th January 1884 Rosina encountered the ghost in a downstairs room. In the way the English often confront a stranger who turns up uninvited,

Rosina asked the woman if she could help her, '*She moved and I thought she was going to speak, but she only gave a slight gasp and moved towards the door.*' Rosina followed the woman and spoke to her again, but still got no reply. The ghost moved on down the hall and, '*seemed to disappear*'.

Rosina tried her hand at ghostbusting, laying tripwires across the stairs at varying heights: the ghost simply passed straight through these. '*I also attempted to touch her, but she always eluded me. It was not that there was nothing there to touch, but that she always seemed to be beyond me, and if followed into a corner, simply disappeared.*' So far, this seems consistent with the 'all in the mind' explanation of ghost sightings.

In the summer of 1882 Rosina's married half-sister Freda sees a woman dressed in black, whom she takes for a nun:

> *My sister was coming down the stairs rather late for dinner at 6.30, it then being quite light, when she saw the figure cross the hall in front of her and pass into the drawing room. She then asked the rest of us, already seated at dinner, 'Who was that Sister of Mercy whom I have just seen going into the drawing room?' She was told that there was no such person, and a servant was sent to look; but the drawing room was empty, and she was sure no one had come in.*

Why one of the Despards, particularly Freda, couldn't be arsed to go and look for the woman themselves is a separate mystery, alongside what actually goes on in a drawing room.

One evening in the autumn of 1883, the housemaid saw what she believed to be an intruder within the house. Her description of the figure matched the appearance of the woman seen by Rosina and Rosina's sister. Just before Christmas 1883 Rosina's younger brother Wilfrid and one of his friends were playing outside when they saw a strange woman crying in the drawing room, close to the window. They ran in to investigate but found no-one.

On 21st July 1884 Rosina had her longest sighting of all:

> I went into the drawing room where my father and sisters were sitting, about nine in the evening, and sat on a couch close to the bow window. A few minutes later, as I sat reading, I saw the figure come in at the open door, cross the room and take up a position close behind the couch where I was. I was astonished that no one else saw her, as she was so very distinct to me. My youngest brother, who had before seen her, was not in the room. She stood behind the couch for about half an hour, and then as usual walked to the door. I went after her, on the excuse of getting a book, and saw her pass along the hall, until she came to the garden door, where she disappeared. I spoke to her as she passed the foot of the stairs, but she did not answer, although as before she stopped and seemed as though about to speak.

The ghost had a favoured route around the house. Around 2 a.m. on the night of 1st August 1884, Rosina followed the ghost from outside her bedroom, down the stairs, into and out of the drawing room and then to the back door, where the woman vanished. The following night the cook and all four of Rosina's sisters heard footsteps on both the top and middle floors of the house, passing and repassing their bedroom doors. Rosina reported that, 'The cook was a middle-aged and very sensible person; she told me that she had heard these footsteps before, and that she had seen the figure on the stairs one night...She also saw the figure outside the kitchen window on the terrace walk, she herself being in the kitchen.' The cook left the job about a year later, and the family lost contact with her, leaving an investigator brought in by the Society for Psychical Research unable to quiz her about the ghost.

A retired general who lived opposite sent his son to call at the house on 6th August 1884 because, Rosina reported, 'he had seen a lady crying in our orchard, which is visible from the road.' Rosina said that the General came over himself that evening, and organised a ghost hunt, which resulted in failure. I can't find a paper trail to support this, but I believe that the old soldier initially agreed to give a sworn statement to back up Rosina's words, but then changed his mind. Nevertheless, the sightings continued. In fact, so many people had seen this ghost by now (I calculate at least ten), that even the dogs started to take notice. The family's retriever slept in the kitchen and according to Rosina had often been found, *'in a state of terror when the cook went into the kitchen first thing in the morning and was also seen more than once coming from the orchard thoroughly cowed and terrified'*. The household's Skye terrier had twice, *'jumped up, fawning as it would if a real person had been standing there, then suddenly shrank away with its tail between its legs and retreated, trembling, under a sofa.'*

The ghostly activity came to a head at 8 p.m. on 12th August. Rosina and Edith Despard both saw the woman in the drawing room, in the bow window. She stayed there for ten minutes, while Rosina tried to entice her to speak. She said nothing in response. Eventually she left the room and headed off in her usual direction, along the hall to the back door. Fourteen-year-old Mabel Despard then, *'came in from the garden, saying she had seen her coming up the kitchen steps outside.'* All three sisters went out in pursuit, and Freda Kinloch then called from a first-floor window to say she'd just seen the woman pass across the lawn, headed for the orchard. This frenzied fifteen minutes marked the high-tide in phantom sightings at the house. Footsteps continued to be heard and bedroom door handles still rattled, but the figure was seen far less frequently over the next three years, and by 1889 all noises and appearances had ceased.

At this point Rosina contacted the Society for Psychical Research to report the hauntings at St Anne's. She filed a full report, under the name of 'Miss R Morton.' The researcher Peter Ackroyd believed she concealed her identity because, *'Captain Despard swore the whole family to secrecy…in case the landlord suffered from depreciation in the value of the property.'*

Frederic Myers, the investigator brought in by the Society for Psychical Research, interviewed everyone he could. Mrs. Twining, who worked at the house as a cleaner, told Myers that she once followed the 'lady' round the house while the family were at tea. '*Just outside the morning-room window she suddenly disappeared. I was quite near her; it was quite impossible that a real person could have got away.*' Mrs. Brown, the parlour maid, told Myers that, '*I saw a dark figure walk round the ottoman and disappear*'. Myer's conclusion was that, '*The phenomena as seen and heard by all the witnesses were very uniform in character.*' People's stories were consistent.

Some modern investigators have concluded that the woman was not a ghost at all, but was instead a real live woman, (perhaps a secret lover of Captain Despard), who covered her face with a handkerchief to avoid identification whenever she bumped into anyone. Rosina Despard gave four reasons why she was certain the figure was a ghost:

1. The woman's ability to pass through the tripwires Rosina had tied across the stairs, leaving them intact.

2. The, '*sudden and complete disappearance of the figure, while still in full view*'.

3. The fact that the figure could never be touched: '*I have repeatedly followed it into a corner, when it disappeared, and have tried to suddenly pounce upon it, but have never succeeded in touching it.*'

4. The woman's sudden appearance in rooms that had all doors shut.

After seeing a photo, Rosina was confident she had identified the ghost: Mrs Imogen Swinhoe, a previous owner of St Anne's, a widow who spent most of her later days in the drawing room and had drunk herself to death. Presumably she had a cold as well.

Although Frederic Myer felt that Rosina was an honest and reliable witness, there's a side to this story that makes me hover over the salt: Rosina and her friend Catherine Campbell held pre-existing beliefs in the paranormal. In giving evidence to support Rosina's story, Catherine wrote a signed statement that while in her own home a hundred miles from Cheltenham, she had had a vision of her friend Rosina's encounter with the ghost:

I seemed suddenly to be standing close by the door of the housemaid's cupboard, so facing the short flight of stairs leading to the top landing. Coming down these stairs, I saw the figure, exactly as described, and about two steps behind Miss Morton [i.e. Despard] herself, with a dressing-gown thrown loosely round her, and carrying a candle in her hand.

Mmmm...so, Rosina had seen something that most people believe can't really exist, and her best friend saw this same something via telepathy, a further something most people believe does not exists. The sceptic-o-meter is now quavering deep in the red.

In fact, Rosina and Catherine later experimented with telepathy, or what the Victorians called 'thought transference'. In these trials the two women would be stationed several miles apart at a pre-arranged time. One woman would 'send' an image of an object she had picked at random, while the receiver or 'agent' tried to guess correctly what the object might be. Some of these experiments were published in the journal of the Society for Psychical Research. One example involved Rosina thinking hard about a scalpel and a pair of gloves while at work. Catherine, in her home, 'sensed' and wrote down both correctly. But considering Rosina was at medical school that day, it only really left forceps and sphygmomanometer to guess, and they're much harder to spell. In fact, the more sceptical side of my brain is now automatically writing the words, 'handkerchief' and 'face'.

Rosina became an honorary consultant of the Society for Psychical Research in 1892, so the question has to be asked, did Rosina see a ghost and then become convinced that ghosts existed or, more likely, did she believe in ghosts and then start seeing one?

So that's probably it then: a tragic backstory, a sexually frustrated army Captain keeping a secret mistress, a smart teenager preoccupied with the supernatural, servants that aren't about to contradict the boss's daughter, and naïve, imaginative younger brothers and sisters. Children grow up and then, as in the case of the Fox sisters in America or the Cottingley fairy sisters in Yorkshire, the cat comes out the bag. Except that's not precisely what happened here. Sixty years after all the excitement, George Gooding, an attorney, wrote to the Society for Psychical Research (SPR) to say that as a boy he had been a friend of one of Rosina Despard's younger brothers. Gooding said he had twice seen the tall figure in black while playing with his friend, once indoors and once outside in bright sunlight. At this second sighting, George and the other boys in the garden had joined hands around the ghost, to capture it. This didn't work: the ghost simply passed through the human chain and then disappeared. Gooding said that the adults weren't afraid of the ghost, but the dogs seemed to be in fear of her.

If George Gooding really was telling the truth, has anyone seen the lady in black since?   Andrew McKenzie spent many years of his life chasing after the Cheltenham Ghost and has collected several 20th Century reports of a phantom woman in black wandering near St Anne's. Here are two of them:

Between 1957 and 1962, John and Paulette Thorne lived on Pittville Circus Road, within sight of St. Anne's. In October 1958, John awoke at approximately 2.30 a.m. to see a figure of a woman in a long Victorian-style dress at the foot of their bed. He dived under the bed clothes. Daring to look again, he found she was still there. He woke up his wife, but by then the woman had gone; he was convinced he had seen a ghost, but the experience was kept secret. In November 1961 John Thorne's brother William and family came to stay overnight. William shared a sofa-bed in the sitting room with his son, also called John Thorne. William was almost asleep when he heard footsteps just outside the room. Thinking it must be his sister-in-law, William called out, '*Is that you Paulette?*' He looked at the open door, but instead of Paulette Thorne, there stood a woman wearing a black dress that reached to the floor. He couldn't get a clear view of the woman's features as she was holding a handkerchief in her right hand, pressed up against her face. William (a customs officer at Heathrow airport) was convinced that he was seeing a ghost; he shut and opened his eyes several times, but the figure remained and was seemingly solid.

John junior heard his dad call out to Paulette, and he too saw a woman in a long black dress standing in the open doorway, but unlike his father, John saw her completely outlined in a glowing light. He had heard no footsteps and did not recall the woman holding a handkerchief to her face. He asked his father, '*Did you see that?*' to which William (no more courageous than his brother in these matters) replied '*Yes, go and close the door*'. Young John dutifully moved to the door, at which point the ghost '*disappeared*'. Andrew McKenzie interviewed William and his son in person and obtained a signed statement from John Thorne senior.

In January 1971, Doreen Jackson from Bishop's Cleeve, Cheltenham, was having a lunchtime driving lesson. As she drove past the garden gate of St. Anne's a tall woman in black stepped off the pavement and into the path of the car, forcing Doreen into an emergency stop. Her instructor asked Doreen why she had braked, to which she replied that a woman had walked out in front of the car. The instructor, however, had seen no-one, and when Doreen looked again the woman had somehow vanished. In reply to questions from Andrew McKenzie, Doreen stated that she'd never heard of the haunting of St. Anne's. The woman was in her view for five or six seconds. Her clothing looked old-fashioned, her dress reaching the floor. She said the woman was holding a handkerchief up to her face.

I've read a lot around this case. Not as much as some ghost detectives, principally Andrew McKenzie, but enough to come to a conclusion. And that conclusion is that I just don't know. Sorry about that. Let's look at a couple of other accounts from the late 19th century.

The following three cases were all reported to, and investigated by, the Society for Psychical Research (SPR).

In 1891, Lucy Dodds, a single London woman in her forties, wrote to the SPR about an experience she had on June 5th, 1887. She said that just before midnight she was in bed but still awake when she heard her name called twice. She thought it was her uncle George, who shared the home, '*but the third time I recognised the voice as that of my mother, who had been dead sixteen years.*' Lucy says her mother entered the bedroom and placed two children in her arms, saying, '*Lucy, promise me to take care of them, for their mother is just dead.*' Lucy begged her mother to stay, but the old woman said, '*Not yet, my child,*' and left. Lucy recalled that she '*was at a total loss to imagine whose children they were,*' but fell asleep, '*feeling the children to be still in my arms.*' On June 7th, Lucy received news from Belgium of her sister-in-law's death. Lucy also learned that she had given birth to her second child three weeks before she died. Lucy had been unaware her sister-in-law was pregnant.

When questioned by a researcher (a Mr C H Cope), Lucy confirmed that when her dead mother 'appeared' to her, she had neither known that her sister-in-law had been ill nor that she'd had a second child. It's difficult to imagine how you could drop off to sleep having just seen a ghost and been given two small children to look after. More likely she'd dreamt the whole thing, but when this point was put to her, Lucy was adamant that she had been '*perfectly awake*' throughout the episode.

In 1885 Caroline Judd wrote to tell the SPR her ghost story.

Caroline's gran had died in her eighties, a tall and calm-natured woman. Although Caroline and her sister Mary missed her, they weren't deeply upset as she'd had a good innings and had been in chronic pain towards the end of her life. Caroline and Mary shared a room next to the old lady's. Beside their bed stood a grandfather clock. She kept it in their room as it was too large for her own. The old woman loved the clock, and at any hour of the day would stand watching its hands move across its face. Grandfather clocks were the ultimate in mid-Victorian home tech: the flat-screen TVs of their day.

'*About three weeks after her death,*' reported Caroline, '*I awoke one morning in October, and saw distinctly the well-known tall figure, the calm old face, the large dark eyes uplifted as usual to the face of the old clock. I closed my eyes for some seconds, and then slowly reopened them. She stood there still.*' When Caroline repeated this test, her grandmother was gone. Fearing judgement from the rest of the family, Caroline kept the vision to herself.

That night, however, her sister said to Caroline, '*I cannot go to bed without telling you something, only don't laugh, for I am really frightened; I saw grandmamma this morning!*' Caroline said, '*I was amazed. I inquired of her the hour, what the vision was like, where it stood, what it was doing, etc., and I found that in every respect her experience was similar to mine. She had preserved silence all day for fear of ridicule.*'

Caroline summed up the experience by saying they, '*even now speak of this incident with awe, though twenty long years have since passed over our heads, and we invariably end by saying, each of us, 'It was very strange; it is impossible to understand it'.*'

At the request of the SPR, Caroline's sister Mary Dear gave a signed statement that supported all that Caroline had written. The story is appealing because nothing much happens; its banal plot (woman looks at clock) gives the claim a prosaic scent of authenticity.

In addition to the home, the English can stumble on a ghost when on their holidays. In September 1886, John Husbands from Melbourne House, Town Hall Street in Grimsby (a red-brick house, now home to the town's

Citizen's Advice Bureau), sent a no-nonsense report of meeting a ghost while on his holidays. *'The facts are simply these,'* begins John:

> *I was sleeping in a hotel in Madeira in January 1885. It was a bright moonlight night. The windows were open and the blinds up. I felt someone was in my room. On opening my eyes, I saw a young fellow about twenty-five, dressed in flannels, standing at the side of my bed and pointing with the first finger of his right hand to the place I was lying. I lay for some seconds to convince myself of someone being really there. I then sat up and looked at him. I saw his features so plainly that I recognised them in a photograph which was shown me some days after. I asked him what he wanted; he did not speak, but his eyes and hand seemed to tell me I was in his place.*

Spooked, John decided to take a foot-forward approach:

> *I struck out at him with my fist as I sat up, but did not reach him, and as I was going to spring out of bed he slowly vanished through the door, which was shut, keeping his eyes upon me all the time.*

A Miss K Faulkner of Church Terrace, Wisbech, was staying at the hotel with her brother and her sister-in-law on the night John Husbands saw his ghost in sporting 'flannels'. She was traced by the SPR and wrote them a signed statement:

> *The figure that Mr, Husbands saw while in Madeira was that of a young fellow who died unexpectedly months previously, in the room which Mr Husbands was occupying. Curiously enough, Mr. H. had never heard of him or his death. He told me the story the morning after he had seen the figure, and I recognised the young fellow from the description. It impressed me very much, but I did not mention it to him or anyone. I loitered about until I heard Mr. Husbands tell the same tale to my brother; we left Mr. H. and said simultaneously, 'He has seen Mr. D.' No more was said on the subject for days; then I abruptly showed the photograph. Mr.*

316

Husbands said at once, 'That is the young fellow who appeared to me the other night, but he was dressed differently' describing a dress he often wore 'cricket suit (or tennis) fastened at the neck with sailor knot.' I must say that Mr. Husbands is a most practical man, and the very last one would expect 'a spirit' to visit. K. FALKNER. October 10th, 1886.

Miss Falkner got her sister-in-law to send her the photograph of the young man who had died ('Mr D'), and an extract from her sister-in-law's covering letter, '*You will see at back of Mr. du F 's photo the date of his decease* [January 20th, 1884]...*Mr. Husbands had to take the room on February 2nd, 1885, as his was wanted. I am clear on all this.*' Edward Gurney from the SPR interviewed both Mr Husbands and Miss Falkner. He judged that they were both '*thoroughly practical, and as far removed as possible from a superstitious love of marvels; nor had they any previous interest in this or any other class of abnormal experiences.*'

John Husbands could easily have made the whole thing up of course, having kept secret a prior knowledge of the tennis-loving dead Mr D. Or it's possible that he, Miss Falkner and her sister-in-law cooked the story up between them. We can never know, but all the same, John Husbands' '*if you see a ghost, punch it*' strategy is one we could all utilise.

Crisis Apparitions

We now reach a particular and fascinating type of ghost experience: a dying or very recently dead person 'visiting' a loved one many miles away. I will refer to these kind of events as 'Wilfred Owen' cases for the following reason.

On 11th November 1918 Harold Owen, a Royal Navy officer, was on his ship, anchored off the coast of West Africa. News had just arrived that World War I had ended, and one of Harold's first thoughts was that his brother, the poet Wilfred, who had been fighting in the trenches, was now safe. Returning to his cabin, Harold pulled back its curtain door and was astounded to see his brother sat in his cabin chair. Years later he wrote about that moment:

> *I saw Wilfred sitting in my chair. I felt shock run through me with appalling force and with it I could feel the blood draining away from my face. I did not rush towards him but walked jerkily into the cabin, all my limbs stiff and slow to respond. I did not sit down but looking at him I spoke quietly: 'Wilfred, how did you get here?' He did not rise and I saw that he was involuntarily immobile, but his eyes which had never left mine were alive with the familiar look of trying to make me understand; when I spoke his whole face broke into his sweetest and most endearing dark smile. I felt not fear – I had none when I first drew my door curtain and saw him there – only exquisite mental pleasure at thus beholding him. He was in uniform and I remember thinking how out of place the khaki looked amongst the cabin furnishings. With this thought I must have turned my eyes away from him; when I looked back my cabin chair was empty.*

Harold added that at that moment he knew, '*with certainty that Wilfred was dead.*'

Wilfred Owen cases are not so rare. The investigator William Barrett was able to uncover 134 personal accounts that involved a deceased person being seen or heard at the precise moment of their death, or very soon after, by someone who stated they were some distance away and completely unaware of that death.

In March 1859 William Howard wrote to the writer and paranormal investigator Robert Owen to tell him of something that happened when he (William) was just a baby. It was a story he had heard from his mother, '*many times*' and was well known to William's family and their neighbours in Heanor, Derbyshire. William takes up the story:

> *One fine calm afternoon my mother, shortly after a confinement* [giving birth], *but perfectly convalescent, was lying in bed.... she was gladdened by hearing footsteps which she took to be those of her brother Frank, as he was familiarly called, approaching the chamber door. The visitor knocked and entered. The foot of the bed was towards the door, and the curtains at the foot, notwithstanding the season, were drawn* [this must have been a four-poster bed], *to prevent any draft.*

Frank pulled back the curtains and looked straight at his sister. He was not his usual cheery self. He said nothing, and when William's mother asked him to come to her side, '*He closed the curtains, as if complying, but instead of doing so, my mother – to her astonishment – heard him leave the room, close the door behind him, and begin to descend the stairs.*' A maid searched the house and surrounding area for him, but no-one had seen Frank either arrive or go. There was then, '*a sudden running and excited talking in the village street,*' and everyone in the house soon learned that Frank had been involved in an argument at the top end of the village and had been stabbed and killed. William's letter concludes by saying that a check on the exact time of the murder and of Frank's strange visit, revealed that, '*the apparition presented itself to my mother almost instantly after her brother had received the fatal stroke.*'

A vicar called Matthew Frost, from Bowers Gifford in Essex, had a similar experience:

> *The first Thursday in April 1881, while sitting at tea with my back to the window and talking with my wife in the usual way, I plainly heard a rap at the window, and looking round at the window I said to my wife, 'Why, there's my grandmother,' and went to the door, but could not see anyone; still feeling sure it was my grandmother,*

and knowing, though she was eighty-three years of age, that she was very active and fond of a joke, I went round the house, but could not see anyone. My wife did not hear it. On the following Saturday, I had news my grandmother died in Yorkshire about half-an-hour before the time I heard the rapping.

Henry Sidgwick from the Society for Psychical Research investigated and was told by Matthew Frost that he'd last seen his grandmother three years before she appeared at the window. It was full daylight at the time, and on 'seeing' her Frost truly believed his grandmother had turned up in the flesh and meant to surprise him.

The writer Carl Watkins records that these kinds of appearances, (at the moment of death), were talked about by village folk in 19th century Yorkshire, and the notion that the dying can appear to the living goes back far earlier, with Chaucer telling the story of King Ceyx, who is drowned at sea but appears to Alcyone his wife back home, at the foot of her bed, to say a last farewell.

Provided the person reporting their vision is not lying, the appealing feature of Wilfred Owen cases is that either (a) the individual had indeed seen the 'spirit' of a loved one, or (b) they had hallucinated a ghost when unaware that the person in question had just died. For the whole experience to be a delusion, an extraordinary level of coincidence would be required. Here's another Victorian one, involving someone who wanted to remain anonymous. He calls himself N.J.S. and his story is told in delightful period prose by Edward Gurney in 1886.

N. J. S. and F. L. were employed together in an office, were brought into intimate relations with one another, which lasted for about eight years, and held one another in very great regard and esteem. On Monday, March 19th, 1883, F. L., in coming to the office, complained of having suffered from indigestion

Come Saturday F.L. was no better and had to take a couple of days off.

On Saturday evening, March 24th, N. J. S. …. said to his wife that he was what he had not been for months, rather too warm; after making the remark he leaned back on the couch, and the next minute saw his friend, F. L., standing before him, dressed in his usual manner. N. J. S. noticed the details of his dress, that is, his hat with a black band, his overcoat unbuttoned, and a stick in his hand; he looked with a fixed regard at N. J. S., and then passed away.

N. J. S. quoted to himself from Job, 'And lo, a spirit passed before me, and the hair of my flesh stood up.' At that moment an icy chill passed through him, and his hair bristled. He then turned to his wife and asked her the time; she said, ' 12 minutes to 9.' He then said, 'The reason I ask you is that F. L. is dead. I have just seen him.'

Mrs N.J.S. thought this was cobblers.

The following afternoon, F.L.'s brother called around. He had been with his sick brother on Saturday evening but F.L. had been OK when he left at 25 minutes to 9 p.m. F. L.'s sister called by at 9 p.m. and found him dead. He had suffered a heart attack. As an added twist, F.L.'s brother had guessed N.J.S. already knew the bad news before he'd called to tell him. *'Because,'* he explained N.J.S. *'you were in such sympathy with one another.'*

I like to think that N.J.S. and F.L. were deeply in love but due to the absurd law and stifling mores of the time could not admit so to themselves and therefore one another. Perhaps somewhere an old tree bears the faintest scar 'N.J.S. 4 F.L.'

With the advent of mobile phones bad news now travels as fast as any would-be apparition, but some Wilfred Owen cases continue to occur here in the 21st century. In 2014, the medical researcher Dr Penny Sartori interviewed Janice Wright, who was visiting friends in Virginia, USA when she *'suddenly snapped wide awake'* in the middle of the night. In her room was her childhood nanny. The two women had remained in touch across the decades, but Janice hadn't seen the old lady for some years. *'In real life, she was well over 80,' said Janice, 'but in the vision, she was ageless and surrounded by an immensely bright light. She smiled at me, put her hand out and telepathically told me all was well. I was shocked and stayed awake. The next morning, I told my hosts I thought my old nanny had died. Later that day, a cousin called from England to tell me that's exactly what had happened.'*

In 2004 Peter Fenwick, a doctor and researcher from London, reported a personal account he had received of a recent Wilfred Owen experience:

> *When I retired to bed I was very restless. I tossed this way and that until suddenly, in the early hours, my father stood by my bed. He had been ill for a long time, but there he was standing in his prime of life. He didn't speak. My restlessness ceased and I fell asleep. In the morning I knew... my father had died late the evening before and had been permitted to visit me on his way into the next life*

Opinions vary on the cause of Crisis Apparitions. The English academic Celia Green groups them with out of body experiences and standard ghost sightings, regarding them collectively as waking dreams. According to Celia, during a Crisis Apparition, the entire visual field and not only the dead visitor is a dream or hallucination. It's true that none of the visitors were physically there, (George Tyrrell points out that ghosts never leave footprints in snow), and it's interesting that while they may say good-bye or thank-you, crisis apparitions do not reply to direct questions. To this extent they are more like very convincing holograms than people. The trickier part to explain is why their appearance to sound-minded friends or relations should coincide with their deaths. Unconscious anxiety within the visited person might play a part: Harold Owen was fully aware that Wilfred Owen was fighting a war at the time, but in some cases the visitor was believed to have been in good health and at no risk at the moment of their appearance.

Deathbed Visions

There are two categories of deathbed vision. In the first, a dying person has a paranormal experience. This involves them either 'seeing' a dead loved one or having a vision of a supernatural light or landscape. In the second category of deathbed vision, it is someone at the dying person's side who sees or hears extraordinary events.

Here is a first category account from a Pauline, a woman who had been sitting with her dying mother. It was reported by the researcher Peter Fenwick in 2004:

> *Suddenly she looked up at the window and seemed to stare intently up at it... this lasted only minutes, but it seemed ages...she suddenly turned to me and said, 'Please Pauline, don't ever be afraid of dying. I have seen a beautiful light and I was going towards it, I wanted to go into that light, it was so peaceful I really had to fight to come back.' The next day, when it was time for me to go home, I said, 'Bye mum, see you tomorrow'. She looked straight at me and said, 'I'm not worried about tomorrow and you mustn't be, promise me.' Sadly, she died the next morning...but I knew she had seen something that day which gave her comfort and peace when she knew she had only hours to live.*

Although their hearing often remains intact, as death nears, a dying person finds it increasingly difficult to speak. Jean Giacomozzi from London, for instance, recalled this about her husband's last moments:

> *My husband never really believed there was a life after death, and watching him die, I saw an expression of puzzlement which I had never seen before on his face. I hope he found out the great mystery...he was 'somewhere else'*

The following case was sent to the Victorian paranormal investigators Edmund Gurney and Frederic Myers by a man who did not want to be identified in print, other than as the 'Vicar of H.' The poor man lost his two eldest sons on consecutive days:

> *On November 2nd and 3rd 1870, I lost my two eldest boys, David Edward and Harry, from scarlet fever, they being then three and four years old respectively. Harry died at Abbot's Langley [Hertfordshire] on November 2nd, fourteen miles from my vicarage at Aspley, David the following day at Aspley. About an hour before the death of this latter child he sat up in bed and pointing to the bottom of the bed said distinctly, 'There is little Harry calling to me.' Of the truth of this fact I am sure, and it was heard also by the nurse.*

The Vicar added that news of Harry's death had been deliberately kept from David. This tragic story would have been helped by a confirming statement from the nurse, but the next very dramatic case includes two such affidavits:

Sir William Barrett was an investigator of psychic reports of the early 20th Century. His wife, Florence, (who William likes to refer to as 'Lady Barrett') was an obstetrician at the Mothers' Hospital in Clapton, East London. On 12th January 1924, Florence, was helping a woman she refers to as 'Mrs B' to deliver her baby. Immediately after giving birth, Mrs B went into heart failure; it soon became clear she would not survive.
Florence Barrett reported that:

> *Suddenly she looked eagerly towards one part of the room, a radiant smile illuminating her whole countenance. 'Oh lovely, lovely,' she said. I asked, 'What is lovely?' 'What I see...Lovely brightness – wonderful beings.' It is difficult to describe the sense of reality conveyed by her intense absorption in the vision.*
> *Then, seeming to focus her attention more intently on one place for a moment, she exclaimed, almost with a kind of joyous cry, 'Why, it's father! Oh, he's so glad I'm coming; he is so glad. It would be perfect if only W [her husband] could come too.' Her baby was*

brought to her to see. She looked at it with interest, and then said, 'Do you think I ought to stay for baby's sake?' Then turning towards the vision again, she said, 'I can't – I can't stay; if you could see what I do, you would know I can't stay.' But she turned to her husband who had come in, and said, 'You won't let baby go to anyone who won't love him, will you?'...I left shortly after, and the Matron took my place by the bedside. She lived for another hour.

William Barrett wrote to a Dr Phillips, who was present while all this was going on. Dr Phillips responded that said she, '*fully agrees with Lady Barrett's account.*' The most interesting evidence was given by Miriam Castle, the hospital's Matron, who wrote that:

I was present shortly before the death of Mrs B, together with her husband and her mother. Her husband was leaning over her and speaking to her, when pushing him aside she said, 'Oh, don't hide it; it's so beautiful.' Then turning away from him towards me, I being on the other side of the bed, Mrs B said, 'Oh, why there's Vida,' referring to a sister of whose death three weeks previously she had not been told.

William Barrett looked into this, contacting Mrs B's mother, Mrs Clark from Highbury North London. Mrs Clark wrote the following to William:

I have heard you are interested in the beautiful passing of my dear daughter's spirit from this earth on 12th January 1924. The most wonderful part of it is the history of the death of my dear daughter, Vida, who had been an invalid some years. Her death took place on 25th December 1923, just 2 weeks and 4 days before her younger sister Doris [Mrs B] died. My younger daughter Doris was very ill at the time and the Matron at the Mothers' Hospital deemed it unwise for Mrs B to know of her sister's death. Therefore, when visiting her we put off our mourning and visited her as usual. All her letters were also kept by request until her husband had seen who they might be from before letting her see them.

Harriet Ogle from Yorkshire wrote to the writer James Alexander MacDonald about her brother John's death. It involved John having a vision of someone he is unlikely to have known to be dead.

My brother John Alkin Ogle died at Leeds, July 17th 1879. About an hour before he expired he saw his brother, who had died about sixteen years before. And John, looking up with fixed interest, said, 'Joe! Joe!' and immediately after, exclaimed with ardent surprise, 'George Handley!' My mother, who had come from Melbourne, a distance of about forty miles, where George Handley resided, was astonished at this and said, 'How strange he should see George Hanley; he died only ten days ago.' Then turning to my sister-in-law she asked if anybody had told John of George Hanley's death; she said 'No one.' My mother was the only person present who was aware of the fact. I was present and witnessed this.

Answering some follow-up questions from the Society for Psychical Research, Harriet said that her brother John Ogle was, '*neither delirious nor unconscious when he uttered the words recorded.*' Harriet added that George Hanley was an acquaintance of John Ogle, but not a close friend.

Stories of deathbed visions have been told in England for centuries (the oldest on record, the death of St Hilda in 680 A.D., is told in Chapter 7, *Back to the Start*). Here's a delightful one from over 300 years ago. It's a combination of a Wilfred Owen and deathbed vision case:

In 1691 the Reverend Thomas Tilson wrote an account about the death of one of his parishioners, Mary Goffe from Rochester in Kent. Seriously ill for some while, come the night of June 3rd 1691 Mary felt she had only hours left. She was unable to leave her sick bed at her parent's house in West Mulling, nine miles from her two children. Between one and two a.m. Mary fell into a kind of coma so deep that Mrs Turner, who was watching over her, couldn't tell if her patient was alive or dead, but Mary awoke the next morning and told her mother she had been back home with her children during the night. When her mother told Mary this was impossible since, '*you have been here in bed all the while,*' Mary agreed, but explained, '*I was with them last night while I was asleep.*' Mary died later that day.

Back in Rochester, a nurse in charge of Mary's children had been startled at two in the morning by a female figure stepping out of the elder child's bedroom. This figure appeared to be Mary Goffe. The nurse was sharing her bed with Mary's younger daughter. The wraith-like Mary stood by their bedside for around a quarter of hour. Her eyes and mouth moved, but no sound came out. The nurse said she was fully awake, looking directly at this ghostly Mary. Eventually, her nerves could take no more and she called out, '*In the name of the Father, Son and Holy Ghost, what art thou?*' At this, the apparition backed away and left the room. The nurse left the house in pursuit of the phantom Mrs Goffe but could find no trace of her. She woke the neighbours and told them exactly what had gone on, later telling the Reverend Thomas Tilson '*If ever I saw her* [Mary Goffe] *in all my life, I saw her this night*'. Tilson went on to interview the neighbours, Mary's mother and the widow Mrs Turner in West Mulling. He concluded by reporting:

> *They all agree in the same story, and every one helps to strengthen the other's testimony. They all appear to be sober, intelligent persons, far enough off from designing to impose a cheat upon the world, or to manage a lie; and what temptation they should lie under for so doing I cannot conceive.*

In a 2011 radio interview, Peter Fenwick gave some background to research he had done into deathbed visions:

> *About a month before you die, you'll start getting visitations from dead family members. We've got enough accounts of these to say who comes, and it tends to be spouses [that] are the highest on your*

list. Then brothers or sisters, and children quite often see their grandparents.

The visitations are most interesting because it produces a...change in language of the dying. They don't talk about 'when I die.' They talk about 'I'm going on a journey,' 'when I'm picked up,' 'I won't be here because I'm leaving.' It's got quite a different sound to it. The visitations usually tell people...that they're going to be there for them and look after them at a certain time.

Peter Fenwick added that it is common for the visited person to die at the exact time of that appointment.

We move now to the other category of deathbed visions: uncanny events experienced by someone at the dying person's side.

Penny Bilcliffe was with her sister when she died. Penny told her story to Peter and Elizabeth Fenwick in 2008:

I saw a fast-moving 'Will o' the Wisp' appear to leave her body by the side of her mouth on the right. The shock and the beauty of it made me gasp. It appeared like a fluid or gaseous diamond, pristine, sparkly, and pure, akin to the view from above an eddy in the clearest pool you can imagine...It moved rapidly upwards and was gone.

Medical professionals can be resistant to reporting unexplained events during patient death. In a 2004 article, Peter Fenwick passed on this anonymous story: *'A doctor who had seen many patients die told me that he was once playing golf when another player had a heart attack. As he was going to help he saw what he described as a white form, which seemed to rise and separate from the body.'* A hospice worker told the American researcher and doctor Raymond Moody that on two separate occasions they had seen, *'a sort of mist that forms around the head or chest. There seems* to be some kind of electricity to it, like an electrical disturbance.' Writing in 2012, Moody added, '*I have spoken to many doctors, nurses and hospice workers who have seen this mist.*'

Peter Fenwick quoted from an unnamed nurse who had been attending to her father in his last hours:

> *When I awoke, the room was pitch dark, but above Dad's bed was a flame licking the top of the wall against the ceiling. . .as I looked...I saw a plume of smoke rising, like the vapour that rises from a snuffed-out candle, but on a bigger scale. . .it was being thrown off by a single blade of phosphorus light. . .it hung above Dad's bed, about 18 inches or so long, and was indescribably beautiful. . .it seemed to express perfect love and peace. Eventually I switched on the light. The light vanished and the room was the same as always on a November morning, cold and cheerless, with no sound of breathing from Dad's bed.*

A woman who also wished to remain anonymous, (seeing the invisible can attract scorn and even uninvited medical attention in modern-day England), described what happened as she sat at her dying husband's side:

> *Suddenly there was the most brilliant light shining from my husband's chest and as this light lifted upwards there was the most beautiful music and singing voices, my own chest seemed filled with infinite joy and my heart felt as if it was lifting to join this light and music. Suddenly there was a hand on my shoulder and a nurse said 'I'm sorry love. He has just gone'. I lost sight of the light and music; I felt so bereft at being left behind.*

The researcher Penny Sartori reported an intriguing event that occurred in a north of England hospital in 2004. An unnamed woman in her seventies was unconscious and nearing death. At her bedside were her husband Peter, son Harry and daughter Gail. Dr Sartori interviewed Peter and Gail separately about what happened next. Peter said he noticed a bright light appear a short distance away. A tall man walked from the light, his arms outstretched. Peter's unconscious wife appeared to rise from her bed and walk towards the man. *'He was waiting there as if to give her a welcoming hug; there was a sense of peace and love,'* said Peter. Daughter Gail, shared the same vision, but 'saw' more detail:

> *All of a sudden, I could see Mum walking into the distance on a path. Around her head was like a sun, and on her right-hand side, I could see the silhouette of some people. [Then] I saw this tall person — I don't know who he was. When she reached him, he took her into his arms as if in a warm embrace that was full of love. Mum's breaths got shallower. And then there were no further breaths and the scene disappeared.*

Throughout all this time, Harry saw nothing unusual at all.

Father and daughter had, in Peter's words, *'big smiles on our faces,'* a bizarre contrast to the sorrow of the moment. He added, *'There'd been such sadness leading up to my wife's death — then this* [vision] *happened...The nurses and ward sister must have thought we were very insensitive because we felt this sense of elation and happiness.'*

It's a mystery why Peter and Gail should have both had this experience, while poor Harry saw nothing. In fact, the whole event is a mystery.

A Dutch man related a similar experience to the researcher Pim van Lommel:

> *I was in a relationship with Anne when she suddenly died in a serious traffic accident. Her son, who'd just turned seven, sustained [a] severe head trauma. Some sixty relatives had gathered around his hospital bed, and since I'd only been his mother's boyfriend, I was standing somewhere at the back by the window. The moment he died, when his EEG flat-lined, I 'saw' that his mother came to collect him. You must bear in mind that she'd died five days earlier. There was this incredibly beautiful reunion...I used to think that I*

knew what was what. But my worldview underwent a radical transformation.

Terminal Lucidity

In the early nineties I worked in a hospital for people with advanced dementia, usually victims of Alzheimer's disease. Most of the patients had lost completely the ability to speak; many others could only talk nonsense: broken fragments of words, random phrases and sounds. It is common for someone with advanced Alzheimer to lose the ability to recognise the faces of their son or daughter, or even their own as it stares vacantly back at them from the bathroom mirror. Large areas of their brains have died. They have become empty shells of their former selves, a detestable fate that can drag on for years.

Yet the staff I worked with told me that as they neared death, some patients, including the most severely brain damaged and mute, would suddenly gather their wits and speak again, chatting eloquently with a startled nurse or very shocked visiting relative. This extraordinary event, known as terminal lucidity, has been witnessed all over the world. Michael Nahm, a German researcher, has identified 83 cases reported by 55 different authors, mostly professionals working in medical settings. Here are three of these cases:

Following two strokes, a 91-year-old woman was left both totally paralyzed and speechless. Her daughter acted as her carer. On the day she died the old woman let out a cry that immediately caught the daughter's attention. Her mother, whose facial expression had been frozen since her second stroke, was *'smiling brightly.'* The woman, *'turned her head and sat up in bed with no apparent effort. She then raised her arms and exclaimed in a clear, joyous tone the name of her husband. Her arms dropped again, and she sank back and died.'*

An elderly woman suffered from Alzheimer's disease for 15 years and was cared for by her daughter:

The woman was unresponsive for years and showed no sign of recognizing her daughter or anybody else. However, a few minutes before she died, she started a normal conversation with her daughter, an experience for which the daughter was unprepared, and which left her utterly confused.

The third case features a grandmother, a long-term sufferer from Alzheimer's disease who:

had neither talked nor reacted to family members for a number of years until the week before she died, when she suddenly started chatting with the granddaughter, asking about the status of various family members and giving her granddaughter advice. Her granddaughter reported that, 'it was like talking to Rip Van Winkle.'

The researcher Penny Sartori interviewed Lyon, a friend:

'My mother, Peggy, while in the latter stages of Alzheimer's, was no longer able to converse with any coherency at all,' said Lyon White, who lives in Sussex. 'Her conversation consisted of what could only be described as 'gobbledygook.'

As Peggy's condition deteriorated, she had to be admitted to hospital. One day, Lyon heard her speaking as he entered the ward. She was having a conversation with her father, a much-loved policeman in Kent who'd been murdered while on duty. Among the things she told him was that she knew that her husband — also deceased — had loved her very much.

Lyon was astounded. It had been a long time since his mother had even been able to form a word, let alone a sentence. But as soon as he interrupted her vision, she once again lost the power to speak

Dreams

In the weeks that follow Jack's death I sleep very little, for fear I will dream Jack is still alive, and must therefore lose him all over again come the morning.

Four months after his death, on 20th April 2010, Debbie has a first and vivid dream about Jack in which he and his good friend Ross are working as film extras in a crowd scene. Jack and Deb are both surprised to see one another. Debbie can smell him clearly as they embrace (she later reflects how strange it was to be able to smell in a dream). Jack walks up to Deb. '*Jack!*' she cries out, '*Deb!*,' he replies, surprised but VERY pleased to see her. He embraces her, and she starts to cry, burying her head in his chest, '*I miss you Jack,*' she says. '*I miss you too Deb,*' he replies. He is fine, and he is happy. The following day Deb hears from her sister Den that she has had a first dream of Jack that same night.

Jack appears in one of my dreams on 8th May. We meet in an empty grey-white space, a no-place. Both he and I know he is dead. '*It would help me if you could wear one or two of my clothes,*' Jack says, his voice flat and his usual smile absent. '*Sure Jack,*' I say, and the dream ends. Every morning for the next year I put on at least one item of his clothing: he said it would help him.

On June 6th Jack shows Debbie a picture of himself in a dream, saying '*I'm almost twenty-two there.*' Jack died aged 21. He has bleached curly hair in the picture, his face distorted and silly. '*It looks like you're out of it there Jack!*' says Deb. The image then changes to Jack grinning in a group photo. On 10th August Debbie has a third dream of Jack as his adult self. In it, Denny and her partner Colin, Deb, myself and Jack decide to watch a Mickey Rourke film. Jack faces the screen with no shirt on. Deb nuzzles up to his back.

After six months or so I have a distressing dream. Deb, Jack and I are together and deeply upset because Rosie has just died. I feel something's not right, and suddenly I know what: '*It's not Rose that's dead Jack,*' I tell him, '*It's you!*' '*Oh yeah,*' says Jack, and before I can stop him, he disappears. I am desolate. Grief doesn't let up. But then I have a wonderful dream. Jack appears and walks up to me. We embrace and gradually meld into a single entity. No longer father or son, we have become nothing but pure joy. I wake to feel a blush of happiness, a first snowdrop in the bleakest winter.

I contact Pim Van Lommel, Europe's leading expert on the Near Death Experience. When I tell him about losing Jack he agrees to an interview. During our conversation Pim asks me if I have had any particularly vivid dreams about Jack. Yes, I reply, I had two a couple of years back. '*And how many other dreams do you remember from two years ago?*' Pim asks me. '*Err, none,*' I answer. '*Well, they weren't dreams then, were they,*' he says. It's a statement, not a question. Pim's view is that Jack had used the dream state to contact me. Our adult selves are too invested in the material world to allow such communication during our waking hours. They banish the possibilities of spirits and invisible friends as we grow up and out of our dreamlike infant years. When we sleep, we are free of this restriction – we travel across time and through reality, joining an improbable cast of characters that might comprise ourselves, our first boss, a long-forgotten classmate and a celebrity chef together in locations that shift and dissolve, breaking several fundamental laws of science. While the guard of reason sleeps, the recently dead may slip into this anything-can-happen night space, to share priceless seconds with us. Could my dream-Jack be real genuine Jack? I don't know if Pim is right. Equally, with all that I am encountering as I research stories about the dead and nearly dead, I don't know he's wrong. I decide Pim has given me a comforting mystery.

Months have turned to years, and I still think of Jack every day. He makes the occasional appearance in my dreams, but always as his very young pre- or primary school self. Adult Jack is now beyond my sleep's reach. Debbie, however, has an unexpected breakthrough. In November 2014 she drove to the Welsh borders for a ten-day Buddhist retreat. All talking between participants and any communication with the outside world are forbidden. It is the last thing Debbie would ordinarily go for, but Jack's death has broken her world into a heap of meaningless pieces. With no prospect of peace of mind, a meditation boot camp emerged as a number one option. Attendees were woken at 4.30, and much of the hours that followed were spent in marathon meditation sessions. As the days of meditation and mental solitary confinement rolled on, Debbie internal world started to change. Her mind began to operate at a pitch that was new to her; when she phoned me at the end of the ten days, I didn't recognise who was calling - even her voice was altered. While in this unique mental state, Debbie had dreamt of adult Jack. He was his usual jokey self, impersonating his uncle Kev. He had bought some trousers that were too long. *'Burt can take them up'*, he said. *'Well, Burt's blind,'* said Deb, correctly.

Caroline, a good and trusted family friend who had known Jack since he was three years old, wrote to Debbie and me in April 2011 to describe two vivid dreams she had had of him:

> *The first dream (which was a few months ago) Jack was about 18 or 19 I would say, and he looked very dashing. It was very vivid, we were by a pond and it was emitting a glow, as was Jack. He was wearing a really cool pair of blue jeans with quite a few pockets and he had a black t-shirt on with a white emblem on it. It was strange as there were other people there, but it was like we were alone. In the dream I felt this was a special moment, but I didn't know he had passed away. He turned to me and smiled, it was a real Jack smile and it was a divine moment. I wasn't close enough to touch him and thinking about it now it was as if I couldn't get any closer, but there was no need. He turned and walked away, and I felt an overwhelming feeling of peace and I woke up feeling happy. I felt as though I had been with Jack and he is happy and in a really good place, I liked it there but I kind of knew I couldn't stay.*

I had the second dream last week. Jack and I were sitting on the floor together, again in a really bright place, a room this time. It isn't anywhere I know or remember form my past. We were on a large colourful rug and it was just like being inside on a sunny day. Jack was a little boy, just as I remember him when I first met him. I knew that Jack had passed away and so I felt as if this was really special. For a moment I felt overpowered with grief and then Jack looked at me, smiled and held up his small hand with his palm facing me. I mirrored him and placed my palm against his. He smiled and I felt a great sense of happiness and calm. When I woke up I knew in myself that I had been with Jack again and that we will meet again in our dreams and beyond.

Dreams give us a potential back door to the brain, where we might catch a clue about the workings of the mind. If – and it's a big if – the mind can leave the body when we sleep, it should be able to manage on its own when we die. But if we dream we are in a supermarket in Mongolia, the chances are very high that we are still at home in bed. Moreover, if we take the trouble to look around as we pass the frozen meat section and note we are totally naked and in the company of two talking Jack Russells, we can be confident that we are 100% not in Mongolia. In short, most dreams are rubbish. For us to have somehow been in the Ulaanbaatar branch of Tesco, we would need a local to swear they'd seen us there and noticed we'd found a pair of uniquely intelligent dogs. We'd need a witness. Here are some accounts from dreamers who reckon they pass this test.

In 1950, William Oliver Stevens published a collection of unusual dreams. Among them was the story of an English mother, (she withheld her name), from Fleetwood, Lancashire. It was 1941, and her son was serving in the RAF. She had a vivid dream that she was in a bar filled with airmen, dressed ready for active duty. '*Suddenly,*' she said, '*I heard my son's voice at my side say, "Well I'm blowed, I have won twelve and six!"*' [62 pence] He'd been sat at a table, playing cards with four other airmen. A siren sounded, and they all ran from the room, with one voice calling out, '*This is it for Hanover!*' On waking she wrote out the details and date of her dream and sent them in a letter to her son. He replied that the scene she had described reflected an actual event in every detail, and when he showed her letter to his comrades, '*they were all amazed.*' She went on to have another dream of 'visiting' her son while he was in a plane on a mission to bomb two ships in Brest harbour. She again wrote to her son, stationed in Slough, giving him details of what she had seen and heard. Again, she reports, her son and his colleagues were astonished by the accuracy of her dream.

On the night of 25th May 1941, she had the last of her RAF dreams. In it she heard her son cry out, '*Mother!*' Her worst fears were confirmed when a telegram arrived two days later to say her son had been reported missing during a mission over France. Her letter to William Stevens was countersigned by six others, who vouched for the truth of its contents.

In 1990 Keith Hearne published the results of his years of research into dreams and dreaming. Among his cases is this one from a woman signing herself M Ellis:

> *I went with my sister to Germany for a two-week stay with my niece and her husband who lived in married quarters. There was to be a party, but the night before I had a dream. All the furniture had been arranged along the walls. A couple came in and asked if we had heard of an accident at the camp that morning; three soldiers had been killed. The dream was so vivid that I asked if such news had been mentioned the previous night, but it had not. That night we arrived at the party. The room was exactly as I had seen it. We sat down for a drink and the same couple came in. I knew straight away what would happen. They said the very words that I had heard in my dream. My niece, her husband and my sister looked at me open-mouthed. 'You mentioned that this morning!' they said.*

The dream is interesting because it looks, on the face of it, to feature travel in time (to a day ahead) as well as place (a room that had its furniture re-arranged). It would have helped if Ms Ellis had included statements from her niece, husband or sister, but Hearne is confident that experiences like this are '*rampant*' in the population. If he's right, then most of us should have bumped into one of these tales in the course of our lives. I believe I have. In 1988 I was working in a hospice in the west country. Two of the nurses there, kindly women called Helen and Carrie, had shared a flat in their student days. Helen told me an unsettling story about a dream she'd had back then. In it she had seen a male friend of theirs called Robbie lying dead beside a railway track. Waking in panic, Helen immediately woke up Carrie to tell her that Robbie was dead. Carrie tried to reassure her, but Helen was distraught and had no doubt about the reality of what she'd seen in the dream. A few hours later, Robbie's dead body was discovered by the side of a railway track.

Keith Hearne is an important man in the English dream world. He invented a lucid dream machine, a slightly clumsy contraption that would give its user a mild electric shock when it sensed, from their breathing pattern, that they had entered a dream state. The jolt would be enough to grab the dreamer's attention, but not so powerful as to wake them. So they remain asleep, but think, '*Oh, that Keith Hearne's dream machine has just zapped me; this means I must be inside one of my dreams.*' They then continue dreaming but are empowered by this insight to attempt some control over the drama. With practice, aware dreamers can manipulate the narrative of their dreams to incorporate favoured real or fictional characters in plots they consciously conjure up. This capacity – known as lucid dreaming – happens naturally to some of us. Jack had been a lucid dreamer from early childhood.

Hearne undertook research work with several lucid dreamers, one of whom decided to find out what would happen should he try to walk 'through' one of the bit-players that inhabit his dreams:

> *I selected a passer-by at random, and moving horizontally, aimed myself at a point just beneath the ribs. My experience was entirely unexpected: on entry, [my] vision stopped, but I felt with a fairly life-like intensity, sensations of warmth and moisture. These lasted a second or two, then I emerged from the other side of the body.*

Another of the dreamers told Hearne that he had found himself at a friend's house:

> *I visited someone (a friend). I knew it was a dream. When I related the story to my friend and told him what I had seen and the rough time* [of my visit]*, he was very surprised, as what I had told him was actually happening at that time.*

This could be no more than coincidence, particularly if the friend had been sat watching telly. More unusual are the experiences of Andrew Paquette, an American based at London University. Andrew has been writing down records of his dreams every morning for the past 20 years. He has a vast collection of 12,000. Some of these involve 'visiting' other people:

> *I saw a person I knew, Dr. David Ryback of Atlanta, Georgia, talking to a tenant in the building they both worked in. Dr. Ryback's acquaintance was telling him how two cars he owned had been severely damaged on two separate occasions in the same week in the same way, by having tree branches fall on and crush their roofs.*

When Andrew phoned David Ryback to ask if this conversation had really taken place, the good doctor confirmed that his neighbour had indeed told him about having two cars hit by falling branches in two separate storms within the same week. The odds on this being a coincidence were so long that Andrew was left to conclude that he really had travelled outside his body that night.

In a dream on 22nd April 1990, (as I say, he writes this stuff down every morning) Andrew 'visited' his mother in her apartment, approximately 2,800 miles' distance from the room where Andrew lay sleeping:

I saw that she was on a date with someone and that they were listening to Schubert while she cooked something in her kitchen. While watching this, I suddenly became very tired and leaned into a wall opposite my mother's position in the kitchen. I then sank to the floor along it, making a kind of scraping noise against the wall. My mother suddenly turned to look directly at me as if alarmed, and then I woke. I called my mother later in the day and verified various elements of the dream. To my surprise, she said that she had been surprised while cooking that night by a strange sound coming from the wall opposite her. She said it sounded like a paper bag being scraped against the wall as it fell to the floor, followed by a thud, but she saw no source for the noise.

Here's an old and charming example of another mother-son dream visit. In 1754 the Reverend Joseph Wilkins, a teaching assistant from Ottery St Mary, Devon, had a peculiar dream.

One night, soon after I was in bed, I fell asleep and dreamed that I was going to London. I thought it would not be too much out of my way to go through Gloucestershire and call upon my family there.

In the dream, Joseph tried his parents' front door. It was locked, but he was able to get in by the back door. He found that his mum and dad were not yet up, so he went upstairs to their bedroom where he saw his dad asleep on his side, but,

I found my mother awake to whom I said these words, 'Mother, I am going on a long journey and am come to bid you goodbye'. Upon which she answered in fright, 'Oh dear son, thou art dead!' With this I awoke and took no notice of it more than a common

dream, except that it appeared to me very perfect.' ('perfect' in this context meaning 'real').

A few days later, a letter arrives in the post from Joseph's mum and dad. Joseph is surprised, because his dad had written to him only very recently. Joseph continues:

> Upon opening it I was more surprised still, for my father addressed me as though I were dead…and gave the reason of their fears. That on a certain night, naming it, after they were in bed, my father asleep and my mother awake, she heard somebody try to open the front door, but finding it fast, he went to the back door, which he opened, came in, and came directly through the rooms upstairs, and she perfectly knew it to be my step; but I came to her bedside and spoke to her these words, 'Mother, I am going on a long journey, and have come to bid you goodbye.' Upon which she answered me in fright, 'Oh, dear son, thou art dead!' – which were the circumstances and words of my dream.

According to Joseph, his mother remained adamant that she had been fully awake when he 'appeared' to her in his ghostly form.

Back here in the 21st century, Chris Hoad from East Sussex recalls an experience his father had at home one day. His father was known to everyone as Nod, due to his love of the power-nap: 'His favourite pastime was kipping in his armchair,' says Chris. On this particular afternoon Nod drifted off in the armchair as usual. He dreamt that he was stood in the living room, looking at his physical body in the chair. He then began to wake up, and in his drowsy state saw his dream-self, looking down at him. His consciousness then switched back inside his upright dream-self, gazing at his armchair-bound self. Realising that he had to decide which version was truly his physical self, Nod awoke in a full panic. This resolved the problem by establishing that he was the man in the chair, and not the other Nod, who had now vanished.

Nod wasn't alone in finding himself in two places at the same time. In February 2003 David R was in his kitchen, making a cup of tea, when he had a heart attack.

> *It is difficult to describe in words but there was a time when I seemed to occupy two different places. I could feel the pain in my body but I was also away from the pain as if floating beside me. I then felt frightened: I could tell I was dying or dead...I remember saying to myself 'If I don't stand up now I will never stand up' so I went back to my body and made me stand up. I remember feeling a rush of life back into my body it was like a sharp gust of wind filling my body and then I was back inside me and I could feel the pain again.*

Unlike Nod, David was far from asleep when he split off from himself. The moment, he said, was '*not dream-like at all, it was very real and direct.*' David summed up his experience in this way: '*The very real and distinct separation of my consciousness and my body is something I will never forget.*'

Near Death Experience

Because energy cannot be destroyed, there has always been something. Or, put another way, there has never been nothing. Even when we are out cold, we can still have vivid dreams, so to believe in nothing is to believe in something for which there is very limited evidence. I used to say with certainty, '*When you're dead, you're dead.*' On reflection I see this statement is no more profound than, '*When you're alive, you're alive.*' Of course you're dead when you're dead. But what exactly is 'dead'? The final part of our search gives us the best shot at answering this question. The accounts given by people who have been clinically dead and then brought back to life are extraordinary tales from the borderland, the absolute edge of life. We can get no closer to death than the Near Death Experience

Near Death Experiences (NDEs) are highly unusual experiences had by persons who are generally, but not always, extremely close to death. I say not always because it is possible to trip into a Near Death Experience at times of great danger or extreme upset. NDEs have the following distinct features that are common to people of any nation who have almost died:

> Separation from the (lifeless) body
> Distortion of time
> Accelerated thinking
> Sense of understanding everything
> Sensation of harmony and joy
> Entry into a marvellous location (sometimes via a tunnel)
> Surrounding of brilliant white light
> Scenes from the past relived (a Life Review)
> Meeting with others (deceased relatives and/or 'spiritual' figures)
> Reaching a border, a point of no return
> Finding oneself back in Birmingham

Most people who are resuscitated have no memory of anything happening while their heart had stopped, but around one in ten will recall an extraordinary experience. Of these ten percent, just about no-one will have accumulated every single item on the above NDE check list, although many will report experiencing most of them.

To remove the risk that Near Death Experiences are restricted to Californians who are confident they are reincarnations of Cleopatra's pet cat, let's start with a down to earth example. David Parsons from London collapsed after a night out and was rushed to hospital. Here he describes heaven in a reassuringly non-spiritual English way.

I'm looking down at my body, thinking 'What on earth are you doing down there?', and I started to think how do I know I'm down there: what's going on? Within an instant I started to travel up towards the ceiling of this room, this hospital area. And I was floating around, almost like Peter Pan – I could go anywhere I wanted to go. And then I noticed a lot of other people, souls or spirit people, around me in a circle, like an upside-down ice-cream cone, going up in a spinning spiral. So I followed them up there, and I was met in this really peaceful, peaceful place. I had no real religious convictions or beliefs at that time, I just lived day to day, enjoying my life…. There were two people that I met with. One was my deceased grandmother on my mum's side, and a friend from High School called Howard from Ceylon [Sri Lanka] who died of leukaemia, and I was so amazed to see these two people…they explained that I was in a safe place, that it was a good place, and they showed me around. So the whole experience…I feel lasted about three of four hours, but I have no way of knowing if that was 2 or 3 seconds of 4 or 5 years [he smiles]. And they introduced me to a light being, a very, very tall energy that shimmered, and it had human-type features to it; very, very nice, very comforting, who then took me into a sort of cinema. It was a big theatre; the seats were like cinema seats – an auditorium – and they sloped down towards a very large cinematic screen…. the 'energy' was behind me, and as I looked around other groups of people were arriving and taking their seats. Each of them had one of these light-beings, or 'guides' or helpers, or angel-beings with them.

And then the film started, and I'm looking, and all I can see is about me, and I'm only assuming now perhaps that these people, when they looked at the screen, were only seeing information about them. So it was almost like Judgment Day that you read about, but I felt that it was like a life review. I was being shown the terrible things I'd done during my growing up, the bad things I'd done, and also a lot of good things that I'd been involved with that I didn't remember too well. And I was given a chance to redress that, to put the balance back into things, make things right.

So the angel-being led me from that theatre, we went round this land, this area and I went into a very tall educational kind of building, with big steps going up to it. And we went in there, and again it was groups of people, with backpacks on, all sorts of races and ages, and each of them had one of these spiritual light-being guides with them. I could hear music being played on a piano, but I could taste the sound. The vibrational notes of the tune, whatever it was, had colour, they had taste, they had substance to them. And I'm experiencing them on such a different level.... each note, each colour was touching a part of my body, my soul, and it was healing it. It was 'encharging' me, it was adapting me, and it was equipping me for the tasks ahead.... a thought came into my mind from the Holy Bible that says, and I don't know who it is, but 'My father's mansion has many rooms', so this is how it seemed, looking back. So this went on for a few hours, then I went back and was joined by my grandmother and my friend Howard.

I didn't want to leave to be honest, it was such a nice place, and they said I had to come back into the human body because there was a job for me to do. And I remember asking them, 'Well, what's this job?', and they said, 'It will all unfold', and I started to slip back into the body, and I was back into the hospital.... It was the following day, in the morning. I was woken up: cup of tea, and then discharged from this place, feeling totally, 'What on earth has happened here?' Gobsmacked. So we went out, found a local cafe, had some food because I was starving, and I just didn't know what on earth had happened; never come across it before. Several months afterwards I started to talk to my old friends and told them this had happened, and I would get laughed at, and so I decided I would hold my own counsel. But then, after six or seven months one or two people explained to me what it was, this experience that I'd had. Everything in my life had changed, my relationship with my parents had changed, my relationship with my close friends had changed, as if I was someone new. I'd walked out, and I'd walked in as a different David. And it was about 15 to 20 years ago I suddenly realised I had been doing 'this job'. My whole life, looking back, had gone from materialist ways to more spiritual, harmonious ways of living.

Heather Sloane from Southampton had never heard of Near Death Experiences when she was rushed into hospital with an ectopic pregnancy. She told her story to the BBC in 2001:

I was aware that I was standing beside a bed, having been a nurse in the past I thought I'd better check how the patient is, and I looked in the bed to see the patient and then realised it was me...there was a voice to the side of me saying, 'Don't worry about that...come with me and move into this light,' and I moved into this tunnel of light. When I got out to the other side it was what I can only describe as pure love really; absolute pure peace. I wasn't even bothered about what I'd left behind, and eventually you meet the only thing I can describe as pure perfection. I cannot describe it in any other way. At that point you think, 'I don't think I should be here', because I didn't really feel that I was worthy to be in front of what was pure perfect. And nobody says you're dying – you are just allowed to become sort of aware of things, and you go into a kind of a review of your past, right back from when you were very tiny. You remember absolutely everything; you feel instantly all the effects that any action had on another person. You just literally felt everything.

I visited Gary M in Essex, to talk to him about his Near Death Experience. Although less involved than David or Heather's experiences, Gary's NDE was still significant enough to undermine his lifelong atheism. Gary was in a car with his sister and mother when he had a brain haemorrhage:

> *I just remember going from room to room or from ward to ward in the hospital, in and out of consciousness…at some point I deteriorated badly and had to be resuscitated…I'm not at all religious, not in the slightest; I do not believe in religion, god, heavens, anything like that. Everything has to be scientific, logical and factual with me. I don't do fantasy; I see religion as fantasy, so that's why it stayed with me, because I'm not religious, but it felt quite different from 'normality'. It was like being somewhere where you are an entire eye, so you can see in every direction at the same time, up, down, sides, everywhere.*

> *You haven't got form, there's no form to you, but you just have this vision of everything. I'd say it was bright light, but it wasn't light. Have you ever had anaesthetic, where you've had the injection and it feels like there's gold running through your veins?…I say this because that is how the light was: it was like gold, but it wasn't gold, it was like the feeling of gold…the light was inside you and you were made up of a part of that light. I remember it being so beautiful and so lovely. It wasn't a feeling; it was a completely new existence. Not a feeling whatsoever: you existed within it rather than experiencing it, if that makes sense…. if time existed, I wasn't conscious of it, not in the slightest. No, it was outside of all of these laws of normality. That's why I was so intrigued by it.*

I asked Gary where was he, the person 'Gary', when all this was happening.

He was dead and gone. The body was dead and gone. This was a different existence, completely different. I knew that others were around me...I also knew that I'd love to share it, but I couldn't share it because there wasn't an existence: I wasn't 'me' anymore.... it's as if you have been entirely dissolved. All that's left is that spark that you started with...pure energy, not a physical spark.

I asked Gary if he believed that spark began at the moment he was conceived.

To me, before then. Which is what confused me, because as I've said, I'm not religious. I've not read up on near death experiences. This is the first time I've properly spoken about this; I've mentioned it to a few people, but I've not read up on near death experiences.... To be honest, I had thought it was a load of bollocks, then this happened and something changed, something was there, and I'm absolutely not afraid of going there again. Not in the slightest: it was a stunningly beautiful place.

Was the light, I wondered, everything?

Absolutely everything. There was nothing else. I suppose I've always assumed that when you die, you die...the only way I could see it now is that maybe these bodies are hosts, we are inside this host body and the body dies and whatever we are inside this host body continues in whatever state of time, space, matter, whatever....all I know is that since that experience I have no fear of being dead...I'd love to go there on holiday: it's REALLY nice!

Gary's ability to see in every direction at the same time finds an echo in other NDE accounts; Anita Moorjani, for instance, lay in a coma in 2006: *'Although I was no longer using my five physical senses, I had unlimited perception, as if a new sense had become available, one that was more heightened than any of our usual faculties. I had 360 peripheral vision....it still felt almost normal.'* PMH Atwater, who has been researching Near Death Experiences for forty years, says *'Reports of 360-degree vision and/or wrap-around sound, taste, touch, smell, and full sensory involvement are commonplace.'*

Both David and Gary lost the usual sense of time, as did Anita Moorjani: *'Everything occurs simultaneously, whether past, present or future.... Without the limitations of my body, I took in all points of time and space as they pertained to me, all at once.'*

The standard flow of time can rupture as someone slips out of consciousness. The English NDE researcher Margot Grey was contacted by a man who had collapsed in his home, at the foot of the stairs. Just before he hit the deck, he managed to call 999:

> *I curled up on the floor waiting for the ambulance...I looked at my watch to see how long it would take them and I realised my watch had stopped, which was most unusual... I then put my hand on my chest and could feel no heartbeat. There was a strange shift in perception at this time and I realized I was above the stairs looking down the stairs and I actually considered throwing myself down the stairs in order to start my heart beating again.*

He was eventually resuscitated by the ambulance staff, and he found that his watch restarted at the exact time he came back into his body.

Like David Parsons at his personal cinema show, many people at death's door have reported witnessing their life replayed in detail. Ex RAF-pilot Allan Pring was on the operating table when his heart stopped:

> *I knew that I was dead and I wasn't bothered, and I felt as if I was waiting for something to happen and it did. In a flash all of my life passed before me. Everything that I've ever done, ever thought, ever said was there and I floated off through this darkness and drifted down into a large, very large room. In each corner there was a figure. They all seemed to have like a monk's cowl, and they all had their*

faces turned away from me and then they started to ask me questions.

For Allan too, time behaved very strangely during this life review, '*Although it took but a moment to complete, literally a flash, there was still time to stop and wonder over separate incidents.*'

A woman signing herself very correctly as Mrs P Morris wrote to Peter Fenwick about her NDE. It appears that rather than taking the form of a Santa checklist of times she'd been naughty or nice, Mrs Morris's Life Review was so complete it amounted to a total memory download: '*All my past life and incidents passed through my mind in a flash, things I had forgotten, right back to about two years of age, when I was given a rag doll.*'

As we've already seen, the Egyptians had a Life Review as the central point of their Books of the Dead, and there are medieval accounts of Life Reviews. The Qur'an assures us that when we die:

> *you will be returned to the Knower of the Invisible and the Visible, and He will inform you of what you used to do. Whoever has done an atom's weight of good will see it. And whoever has done an atom's weight of evil will see it.*

We don't have to be just about dead to have a near death experience; we can have one by falling off a mountain, at which point we can reasonably believe death to be imminent. On a January night in 1865 a Church of England vicar, Edmund Donald Carr, went missing on the top of Long Mynd in Shropshire. Lost in the pitch black, he stepped over a precipice and plunged through the air. Reverend Carr somehow survived the fall, and was moved to write about the experience:

> *The pace I was going in this headlong descent must have been very great, yet it seemed to me to occupy a marvellous space of time, long enough for the events of the whole of my previous life to pass in review before me.*

Albert Heim had a very similar experience when he fell while climbing in the Alps:

> *Mental activity became enormous, rising to a hundred-fold velocity...I saw my whole past life take place in many images, as though on a stage at some distance from me*

Avon Pailthorpe, a social worker, had a similar experience when her car spun wildly out of control on a motorway in June 1986. Strangely, the experience concluded before her actual crash:

> *Around me, as the tunnel began to lighten, there were presences. They were not people, and I didn't see anything, but I was aware of their minds. They were debating whether I should go back. This was what made me so safe; I knew that I had absolutely no responsibility to make the decision...There was total wisdom and goodness in them*

They did send Avon back, and she was again behind the wheel and fully conscious at the moment a car broadsided her at seventy mph:

> *The crash knocked me deeply unconscious, but when I came around the second time I was not surprised because I knew it was all right. I was only surprised later, in the hospital, that the doctors were so worried and dashed around and worked so feverishly on me, because I knew it had been decided I should live. I tried to tell them...but they didn't understand.*

Modern advances in resuscitation and emergency surgery have snatched growing numbers of people from the jaws of death. This is good news on two fronts: alongside the saving of more lives, improved emergency care has produced a large and growing population of people with near death experiences to recount.

Margot Grey fell seriously ill during a travel tour of India. She was pretty sure she was dying; next thing she found herself in a '*world of light*'. While she was there, Margot was convinced she had a telepathic conversation with a *'being of light'*. Looking back on the experience, Margot wrote that, *'the feeling of one-ness, the sense of beauty is totally beyond anything that one can imagine here'*. Margot was so struck by what had happened that she decided to research Near Death Experiences in the UK, seeking out and interviewing others who with a baffling story to tell. She published the results in her 1985 book *Return from Death*.

The following sample of cases collected by Margot all relate to the initial stage of a Near Death Experience: leaving the body.

> *They took me into the emergency room...I was unconscious when they brought me in. I was above the room and I could see the doctors as clear as a bell....About a month later I wanted to make sure this was not a hallucination or something of that sort and I went back to the hospital and I asked the nurse to show me this room which I had never seen in my life before and I walked in there and I knew everything was. It was all there, the table, the lights, the cabinet, everything, like I remembered.* [Adult male, after heart attack].

> *I was in the intensive care unit of Worthing Hospital. I found myself looking down at myself. I heard and saw two doctors and a nurse running towards the bed and heard them say, 'Quick, quick'. I am sure I had died.* [Adult female, heart attack]

> *Suddenly I realised I was standing up by the door and could see my body lying on the floor. I could see everything that was going on...the pain had ceased.* [Adult female with breathing problems]

It's interesting so many interviewees chose to conceal their identity, as though they'd been involved in a criminal act. Talk of leaving one's body amounts to modern sedition.

People often feel at complete ease on discovering they are clinically dead:

I remember...finding myself out of my body, looking down at my carcass.... I was neither a woman nor a man, just pure spirit. I could see doctors and nurses round my bed, frantically trying to give me a blood transfusion...I was amused at all this fuss going on with my body as it did not concern me a bit.

Reflecting on her own near death experience in India, Margot Grey wrote:

I remember looking at my body lying on the bed and feeling completely unperturbed by the fact that it seemed likely that I was going to die in a strange country...thinking that it was totally unimportant where I left my body, which I felt had served me well and like a favourite worn-out coat had at last outlived its usefulness and would now have to be discarded.

In 1949, Edmund Wilbourne came down with a serious case of pleurisy and was declared dead by the medical team at the Crumpsall Hospital in Manchester.

I can still picture the scene. I saw myself lying on the bed. I saw a young nurse. She was preparing me for the mortuary. I remember thinking at the time how young she was to have to do such a thing as getting me ready and even shaving me. I actually saw it taking place...I felt no emotion, just nothing, like looking at a picture. I was clinically dead about two hours...and I woke up at the mortuary of Crumpsall Hospital, and it was the mortuary attendant who nearly had a heart attack. I know it wasn't a dream.

Anita Moorjani was comatose in her hospital bed on 2nd February 2006 when she began to break loose:

I was tasting freedom for the first time! I began to feel weightless and to become aware that I was able to be anywhere at any time ...I didn't even think it was odd that I was aware of my husband and the doctor speaking to each other outside the ICU, some 40 feet down a hallway....There I was, without my body or any of my

physical traits, yet my pure essence continued to exist…it felt far
greater and more intense and expansive than my physical being.

After they 'leave' their unconscious bodies, many people are able to describe details of the accident scene, an operating theatre or A&E department, which they claim to see from an unusual vantage point: a ceiling, or the roof of an ambulance. Their reports include the layout of equipment, the names of people gathered around their apparently lifeless body, and the actions and words of these professionals. Janice Holden, an American psychologist, was able to contact medical staff and other independent witnesses who were present at the time of 40 separate incidents of near death that featured the claim of an out of body experience. Holden found that 88% of details reported by these out-of-body 'experiencers' were completely accurate, 10% contained some error, and only 3% were completely wrong. Although this is a very high strike rate, it is not proof a person floats to the ceiling above their own body and watches and listens from up there. Of our five senses, hearing is usually the last to go, allowing the mind to construct a visual 'memory' from all that it hears: the urgent words of a doctor, the sounds of a door closing to one side and a medical cabinet opening opposite…as we have already established, our brains don't always need open eyes to produce convincing pictures. But research has shown us that as time progresses we generally fail to recall events, even personally important ones, with any degree of accuracy. Facts begin to fray and jumble, to the point where five, ten and fifteen years after it has occurred, we give three quite different accounts of the same incident. As Holden and others have discovered, this natural shakiness of memory doesn't appear to apply to Near Death Experiences. Recalling the several conversations he had over the years with his aunt about her near death experience when she almost drowned, Thomas de Quincey wrote:

Forty-five years had intervened between the first time and the last
time of her telling me this anecdote, and not one iota had shifted

its ground amongst the incidents, nor had any of the most trivial of the circumstances suffered change.

Light features heavily in NDEs. This light is super-bright but never dazzling:

I found myself in a place full of radiant light. It's quite unlike anything you could possibly imagine on this earth. The light is brighter than anything you could possibly imagine...but it doesn't hurt one's eyes a bit

The light is brighter than anything possible to imagine. There are no words to describe it, it's a heavenly light.

Higher intensity of colour is also often reported

I was in a beautiful landscape, the grass is greener than anything seen on earth, it has a special light or glow. The colours are beyond description; the colours are so drab here by comparison.

In addition to its brightness and intensity, people often recall the light as having a personality, a kind of consciousness of a super-brilliant variety:

You can't compare it to the love of your wife, or the love of your children, or sexual love. Even if all those things were combined, you cannot compare it to the feeling you get from this light

In 1999 a middle-aged woman wishing only to be known as Mary recounted her story to the Near Death Experience Research Foundation. While living as a young single woman in London, Mary fell pregnant. She decided to go for a back-street abortion. It went badly wrong and she was rushed to hospital and almost bled to death in the A&E department. At this point, Mary found herself within inches of the ceiling:

I was totally conscious even though I had heard a nurse, the only one in a blue smock, tell the doctors I had lost consciousness soon

355

after entering the emergency room. I was very aware of every detail of the events and the room

A tunnel appeared, and Mary was drawn through it:

I finally came to the end and floated into a place which was overwhelmed by a radiant white light. ... It seemed like a giant force field or energy that radiated all the good and noble emotions known to man.

May met a '*warm joyful presence*' there, who,

showed me a beautiful shiny bubble which floated next to me. In it I saw a tiny baby nursing at a breast. The baby became a toddler and began walking toward me still inside the bubble. Then the image of a young boy turned into a teenager and he continued to age until he was a full-grown man. 'Who is that?' I asked. 'Your son Michael', was the reply. I recall feeling very relieved that I hadn't destroyed his chance at life.

Mary immediately found herself back in her body in the A&E treatment room:

While out of my body in the Emergency Room I noticed a red label on the side of the blade of a ceiling fan facing the top of the ceiling. When I was taken to the recovery room, I was told that my baby was saved. I said, 'Yes, I know'. I asked if someone would please listen to my incredible experience and was told that they had no time.....Only one nurse in the hospital listened to me.....I finally convinced her to get a tall ladder and see for herself the red sticker whose appearance I described in great detail on the hidden side of the emergency room ceiling fan. The nurse and an orderly saw the sticker, confirming all the details of its appearance I described. I knew what I knew, but I felt better that at least two people believed me.

Her baby survived. She called him Michael and he grew to become a man. Looking back, Mary said, '*The experience remains as real and vivid now as it did 34 years ago.*'

Influenced by stories like Mary's, medical researchers have tried putting cards bearing words and pictures on top of very high shelves in emergency rooms, face up, in the hope that a revived patient will be able to tell staff what she/he had seen on the card. To date, no-one has been able to recall seeing any of these out-of-view cards.

Among the many NDE stories that involve leaving the body, several mention a cord linking the very-nearly-dead body to its floating owner. E. A. Hearn-Cooper was 13 years old in 1918, and very ill with Spanish flu:

> *I felt myself rise up, float up into the highest part of the room and look down on myself lying there 'asleep' on my bed…I realised that I had a 'cord' linking me with my body below me, and while I felt very happy floating there, I somehow knew that if I moved too violently I would break the cord and I would never be able to return to my body. I decided to return.*

When he almost died, James Carney believes he caught sight of a similar cord: '*When I looked down, although I could not see my body, I could see I was attached by a light grey rope.*'

Frances Barnshey seemed to have bagged a place in heaven, but her 'cord' pulled her away. Her consolation prize for landing back in England was a decent cup of tea:

> *I was in bed, recovering from the 'flu, reading. I began to feel very relaxed and peaceful. I've never felt like that either before or since that experience. I put down my book and I could hear my husband and two children moving about downstairs, getting tea ready, and I remember thinking, 'Lovely, there's going to be a cup of tea in a*

minute,' and just at that point I felt myself shoot up out of my body at terrific speed, like being fired from a rocket.

I was out in space, no dark tunnel, and I thought, this is how the birds must feel, so free. I was actually like a kite on an endless string, which I could feel attached to my shoulder blades. I couldn't see any kind of body belonging to me, I seemed to be mind and emotions only, but I felt more vital, more myself than I've felt in my life at any time before or since. I found myself travelling towards this tremendous light...I saw no one and heard no one, but I knew I wasn't alone, and I felt this wonderful love enfolding me and understanding me. No matter what my faults, what I'd done or hadn't done, the light loved me unconditionally. I so wanted to stay there, but I was told neutrally that this couldn't be, I had to go back, and then I felt this cord on my back – the biblical silver cord? – pulling me back and the next thing I knew was that I was back in my body and my son was coming into the bedroom with my cup of tea.

Some people come back from the edge with the impression that they had, for one glorious moment, been given the answers to everything:

I knew the answer to every mystery – I was not told, I just knew; the light held all the answers. (N Baker, writing to Peter Fenwick)

I was going upwards and had great mental awareness, a sense of great excitement. All around me were the answers to everything (Audrey Organ, writing to Peter Fenwick)

In addition to answers to every current mystery, insights into future events are sometimes provided. The American researcher Kenneth Ring interviewed an elderly Englishman who recalled an experience he had when suffering from acute appendicitis as a ten-year old in 1941. While he was dead to the world, the boy encountered some robed characters, who gave him to understand that he would be married at 28 (he was, despite not meeting the woman he would marry until he had reached his 28th birthday). The mysterious folk from 'over there' went on to show him a scene from his future, featuring his adult self and his wife in a room with their two children. He told Kenneth Ring that this scenario played itself out many years later, like a decades-long case of Deja-vu.

Whatever and wherever 'over there' is, most people reckon it's unbeatable:

> *It was a lovely feeling. In the peace, beauty, joy and, above all, love, I felt more truly alive than I ever have before'.* [Adult male, clinically dead for two hours, quoted by Margot Grey]

> *There are no words to describe it. I was so happy, it's impossible to explain. It was such a feeling of serenity; it was a marvellous feeling.* [Adult female, medical complications following surgery]

As one survivor struggled to explain, the emotional heights of the near death experience are of a different order to earthbound joy: '*When you try to recapture the feeling, however happy you are, it's just not the same.*' Speaking to Peter Fenwick, Ashley Coleman had this to say about his NDE:

> *The only way I can explain it is: think of the happiest moment of your life, and when you do, [that] happiest moment is awful pain compared to what you feel, and I will swear to that*

The following checklist of delights gives a clue as to why it's so great 'over there':

> *All pain disappeared; comfort seized me. Only my essence was felt. Time no longer mattered, and space was filled with bliss. I was bathed in radiant light and immersed in the aura of the rainbow. All was fusion. Sounds were of a new order, harmonious, nameless*

One person rated the bliss they experienced while clinically dead as 1,000 times greater than the best feeling one can get in this world. But when I put this figure to Gary, who had his own vivid NDE a few years ago, he firmly disagreed: '*I'd say that's a gross underestimate*' was his response.

Justin U had a serious accident that left him in a coma. As his condition worsened, Justin was transferred from one hospital to another via ambulance:

> *I had a clear recollection of flying above the scene going backwards looking down on the ambulance, keeping pace with it. I also remembered clearly a family member in the front of the ambulance going with me being sick into a bag. This was verified afterwards and the only part of the experience that I can put an actual exact time on.*

Justin found himself in another world, among relatives who had died:

> *I saw my Aunty who died at age 7 one year before I was born. I described to family members the exact clothes, and certain jewelry she had on the day she died, which was confirmed. It was impossible to have this information without seeing it.*

In answering a question about the reality of his experience, Justin said that it was, '*Definitely real, more intense, powerful and profound than any material experience I have ever had.*'

Leaving aside the question of how Justin might have known how his young Aunt used to dress, (from a forgotten photograph?), the side of his and perhaps other NDEs that hold the most interest are the recalled impressions that they are more real than reality itself, with the just-about-dead folk feeling '*more alive*' than they ever felt in this world. Wonderful if you're having a wonderful time, but very hellish if you're not. A woman interviewed by Margot Grey said:

> *I found myself in a place surrounded by mist. I felt I was in hell. There was a big pit with vapour coming out and there were arms and hands coming out and trying to grab mine...I was terrified that*

360

these hands were going to claw hold of me and pull me into the pit with them.

I spoke with Michelle from Bristol. In 2013 she fell seriously ill with meningitis and was rushed to hospital in Bristol. *'I was told I was dying. I was pleading with them to take care of my daughter. At that point I was quite delirious.'* Michelle slipped into coma for almost two weeks, during which time she found herself in a hellish scenario: *'I remember being thrown into the water. And raped.'* Despite the terror of this experience, it seems to have benefitted Michelle. *'I never used to be a positive person. I used to go to the negative. The previous Michelle would have gone mad and shouting; outwardly I'm very calm now.'*

And a man wrote to Peter Fenwick to describe his frightening near death experience:

> *It was really like all the images I had ever had of hell. I was being barbecued. I was wrapped in tinfoil, basted and roasted. Occasionally I was basted by people (devils) sticking their basting syringe with great needles into my flesh and injecting my flesh with the red-hot fat. I was also rolled from side to side with the long forks that the 'devils' used to make sure I was being well and truly roasted....I was overcome with the feeling of utter doom and helplessness.*

Poor fella. But his experience had a rational explanation. It turns out that all this happened while he was in hospital, where, *'I was wrapped in a tinfoil blanket, an electric cage was put over me and during that time I was turned several times and innumerable injections were given.'* So where does this leave all the heavenly NDEs? Are they just vivid hallucinations too? We will need to address this critical question at the end of the chapter.

Some hellish Near Death Experiences are associated with the nearly dead subject living the wrong kind of life: addiction, crime, etc., while others happen to people who seem to have kept to the straight and narrow. There doesn't seem to be a solid pattern to it. It could be an internal thing. As John Milton puts it in Paradise Lost:

> *The mind is its own place, and in it self*
> *Can make a Heav'n of Hell, a Hell of Heav'n*

Edmund Leversedge, born in Frome, Somerset in the 15th century, had an NDE from hell, and perhaps it was no more than he deserved. As a younger bloke Edmund was a bit of a poser, with a weakness for showy clothing. Looking back, he describes himself as a *'wretched and sinful creature'*.

All that changes in May 1465, when he's suddenly struck down with the plague. His face and tongue turn black, and Edmund finds himself at death's door. Worse still, he's seized by a group of well-dressed demons who take him in spirit form to some horrible underworld. In desperation, Edmund calls upon Jesus's mother, the Virgin Mary, to rescue him. She turns up but tells him straight that he is headed for *'eternal damnation'* on account of his sinful ways, particularly the fancy clothes addiction.

As part of his rehabilitation, Mary orders Edmund to wear plain clothes for the rest of his days and to go and study at Oxford University for the next three years. She adds that he'll have to give up sex too. Edmund is OK with the first two preconditions, but deeply fed up by the third. At this point he comes upon an area of brilliant white light that contains the sound of heavenly voices. He sees ladders leading up to this inviting world, but Edward isn't on the guest list. Instead, he finds himself back in Somerset with instructions to be a very good boy in future and – thanks to his Oxford education – a strange story to tell us.

A number of people report that attempted suicide is generally frowned upon in the next world. Here's an account from a man who almost managed to take his own life:

I found myself floating about six inches above my body. The next thing I remember is being sucked down a vast black vortex like a whirlpool and I found myself in a place that I can only describe as being like Dante's Inferno. I saw a lot of other people who seemed grey and dreary and there was a musty smell of decay. There was an overwhelming feeling of loneliness about the place.

Most suicide NDEs do not, however, involve a trip to hell. In 1978 David Ayre, an engineer from Bristol, was severely depressed following the breakup of his marriage, and decided to end it all. He swallowed a pile of tablets, drank loads of whisky, switched off the electricity supply, sealed himself in his bathroom and opened the valve of a propane gas bottle. He clearly wanted out. As David took his final gulps of poisoned air, he felt despair give way to a huge sense of peace and warmth. He found himself rising from his lifeless body *'like the thought bubble of a cartoon character.'*

David drifted through the external wall of the locked bathroom and rose up above the city's rooftops. He then found himself moving through a tunnel that emerged into a lovely golden light. He seemed to have companions: *'I can't describe them – it was just that I was aware of the presence of others.'* David was greeted by his father, who had died two years earlier. He was younger and healthier than he had been prior to his death. They communicated telepathically. *'It was incredible, as if he knew everything I knew, and I knew everything he knew'.* Ayre eventually *'came into the presence of the Being of Light...It was like being inside a soft gold neon tube...one I don't hesitate to call God.'* David was given a review of his life, which featured the effects his actions had had on the feelings of others. Although not judgmental, the god-like being was pretty direct, saying to Ayre: *'You see what you did there? That wasn't very helpful, was it? Now will you go back?'* David could hardly refuse and rousing himself from a collapsed state back in his home in Bristol, he just about managed to phone 999. The emergency services broke down his door and David's life was saved.

In some cases, people recognise the landscape of their near death experience:

> *It suddenly looked extremely familiar. I came to the startling conclusion: I've been here before. It felt like a homecoming...this state of being is a reality that feels more real than what we call reality.*

More commonly, they come upon people they've known:

> *There was my father standing before me as large as life. He had died of a heart attack fifteen years before. He was dressed just like he used to be in grey trousers and a cardigan. He hadn't changed a bit. We chatted quite naturally, and he joked with me about my brothers.*

It's pleasing to learn there's room in paradise for casual knitwear. One returner reported meeting his greatly rejuvenated mother

> *I saw my deceased mother – not the mother I had known, but I knew she was my mother, a young mother....I had nearly got to her when I felt myself being pulled away from her...It was no hallucination. How can you hallucinate a mother whom you knew and loved and remembered when she died, and see an entirely young beautiful girl, and each know who the other is?*

The following experience was reported to the Dutch researcher, Pim van Lommel:

> *During my NDE following a cardiac arrest, I saw both my dead grandmother and a man who looked at me lovingly but whom I didn't know. Over ten years later my mother confided on her deathbed that I'd be born from an extramarital affair; my biological father was a Jewish man who'd been deported and killed in World War II. My mother showed me a photograph. The unfamiliar man I'd seen more than ten years earlier turned out to be my biological father.*

364

Encounters with a divine beings represent another NDE theme. Mr G Thomas had a heart attack when aged 55. He floated through a tunnel and emerged into a '*most wonderful*' light, where he came upon someone with long hair dressed in a robe with wide sleeves that touched the ground. They seemed to be getting on famously until another '*being*' came along and had a word with the robed figure:

> *Slowly he waved towards me in such a way as to indicate, go away, go back, but when he did this I felt, 'Oh no, I don't want to leave this place, please don't send me away, let me be with you forever.'*

Plainly he liked the wizard-guy.

> *I woke up and found I was wired up to the heart machine...When I got home ten days later, I had to tell my wife what happened...I nearly burst into tears because I wanted everyone to have the same experience. It was wonderful.*

Ella Silver was equally heartbroken at being sent back to the land of the living by two long-haired entities:

> *I assumed it was two men, although both had long hair to the shoulders....One suddenly turned towards me....in a beautiful voice, very loud, he said, 'She must go back'. Oh the terrible feeling. I didn't want to go back. I didn't feel they rejected me, because they loved me. It just wasn't for me to decide...I have never before or since known such a feeling of 'knowing' for sure I would know joy. It was totally different from happiness.*

A Mrs Holyoake encountered a being who she identified as Jesus.

> *He was dressed in a long white robe, his hair to his shoulders, ginger-auburn. He had a short beard...I was trying so hard to tell him that I couldn't leave until I had kissed my husband and three children goodbye. Jesus heard me and understood, he smiled and*

*started to walk backwards, taking his magnificent garden with him
and the light.*

NDE sightings of known religious figures are comparatively rare, but Allan
Pring also had such an encounter:

> *I was met by a figure of light, and it was what can only be described
> as a 'Jesus' figure. But I 'knew' that the appearance of the figure was
> to make me feel comfortable in this new place.*

All good things come to end, and eventually every near death experiencer
must return to earth. Often the 'dead' person has some say in the decision
to stay or go. Heather Sloane was emphatic about getting back to the land
of the living, but in negotiating with the divine beings, she remembered her
manners:

> *I said, 'I'm sorry, I can't stay', and I got very, very distressed because
> I was thinking I had an 18-month-old baby at home, with a
> husband at sea and no family living anywhere near, so who is going
> to look after her? And I was really, really upset, and basically it was
> gradually a discussion of 'OK, we'll let you come back', and there
> was a massive jolt and I was back with the nurses, fiddling around,
> checking my wellbeing.*

Pim van Lommel offers an account from a boy who was born deaf and
almost drowned as a ten-year-old:

> *I reached a border. Even at the age of ten I needed no further
> explanation. I simply understood that I'd never be able to return if
> I crossed this border. But some of my ancestors were on the other
> side, and they caught my attention because they were
> communicating through a kind of telepathy. I was born profoundly
> deaf. All my relatives can hear, and they always communicate with
> me through sign language. Now I had direct communication with
> about twenty ancestors via some kind of telepathy. An
> overwhelming experience.*

Judith Smith found herself moving through a tunnel and approaching some weird but kindly beings:

> *As we approached the light, one of the voices said, 'Are you coming or staying?' and I knew that if I went I would die. I thought about it – certainly there was no fear – but I said, 'No, I haven't finished my life yet.' Instantly I was whisked back (I can only describe it as being like when you blow up a balloon and let the air out) and I was in the recovery room and a nurse was saying, 'She's not coming round, she's not coming round – oh, it's OK, she's all right.'*

Joan Hensley was deeply tempted to stay:

> *I saw someone, but no one I knew. He held out his arms to me…I felt very comfortable and secure…I knew I only had to touch his hands and I would join him….I felt reluctant to go.*

Others are so happy with their deal up there that they are more than glad to stay, despite the sorrow this will cause folks back home. Elizabeth Rogers, for instance, had no intention of returning to England:

> *I saw a group of people between me and the light. I knew them; my brother, who had died a few years before, was gesticulating delightedly as I approached. Their faces were so happy and welcoming. Then somehow my mother became detached from the group. She shook her head and waved her hand (rather like a windscreen wiper) and I stopped, and I heard the doctor say, 'She's coming round,' and I was in my bed and the doctor and my husband were there. My first words to the doctor were, 'Why did you bring me back?'*

Bit tough on Mr Rogers:

> *I love my husband dearly and it now seems very strange that there was no 'pull', no regrets at leaving, nothing: only pure joy and peace.*

Ella Silver was equally happy to give up on loved ones down here:

I never once thought of my husband or my children, who were quite young then...Later, I was riddled with guilt because I had not considered my family.

Being sent back can be tough, particularly when so many loved ones are up there:

I found my mother and father and my grandparents. My daughter who had also passed on was there too. I asked them where I was and what I was doing there. They told me I was in the spirit world. When I asked if I was there to stay, my father said, 'It's not yet time for you to join us.'

Allan Pring was given the choice of returning to terrestrial England or remaining in the great fish and chip shop in the sky. He decided to come home ('*I was very much in love with my wife and I wanted to be able to tell her that you can't die, it's impossible to die*'). But the decision came at some cost to Allan: '*Leaving was the worst experience of my existence and it will affect me for as long as I live.*' He had to turn his back on a place of '*absolute happiness, utter bliss, complete love, perfect peace, and total understanding*'. A sort of celestial Croydon.

My personal favourite sent-home story comes from a London woman who told Margot Grey of the day she almost died and found herself outside a beautiful little house her mother occupies in the after-world. It shows that even in paradise, some family members can still get on our nerves.

I could see my Uncle Alf inside; I never cared for him much in this life....I said, 'Can I come in?' It looked so nice and welcoming, but my mother said, 'No, you can't, it's not your time to stay... We are getting ready for your Auntie Ethel'...the next thing I remember is finding myself in bed at the hospital. I had been unconscious for three days...A day or two later my family were allowed to see me...they said that since I had been in hospital my Auntie Ethel had unexpectedly died of a sudden heart attack. I thought, well, I could have told them that.

To be fair, she seemed to have buried the hatchet with Uncle Alf, which is just as well if Anita Moorjani's 2006 near death experience is anything to go by:

> *I became aware that we're all connected. This was not only every person and living creature, but.... everything in the universe – every human, animal, plant, insect, mountain, sea, inanimate object, and the cosmos...we're all One.*

Shelley and Wordsworth would have loved her.

Hindus, Buddhists, Sikhs and Jains all believe that with a lot of meditation, it's possible to tune the mind to the point where it leaves ordinary consciousness, and reaches samadhi, a super-conscious state. It is a light-filled world where everything is pure and blissful. It is so great up/out/in there, that when someone enters samadhi, they often don't want to come back. It is possible to stay there for a few days, but the longer someone remains, the higher the chance they'll never come back. There are clear similarities between this super-brilliant state and the near death experience.

We must now return to the question of illusion, whether NDEs might be no more than a trick of the brain. Edgar Alan Poe (and Marvin Gaye) advised us to only believe half of what we see and none of what we hear. For some reason they, and we, have more faith in vision than the other senses. We will ask others, *'Is it just me, or is something burning?'*, when we definitely smell burning. Or, on hearing a noise, we'll ask someone next to us, *'Did you hear that?'*, and if they say no, we are willing to consider we imagined the whole thing. But, if we see something that others doubt, we are far more likely to stick to our guns: (*'I saw it with my own eyes. It was there for sure'*). Society goes along with this league table of believable sensations: if you hear voices then you are schizophrenic, but if you see UFOs there's nothing wrong with you and the government is probably concealing the truth about alien visitors to avoid global panic. Seeing is believing.

We don't really see with our eyes, (although we'd be stupid not to involve them); We 'see' at the back of our brains, in the visual centre. Our eyes take in impressions of colours and shapes, but it is the brain that turns these into 3-D moving pictures. Similarly, vibrations picked up by the ears are turned into sound inside the brain. We can therefore see richly detailed scenery with our eyes shut, when we dream, or when our brain goes on the blink. We can also hear the voices of people who aren't present when we dream or when areas of our brain malfunction.

The brain disorder Temporal Lobe Epilepsy (TLE) can generate very convincing world of places, people and assorted wildlife, including sounds and even smells. During an attack, sufferers from TLE may suddenly zone out, their eyes fixed in a faraway stare, or they might collapse, losing consciousness altogether. While having one of these seizures, a person may have a powerful sense of déjà vu, experience convincing religious hallucinations, or even see their own body from an external vantage point.

In the 1990s, Rudi Affolter, then aged 43, was in hospital in Croydon when he had a vivid supernatural experience. A cast-iron atheist, Rudi found himself in hell: '*I was told that I had gone there because I had not been a devout Christian, a believer in God. I was very depressed at the thought that I was going to remain there forever.*' It turned out that Rudi suffered from TLE, and during a seizure his brain had manufactured a totally convincing trip to the underworld.

Ellen G White was a key founder of the Seventh-day Adventist movement. During her lifetime, Ms White had hundreds of dramatic religious visions that featured messages from God which she dutifully wrote down and shared with others, leading her followers to believe Ellen was in direct contact with the almighty. At the age of nine Ellen had been hit on the head by a rock. The assault left her in a near-coma for several weeks, and it is probable that the injury caused her long-term brain damage. When entering a religious trance Ellen was said by observers to have a fixed and faraway look, or to make repeated automatic movements. There seems a real possibility here that Ellen, and perhaps many other saints and prophets throughout history, suffered from TLE.

Although only a limited number of people with TLE have visions of heaven or hell, we can say that supernatural experiences can be the result of the brain's bio-electrical system messing up. And we can also say that when people are very close to death, their brains are likely to have a tough time keeping their minds straight. In other words, near death experiences may simply be random stories our brain throws out as it begins to fail and shut down. This explanation holds true for many NDEs, and people reporting NDEs have been found to be more likely than the average citizen to have unusual brain activity in the temporal lobes (the part of the brain that produces TLE).

But there are some experiences that don't seem to fit this 'all in the (failing) brain' theory for NDEs. Some NDEs, for instance, are experienced by people whose brains are a long way from death (the mountaineers who are plunging through the air, or cases like Avon Pailthorpe's, that involve a calm visit to another world in the split seconds before a car crash). There are also many accounts of people 'knowing' a healthy-when-last-seen family member had died while the subject was clinically dead, an occurrence inconsistent with brain malfunction.

There's also an explanation that people have NDEs because they already know about them: their brains are therefore conditioned to click into an NDE when they near the edge of existence. This may be so in some cases, but Peter Fenwick has seen little evidence of this in his research:

In 1987, I was involved in…. the first TV programme to describe the near death experience in this country, I received over 2000 letters from people who had had such an experience. I sent out a questionnaire to 500… What we found was that over 98 percent of people who wrote to us had not heard of NDEs when they had their own experience.

For the brain to be wholly responsible for the generation of a Near Death Experience, manufacturing a grand end-game delusion, it would need to rely on its stock of memory and imagination. One category of NDE that appears to go beyond the brain's personal inventory are reports from people who had been blind yet find themselves able to 'see' during their brush with death. Among these is the case of Vicki Noratuk, who was interviewed by the BBC in 2001. Vicki had been totally blind from birth.

I've never seen anything, no light, no shadows nothing. A lot of people ask me if I see black. No, I don't see black; I don't see anything at all.

Vicki has never had a visual dream.

In 1973, when aged 22, she was involved in a serious car accident. She takes up the story:

The next thing I recall I was in Harborview Medical Centre and looking down at everything that was happening; and it was frightening because I'm not accustomed to see things visually, because I never had before. And initially it was pretty scary! And then I finally recognised my wedding ring and my hair. And I thought: 'Is this my body down there? And am I dead or what?' They kept saying, 'We can't bring her back, we can't bring her back!', and they were trying to frantically work on this thing that I discovered was my body and I felt detached from it and sort of 'So what?', and I was thinking 'What are these people getting so upset about?'. Then I thought 'I'm out of here – I can't get these people to listen to me', and as I thought that I went up through the ceiling

372

as if it were nothing. And it was wonderful to be out there and be free, not worry about bumping into anything, and I knew where I was going.

I heard this sound of wind chimes that was the most incredible sound that I can describe...as I was approaching this area, there were trees and there were birds and quite a few people, but they were all, like, made out of light, and I could see them, and it was incredibly, really beautiful, and I was overwhelmed by that experience because I couldn't really imagine what life was like. It's still...a very emotional thing when I talk about this...because there was a point at which...I could bring forth any knowledge I wanted to have.

Vicki told researchers Kenneth Ring and Sharon Cooper that she then met up with two friends from blind school, Debbie and Diane, who had both died in childhood. They were no longer children and had been cured of blindness and their other significant handicaps. She also had a joyous reunion with two of her adult carers and her grandmother. Everything was going great, but then she was resuscitated, forcing her back to earth and a return to sightlessness. She had been clinically dead for four minutes. Given that Vicki had never so much as dreamt of a visual world, it is difficult to write off her experience as a hallucination: her brain had no stock of images to produce such a movie, and in years of dreaming had never demonstrated any ability to picture the appearance of forms and persons.

There is a way that might help us decide if NDEs are real or just imagined. If NDEs are delusions, it is likely that people who have one will tell a few people, then carry on living life the same way they had before their near miss. If, however, a person comes to believe that their NDE was truly a preview of the next world, it is likely that they'll be profoundly changed by it. There's nothing more life-changing than death.

Taking this idea further, Cardiologist Pim van Lommel interviewed patients that he and his team at Arnhem hospital in the Netherlands had brought back to life following heart attacks. He got them to give details about their attitudes to life. Some of these patients reported having a near death experience when their hearts had stopped, but many could remember absolutely nothing of their brush with death. Pim interviewed these same people eight years later, to see if their near-fatal cardiac arrest had acted as a lasting influence on their approaches to life.

He found that for those who had recalled nothing of the time they were clinically dead, life had gone back to normal, while patients who had reported NDEs had become '*transformed*'. After the eight years, people with an NDE had become far freer at showing their emotions and more accepting and compassionate towards other people. They had lost much of their previous appetite for money and possessions, and had developed an increased interest in nature, the environment and social justice. NDE ex-patients had also reduced their church attendance, but had become more drawn to '*spirituality*', Buddhism in particular. Their fear of death and dying had reduced and their belief in life after death had increased.

By contrast, the ex-patients who hadn't had an NDE showed very little change in their lifestyles, beliefs or attitudes eight years on from their heart attack.

Three of the ex-patients who'd had an NDE had this to say:

'It's possible to be physically dead while your mind lives on. Only one thing matters: your attitude toward other people. I think about everything now.'

'It had such a profound effect on the rest of my life: the timelessness that I experienced; the knowledge that my consciousness will survive my body. It was enough to destabilize my life.'

'It felt like I'd become another person, but with the same identity.'

In his autobiography, Queen Victoria's doctor Benjamin Collins Brodie gives a cute example of the change an NDE can inspire:

A sailor who had been snatched from the waves, after lying for some time insensible on the deck of the vessel, proclaimed on his recovery that he had been in Heaven, and complained bitterly of his being restored to life as a great hardship. The man had been regarded as a worthless fellow; but from the time of the accident having occurred, his moral character was altered, and he became one of the best conducted sailors in the ship.

Moving forward to 21ˢᵗ Century Bristol, Michelle has this to say about the impact of her NDE:

I hadn't spoken to my mother for about eight years. I am talking to her now. It's all about letting go of things in the past, trying to forgive people. Before, I was probably an unforgiving person. Angry.

Several other people told English researcher Margot Grey of the lasting influence of their NDEs:

'I developed a great compassion for people that were ill and facing death and I wanted so much to let them know, to somehow make them aware that the dying process was nothing more than an extension of one's life.'

'Since then…the sky is so blue, and the trees are much greener; everything is so much more beautiful. My senses are much sharper. I can even see auras round trees.'

'My character and thinking etc. drastically changed and I am certainly not the man I was, thank God.'

'I have lost all fear of death. I almost welcome it, but at the same time I would never do anything to precipitate it. I feel we are here for a purpose and we cannot avoid what we have come here for'

'Before the experience I always thought death was the end, that there was nothing more. It had a very profound effect on me.'

'I do not fear death anymore as I now know that there is a wonderful life after death'

They'll all be a bit sick if it turns out there's a big nothing beyond the grave, but to give them their due, they've each been closer to the edge than almost all of us.